MORE PRAISE FOR *MESTIZA RHETORICS*

"*Mestiza Rhetorics* not only gives the field of feminist rhetorical and archival studies new primary works of Mexican rhetors; it also gives us ways to reexamine our assumptions about what rhetorical texts, texts in translation, and recovery work *should* look like. Kudos to Cristina D. Ramírez and Jessica Enoch for providing feminist rhetorical scholars with such a rich resource."
— Jen Wingard, editor of *Peitho: The Journal of the Coalition of Feminist Scholars in the History of Rhetoric and Composition*

"A rich and important example of the transborder feminist work of mexicana rhetors in the latter part of the twentieth century and the early twenty-first. This collection stunningly captures how these feminist rhetors had to engage a *mestiza* project to negotiate cross-border relationships, politics, national identities, and culture to enact their political projects. *Mestiza Rhetorics* is an important read not only for rhetorical scholars of history but also for those who want to better understand the history of our current political moment."
— Rebecca Dingo, author of *Networking Arguments: Rhetoric, Transnational Feminism, and Public Policy Writing*

"*Mestiza Rhetorics* presents an important collection of Mexican newspaperwomen's original writings and their translations. Readers will appreciate this rich array of genres and styles that address women's rights, border politics and nationalism, and the role of Spanish language and the arts. Enoch and Ramírez offer multiple avenues for the analysis of these readings, making the collection both a necessary intervention in the rhetorical canon and a valuable scholarly resource."
— Ellen Cushman, author of *The Cherokee Syllabary: Writing the People's Perseverance*

Studies in Rhetorics and Feminisms

Series Editors, Cheryl Glenn and Shirley Wilson Logan

MESTIZA RHETORICS

An Anthology of Mexicana Activism in the Spanish-Language Press, 1887–1922

Edited by
Jessica Enoch and
Cristina Devereaux Ramírez

Translations by
Joel Bollinger Pouwels and Neil J. Devereaux

SOUTHERN ILLINOIS UNIVERSITY PRESS
Carbondale

Southern Illinois University Press
www.siupress.com

Copyright © 2019 by the Board of Trustees,
Southern Illinois University
All rights reserved
Printed in the United States of America

22 21 20 19   4 3 2 1

Cover illustration: Jovita Idar (*center*), image cropped and tinted; University of Texas at San Antonio Libraries Special Collections

Library of Congress Cataloging-in-Publication Data

Names: Enoch, Jessica, editor. | Ramírez, Cristina Devereaux, 1971– editor.

Title: Mestiza rhetorics : an anthology of Mexicana activism in the Spanish-language press, 1887–1922 / Jessica Enoch, Cristina Devereaux Ramírez.

Description: Carbondale, IL : Southern Illinois University Press, 2019. | Series: Studies in rhetorics and feminisms | Includes bibliographical references and index.

Identifiers: LCCN 2018054891 | ISBN 9780809337408 (paperback) | ISBN 9780809337415 (ebook)

Subjects: LCSH: Women—Mexico—Political activity—Sources. | Feminism—Mexico—History—Sources. | Women—United States—Political activity—Sources. | Feminism—United States—History—Sources. | BISAC: LANGUAGE ARTS & DISCIPLINES / Rhetoric. | SOCIAL SCIENCE / Women's Studies. | LANGUAGE ARTS & DISCIPLINES / Journalism. | SOCIAL SCIENCE / Ethnic Studies / Hispanic American Studies.

Classification: LCC HQ1463 .M49 2019 | DDC 305.420972—dc23
LC record available at https://lccn.loc.gov/2018054891

Printed on recycled paper ♻

Contents

ACKNOWLEDGMENTS ... ix

INTRODUCTION: *UNA INVITACIÓN* ... 1
   Cristina Devereaux Ramírez and Jessica Enoch

LAUREANA WRIGHT DE KLEINHANS ... 23
   Saludo y prospecto (Greeting and Prospectus), *Las Hijas del Anáhuac*, Mexico City, Mexico, 1887 ... 27
   Capítulo xxi. La lectura (Chapter 21: Reading), *La Gaceta Popular*, Mexico City, Mexico, 1892 ... 31
   La mujer artista y artesana (The Woman Artist and Artisan), *El Tiempo*, Las Cruces, New Mexico, 1891 ... 37

CATALINA ZAPATA DE PUIG ... 43
   La mujer de este siglo (The Woman of This Century), *Violetas del Anáhuac*, Mexico City, 1888 ... 46
         Writing from San Juan Bautista, Tabasco, México

CONCEPCIÓN MANRESA DE PÉREZ ... 53
   Mujeres de nuestra época (Women of Our Era), *Las Hijas del Anáhuac*, Mexico City, Mexico, 1887 ... 55

PAZ ... 61
   Carta abierta a las damas de *Las Violetas del Anáhuac* (An Open Letter to the Ladies of the Violets of Anáhuac), *Violetas del Anáhuac*, Mexico City, Mexico, 1888 ... 63
         Writing from New Orleans, Louisiana

JUANA BELÉN GUTIÉRREZ DE MENDOZA AND
ELISA ACUÑA Y ROSSETTI ... 67
   A los mexicanos (To All Mexicans), *Vésper: Justicia y Libertad*, Mexico City, Mexico, 1903 ... 71

JUANA BELÉN GUTIÉRREZ DE MENDOZA
   ¡Ecce homo! (Behold the Man!), *Vésper: Justicia y Libertad*, Mexico City, Mexico, 1903 ... 79
   "Vesper" siempre ocupará su puesto ("Vesper" Will Always Occupy Its Post), *Vésper: Justicia y Libertad*, Mexico City, Mexico, 1910 ... 82

HERMILA GALINDO — 85

¡Laboremos! (Let Us Labor!), *La Mujer Moderna*, Mexico City, Mexico, 1915 — 88

La mujer como colaboradora en la vida pública (Woman as Collaborator in Public Life), Sunday supplement of *El Pueblo*, Veracruz, México, 1915 — 91

JOVITA IDAR (A. V. NEGRA AND ASTREA) — 96

A. V. NEGRA

Por la raza: la niñez mexicana en Texas (For the Mexican People: Mexican Children in Texas), *La Crónica*, Laredo, Texas, 1911 — 98

Por la raza: la conservación del nacionalismo (For the Mexican People: The Preservation of Nationalism), *La Crónica*, Laredo, Texas, 1911 — 101

ASTREA

Para la mujer que lee (To the Woman Who Reads), *La Crónica*, Laredo, Texas, 1911 — 104

Debemos trabajar (We Must Work), *La Crónica*, Laredo, Texas, 1911 — 107

LEONOR VILLEGAS DE MAGNÓN — 110

Evolución mexicana (Mexican Evolution), *La Crónica*, Laredo, Texas, 1911 — 112

Adelanto de los mexicanos de Texas (The Progress of the Mexicans in Texas), *La Crónica*, Laredo, Texas, 1911 — 115

SARA ESTELA RAMÍREZ — 119

¡Surge! A la mujer (Rise Up! To Womankind), *La Crónica*, Laredo, Texas, 1910 — 120

ANONYMOUS WRITINGS ON LA LIGA FEMENIL MEXICANISTA (THE MEXICANIST FEMININE LEAGUE) — 122

Liga Femenil Mexicanista (Mexicanist Feminine League), *La Crónica*, Laredo, Texas, 1911 — 123

La Liga Femenil Mexicanista (The Mexicanist Feminine League), *La Crónica*, Laredo, Texas, 1911 — 126

MARÍA RENTERÍA — 128

Leona Vicario y Rafaela López (Leona Vicario and Rafaela López), *La Crónica*, Laredo, Texas, 1911 — 130

Contents

ANDREA VILLARREAL GONZÁLEZ — 135
  A qué venimos (What We Have Come For), *La Mujer Moderna*, San Antonio, Texas, 1909 — 137

ISIDRA T. DE CÁRDENAS — 140
  ¡Unifiquémonos! (Let Us Unite!), *La Voz de la Mujer*, El Paso, Texas, 1907 — 142

ARTEMISA N. SÁENZ ROYO (XÓCHITL) — 146
  La mujer en el pasado, en el presente y en el porvenir (Women in the Past, Present, and Future), *La Época*, San Antonio, Texas, 1920 — 148

Writing from Veracruz, México

MARÍA LUISA GARZA (LORELEY) — 154
  [¿]Feministas . . . ? [¡]No! Femeninas (Feminist Women . . . ? No! Feminine Women), *La Época*, San Antonio, Texas, 1920 — 157
  Las mujeres que escriben (Women Who Write), *La Época*, San Antonio, Texas, 1921 — 163

Reprinted from "El Informador," Guadalajara, México

ARIANA — 167
  La mujer moderna y el hogar (The Modern Woman and the Home), *La Prensa*, San Antonio, Texas, 1920 — 169
  Lo que no es el feminismo (What Feminism Is Not), *La Prensa*, San Antonio, Texas, 1920 — 173

ANONYMOUS FEMINIST WRITINGS FROM *LA PRENSA*, SAN ANTONIO — 177
  Opiniones de algunas de las feministas que han concurrido al Congreso de La Haya en favor de la paz (Opinions of Some of the Feminists Who Attended the Congress of The Hague in Favor of Peace), *La Prensa*, San Antonio, Texas, 1916 — 179

ANONYMOUS FEMINIST WRITINGS FROM *LA PRENSA*, LOS ANGELES — 186
  Mujeres mexicanas notables (Notable Mexican Women), *La Prensa*, Los Angeles, California, 1919 — 188

AURORA LUCERO-WHITE LEA — 196
  Shall the Spanish Language Be Taught in the Schools of New Mexico, *New Mexico University Bulletin*, Albuquerque, New Mexico, 1911 — 198

ELENA ARIZMENDI MEJÍA 203
El feminismo y la Liga Internacional de Mujeres Ibéricas e
   Hispano-Americanas (Feminism and the International League
   of Iberian and Hispanic-American Women), *El Heraldo de
   México*, Los Angeles, California, 1922 205

CATALINA DULCHÉ ESCALANTE (CATALINA D'ERZELL) 217
La mujer y el arte. Teresa Farías de Isassi (The Woman and Art:
   Teresa Farías de Isassi), *El Heraldo de México*, Los Angeles,
   California, 1920 219

NOTES 225
WORKS CITED 235
INDEX 245

Acknowledgments

In all respects, *Mestiza Rhetorics* is a collaborative endeavor. First, we want to thank our translators Joel Bollinger Pouwels and Neil J. Devereaux. Joel Bollinger Pouwels carefully and meticulously transcribed and translated over 280 pages of Spanish-language text. We attribute a great deal of this project's success to Joel's turn-of-the-twentieth-century Spanish-language expertise and extensive knowledge of mexicana history. Her help was indispensable. Even a translator needs an editor, and Neil J. Devereaux, who is also an expert in twentieth-century Spanish linguistics and Hispanic literature, dedicated himself to editing and revising Joel's translations. Throughout the project, they answered our questions about turn-of-the-century history, language accuracy, and bilingual fluency. Beth Chapple helped move the anthology through its final stages, and her editorial translations were meticulous and thorough. Without all of their work, this project would have remained a dream.

We also must thank the archivists and librarians, as well as acknowledge the archives that were central to this project. The archivists at the University of Arizona helped to secure and find primary documents and also direct us to resources we did not know. Throughout this project, we consulted and drew from the digital archives at Arte Público Hispanic Historical Collection Series 1 and 2, and the subsidiary database Hispanic American Newspapers, 1808–1980, under the direction of Nicolás Kanellos at the University of Houston. Other important databases for this anthology include America's Historical Newspapers, Latin American Newspapers, Latin American Women Writers (LAWW), and the Hemeroteca Nacional Digital de México. We deeply appreciate those who create, maintain, and grow these archives, and we are grateful for the permissions we received to publish the materials we culled from these resources.

While most of our collected entries were drawn from these archives, others were preserved by scholars through their individual collections and publications. Scholar Dra. María de Lourdes Alvarado y Martínez Escobar at Universidad Nacional Autónoma de México gave us access to Laureana Wright de Kleinhans's "Capítulo XXI. La Lectura," and we gained permission to publish this piece from the Instituto de Investigaciones sobre la Universidad y la Educación. Dra. Rosa María Valles Ruiz at Universidad Autónoma del Estado de Hidalgo allowed us to use her transcription of Hermila Galindo's "¡Laboremos!" Dra. Patricia Galeana, Directora General del Instituto Nacional de Estudios Históricos de las Revoluciones de México, gave permission to publish "¡Ecce Homo!" by Juana Belén Gutiérrez de Mendoza and "A qué venimos" by Andrea

Villareal—two pieces published in *Mujeres y Revolución, 1900–1917*, edited by Ana Lau Jaiven and Carmen Ramos-Escandón. The capacious intellectual generosity of these scholars was one of the most heartening and affirming aspects of this project.

In 2014, we were awarded with the Conference on College Composition and Communication's Research Initiative Grant that propelled our work forward and funded every aspect of this project. We especially want to note how expensive translations are and can be: *Mestiza Rhetorics* would not have been possible without this grant. We hope CCCC continues to support translation and bilingual scholarship such as this.

Editors of the Feminisms and Rhetorics Series Cheryl Glenn and Shirley Wilson Logan championed this anthology and offered critical and helpful guidance from 2014 to the book's completion. We deeply thank them for their support. Two anonymous reviewers offered insightful recommendations. We did our best to attend to each and every one, and the anthology is better for their suggestions. We especially want to acknowledge the hard and thoughtful work of Kristine Priddy, who saw this project through from beginning to end; it's been a long process, and we appreciated (and even enjoyed!) taking every step with her.

We both depended on our families as we made our way through this project. Jess's three children have spent their early years hearing about *Mestiza Rhetorics*, watching their mother work and collaborate on it—even popping in to video conferences to say "hello" to Cristina. Their comic and loving relief in addition to the intellectual space and support from Scott Wible were invaluable to Jess. Cristina consistently turned to the Mexican linguistic and cultural heritage that grounds her immediate family. Her fluency in Spanish allowed her access to Mexican archives, archival documents, and connections with scholars and institutions in Mexico. Most importantly, she received endless support throughout this project in time and encouragement from her husband, Alejandro Ramírez.

Finally, we want to make clear the collaboration, respect, and friendship that sit at the center of this project. *Mestiza Rhetorics* was composed through rigorous and dedicated effort from both editors, with each person's unique contributions giving this anthology its character and form. Neither of us could have completed this project alone. There is no lead or secondary editor; instead, this book is a partnership to which both scholars contributed time and expertise equally. We mark this shared investment in the project by changing the order of authors for the anthology and the introduction. We hope this reordering signals our collaboration, our shared investment, and even our interdependence.

Mestiza Rhetorics

Introduction: *Una Invitación*
Cristina Devereaux Ramírez and Jessica Enoch

Mestiza Rhetorics is an invitation for readers to learn about the rhetorical achievements of mexicanas writing in Mexico and the United States from 1887 to 1922. More specifically, this critical anthology focuses attention on Mexican newspaperwomen and recovers the journalistic contributions of those who used the press to forge the early feminist[1] movement in Mexico and southwestern United States, confront the hypocrisies of their particular patriarchal systems, and engage in important debates concerning education and women's rights, as well as local and national politics. By including thirty-three readings originally published in Spanish-language presses,[2] *Mestiza Rhetorics* also invites readers to investigate these women's contributions to periodicals such as *Las Hijas [Violetas] del Anáhuac*,[3] *Vésper, La Crónica, La Prensa, El Heraldo de México, La Mujer Moderna*, and *La Voz de la Mujer*.[4] And because these presses were located in both Mexico and the United States, the readings herein offer opportunities to explore the concerns, struggles, and triumphs of mexicanas in U.S. cities such as El Paso, Laredo, Los Angeles, San Antonio, and Las Cruces, as well as in cities across the border like Veracruz, San Juan Bautista, Mexico City, and Durango. Within this volume, newspaperwomen reflect on the importance of labor and art, debate education and language instruction, and define and redefine their rights and roles. These women protest injustices within society and construct possible solutions. They celebrate the Mexican woman's past, and they look out internationally to identify the strides women have made in such places as France, Italy, the Netherlands, and Russia. They write collaboratively and alone. They rely on styles ranging from simple to florid. They sign their names to their writings, use pseudonyms, and remain anonymous. Significantly, these women leverage diverse and compelling rhetorical strategies to make their case.

Mestiza Rhetorics thus invites readers to explore this richness. With this invitation, we do not offer detailed assessments of these women writers or their work. Instead, as an anthology, the purpose of this volume is to create opportunities for readers to think critically about these pieces and conduct more writing and research. The goal is to set the groundwork for new arguments to be made about Mexican women's rhetorics. Our introduction initiates this invitational process by contextualizing the collected writings, explaining our editorial decisions, and identifying the scholarly context from which this anthology emerges. By articulating our goals and motivations as well as our choices and decisions, we hope to enable readers to engage with these women's words carefully, critically, and imaginatively.

MEXICANA RHETORS / MESTIZA RHETORICS

Throughout this introduction and the anthology as a whole, we define these women as Mexican women rhetors or mexicana rhetors. We do so because we want to signal the geographic roots of the women whose work is collected herein. We use this terminology because, most obviously, many of these women lived within Mexican territory, or, if they were located on the U.S. side of the border, they were of Mexican descent and identified in their writings with the Mexican nation, language, and culture.[5] We also choose to designate these women as mexicanas because that is how they often named themselves in their work, regardless of their location within a particular nation-state. Furthermore and more particularly, many of these women, such as María Luisa Garza (Loreley), Catalina Dulché Escalante (Catalina D'Erzell), and Andrea Villarreal, identified with the intellectual collective "El México de Afuera" (Mexico on the outside). This collective was made up of Mexican citizens who were exiled—some voluntarily, others forcibly—for their political beliefs during the Mexican Revolution. Those who formed this group used their writing to express a strong connection with and longing for the Mexico they left behind, and they created this connection through selective rhetorical practices, one of which was writing in Spanish.[6]

While we call the women in this collection mexicanas, we choose to define their writings as *mestiza* rhetorics, and we do so for a number of reasons. We use the term *mestiza* to link to the concept of *mestizaje*, which was an especially popular concept during the time period of this anthology. *Mestizaje* served, for many of the women anthologized here, as both a way to name the mixed identity of the Mexican people and a tool for the formation of the modern Mexican nation-state. More specifically, *mestizaje* references the racial comingling that began in the sixteenth century between the indigenous tribes of Latin America and the Spanish conquistadores, due in great part to the subjugation and rape of indigenous women. After the Conquest, the Spanish imposed a detailed *sistema de castas*, or caste system, in Mexico that relied on assessments of blood purity and ethnicity to create hierarchical status.[7] Scholar Jake Frederick notes, "Racial categories such as *mulato*, *español*, *mestizo*, and *pardo* were conceived to identify the ancestral mixture of a given individual, thus supporting a system that privileged those of undiluted Spanish ancestry" (497).[8] While many of these terms fell out of use in the later nineteenth century, the concept of *mestizaje* prevailed, describing a process of racial and cultural mixture, and *mestizo* continued to identify people born of indigenous and European heritage.[9] Thus, we title our anthology *Mestiza Rhetorics* because the terms *mestiza* and *mestizaje* resonated powerfully for the women whose writings are collected here as part of their national connections and sense of ontology. The terms' adoption and circulation enabled these rhetors to consider, discern, and argue for their ethnic identities.

We also, however, choose to title our anthology *Mestiza Rhetorics* as a way to bring into conversation and indeed tension the turn-of-the-twentieth-century understandings of the term *mestiza* with our twenty-first-century ones. Due to the work of scholars such as Gloria Anzaldúa, Paula Moya, Damián Baca, and Cristina D. Ramírez, *mestiza* rhetorics have been defined as those that create an alternative and gendered rhetorical space for rhetors to explore their hybrid lived experiences, which were often, but not always, a mix of indigenous, Mexican, European, and Anglo. Calling the rhetorics of the women in this volume *mestiza* rhetorics emphasizes the ways they used their intersecting social, political, cultured, linguistic, and gendered locations as heuristics for rhetorical invention and intervention.[10]

It is critical to note, however, that the rhetors in this volume engage the *mestiza* project in vastly different ways. That is, one woman's version of *mestiza* rhetoric does not align directly with another rhetor's, nor even with Anzaldúa's or Baca's. So, for example, while the anonymous writer of "Mujeres mexicanas notables" ("Notable Mexican Women") recovers both Aztec and Mexican women as exemplars for Los Angeles's *La Prensa* readers to emulate, Jovita Idar argues for the educational rights of Mexican children living in the border city of Laredo, and Juana Belén Gutiérrez de Mendoza and Elisa Acuña y Rossetti speak from their position as persecuted women journalists to critique the political regime of Mexican president Porfirio Díaz. Thus, all the rhetors in this volume take up a *mestiza* project because they negotiate the multiple and complex demands of gender, geography, national identity, politics, and culture to consider who they are as mexicanas and what their sociopolitical agenda should be. Each rhetor crossed, recrossed, and even situated herself at borders that were ideological, gendered, linguistic, rhetorical, and geographic.[11] Hence, we choose to use this term *mestiza*—in all its provocative complexity—as a way to link the rhetors in this volume to one another and the *mestiza* tradition as well as to foreground the intricate negotiations mexicanas have made while living and writing in the United States and Mexico.

SCHOLARLY FOUNDATION AND CONVERSATION

Mestiza Rhetorics is a feminist rhetorical recovery project. As such, it contributes most directly to a central prerogative of feminist historiographic research: to challenge *the* rhetorical tradition that has until recently only included the writings of elite, enfranchised, Western men. However, with great effort, researchers are beginning to shift the terrain. Emboldened in great part by Cheryl Glenn's groundbreaking research in *Rhetoric Retold*, feminist scholars have "remapped" the landscape of rhetorical history with the goal of forging new paths to figures and sites that the well-trodden highways of the Western tradition have bypassed (3). For over twenty years, feminist historiographers of rhetoric have taken up this work with great interest, with studies such as Jacqueline Jones Royster's *Traces of a Stream*, Lisa Shaver's *Beyond the Pulpit*, and Katherine Kelleher Sohn's *Whistlin' and Crowin' Women of Appalachia* recovering the words and work of African American, Methodist, and Appalachian women, just to name a few.[12] *Mestiza Rhetorics* advances this initiative by collecting the writings of mexicana newspaper contributors at the turn of the twentieth century and prompting readers to assess their rhetorical power.

While *Mestiza Rhetorics* is decidedly feminist due to its focus on its recovery of mexicanas and their rhetorical significance, it also speaks to historiographic scholarship dedicated to cultural rhetorics writ large. Studies such as Xiaoye You's engagement with the Chinese rhetorical tradition (*Writing in the Devil's Tongue*), Janice Fernheimer's investigation of Jewish rhetorics ("Talimidae Rhetoricae"), and Malea Powell's recovery of Native American rhetorics ("Rhetorics of Survivance") are a small sampling of the many projects that blaze trails beyond the much-visited locations of the Greco-Roman tradition to explore how rhetors from varied cultural traditions have made meaning in their worlds.[13] Especially important to the work of this collection is Damián Baca and Victor Villanueva's *Rhetorics of the Americas: 3114 BCE to 2012 CE* and the 2015 special issue of the *Rhetoric Society Quarterly* dedicated to Latin American rhetorics, edited by Christa Olson and René Agustín De los Santos. Together, these volumes "urg[e]" scholars toward "a wider notion of *Américan* rhetoric grounded in long histories of hemispheric interaction" (Olson and De los Santos 194).[14] *Mestiza Rhetorics* furthers this line of inquiry but also distinguishes itself by focusing on how questions of gender animate discussions about rhetorical activity in the Americas.

Most specifically, however, *Mestiza Rhetorics* builds on and contributes to the small but growing conversation regarding *mestiza*, mexicana, Chicana, and Latina rhetorics and rhetorical historiography. To be sure, scholars such as Julie Bokser, Damián Baca, Jessica Enoch, Andrea Lunsford, Kendall Leon,

Cristina D. Ramírez, Tricia Serviss, and Susan Romano have begun to recover these women's rhetorical significance. Additionally and importantly, the work of two particular figures have been anthologized and thereby frequently studied: the writings of Sor Juana Inéz de la Cruz and Gloria Anzaldúa are now featured in the second edition of Patricia Bizzell and Bruce Herzberg's *The Rhetorical Tradition: Readings from Classical Times to the Present*, as well as Joy Ritchie and Kate Ronald's *Available Means: An Anthology of Women's Rhetoric(s)*. Inclusion in these volumes is significant, because here we see Sor Juana's and Anzaldúa's writings next to Aristotle's, Diotima's, Michel Foucault's, and Sojourner Truth's. However, there is also an unfortunate consequence. By dedicating scholarly attention to Sor Juana and Anzaldúa, these oft-read and assigned anthologies implicitly suggest not only that there were just two "great" mexicana/Chicana rhetors, but also that women from this cultural group were not consistently intervening in public discourse between 1691 (Sor Juana's "Respuesta") and 1987 (Anzaldúa's *Borderland/La Frontera*).

Mestiza Rhetorics offers a corrective. By recovering little known rhetors such as Catalina Zapata de Puig, María Rentería, María Luisa Garza, Elena Arizmendi, Artemisa Sáenz Royo, and Ariana, this volume demonstrates the fact that numerous mexicanas have voiced their varied concerns in rhetorically important ways. Furthermore, by centering attention on mexicana rhetors publishing between 1887 and 1922, this anthology challenges the almost three-hundred-year temporal lacuna implicitly created through present-day scholarship and anthology production. Ultimately, the access *Mestiza Rhetorics* provides and the diverse collection it presents disturb the idea that the history of mexicana rhetorics is marked by just a few rhetorical achievements. *Mestiza Rhetorics* signals instead a rich mexicana tradition that extends far beyond the writings gathered within its pages.

Indeed, we hope readers pursue the rhetorics anthologized here and are inspired to learn even more. To do so means that readers would complement the writings in *Mestiza Rhetorics* by consulting not only the growing body of scholarship within rhetorical studies but also the scholarship *outside* the field in areas such as mexicana history and Chicana studies. Most particularly, readers might turn to texts such as Jennifer Browdy de Hernandez's *Women Writing Resistance: Essays on Latin America and the Caribbean*; Debra A. Castillo and María Socorro Tabuenca Córdoba's *Border Women: Writing from La Frontera*; Clara Lomas's "Revolutionary Women and the Alternative Press in the Borderlands"; Anna Macías's *Against All Odds: The Feminist Movement in Mexico to 1940*; Emma Pérez's *The Decolonial Imaginary: Writing Chicanas into History*; Pilar Melero's *Mythological Constructs of Mexican Femininity*; Joel Bollinger Pouwels's *Political Journalism by Mexican Women during the Age of Revolution, 1876–1940*; Vicki L. Ruiz's *From out of the Shadows: Mexican*

Women in Twentieth-Century America, and Julia Tuñon Pablos's *Women in Mexico: A Past Unveiled*. Readers might also consult the wealth of primary resources dedicated to Spanish-language newspapers available through the digital archives America's Historical Newspapers; Hispanic American Newspapers, 1808–1980; Hemeroteca Digital Nacional de México; Hemeroteca Digital de Chihuahua; and Arte Público Hispanic Historical Collections Series 1 and 2.

Furthermore, an additional and critical avenue of exploration would be to engage the work of feminist scholars publishing outside the United States and in Spanish. Some of the scholars who have led feminist recovery efforts in Mexico and indeed researched many of the women's writings collected here include Lourdes Alvarado (*Educación y superación femenina en el siglo XIX: dos ensayos de Laureana Wright* [Feminine education and overcoming in the nineteenth century: Two essays by Laureana Wright]), Gabriela Baeza Ventura (*La imagen de la mujer en la crónica del "México de afuera"* [The image of woman in the chronicle of "Mexico on the outside"]), Gabriela Cano (*Se llamaba Elena Arizmendi* [She was called Elena Arizmendi]), Gabriela Cano and Georgette José Valenzuela (*Cuatro estudios de género en el México urbano del siglo XIX* [Four studies of gender in urban Mexico of the nineteenth century], Rosa María Vallez Ruiz (*Sol de libertad Hermila Galindo: Feminista, constitucionalista y primera censora legislativa en México* [Sun of liberty Hermila Galindo: Feminist, constitutionalist and first legislative censor in Mexico], Ana Lau Jaiven and Carmen Ramos-Escandón (*Mujeres y Revolución, 1900–1917* [Women and revolution]), and Julia Tuñon Pablos (*Voces a la mujeres: Antología del pensamiento feminista mexicano, 1873–1953* [A voice for the women: Anthology of Mexican feminist thinking]). By reading beyond this anthology and placing texts such as these in conversation with *Mestiza Rhetorics*, readers could deepen and complicate their understandings and analyses of the writings collected here.

SELECTION

Mestiza Rhetorics brings together thirty-three writings of mexicana newspaper contributors who lived and wrote in Mexico and the United States. To make our selections, we used the newspaper and specifically the Spanish-language press as our primary touchstone. We did so for two major reasons. First, between the years 1887 and 1922 there were hundreds of Spanish-language newspapers in print throughout Mexico and the United States, and these publications were often overtly political in nature, functioning as outlets for protest and rhetorical intervention. As Nicolás Kanellos writes in "A Socio-Historic Study of Hispanic Newspapers in the United States,"

> Most of the Hispanic press, whether a small weekly or a large city daily,
> ... had to assume a leadership role in cultural (if not political) resistance and, beyond that, in the battle to protect the very real economic and political interests of the Hispanic community, whether envisioned as a community, an internal colony, or a racial-minority ghetto. (107)

To be sure, mexicana contributors faced gendered constraints regarding publication opportunities, but even so, the Spanish-language press was the venue most available to them for publishing their writings. In the face of gendered discrimination, women such as Laureana Wright de Kleinhans, Jovita Idar, Hermila Galindo, Elena Arizmendi, and María Luisa Garza took on leadership roles within these newspapers, working as both contributors and editors. Especially in their positions as editors, these women not only accessed publication opportunities themselves, but they also created them for others, enabling their sister-rhetors to contribute to these presses.

Wright de Kleinhans helps to make an additional point about the part the press played in mexicana rhetorical production: these newspaperwomen *started* presses of their own that focused on women's concerns. Wright de Kleinhans acted as literary director of *Las Hijas del Anáhuac* (1887–89), a newspaper that, in January of 1888, changed its name to *Violetas del Anáhuac*. Similarly, Juana Belén Gutiérrez de Mendoza started *Vésper: Justicia y Libertad* in Guanajuato, Mexico; Andrea and Teresa Villarreal initiated their own feminist newspaper titled *La Mujer Moderna* in San Antonio, Texas; and Hermila Galindo instituted her identically named but distinct newspaper *La Mujer Moderna* out of Mexico City. Not surprisingly, newspapers that were founded by women and that centered attention on women's issues offered greater rhetorical opportunities for mexicana writers.

Second, we turn to the press and especially the Spanish-language press because it often published the speeches of mexicana rhetors on the (rare) occasion when these women could speak publicly. For example, included here is María Rentería's speech "Leona Vicario y Rafaela López." Rentería delivered this speech at a meeting of La Liga Femenil Mexicanista, a women's group based in Laredo, Texas. Her presentation was then published in the city's Spanish-language newspaper, *La Crónica* (The Chronicle), a newspaper owned and operated by Idar and her family. A similar situation occurred with Aurora Lucero-White Lea. Lucero-White Lea delivered her speech "Shall the Spanish Language Be Taught in the Schools of New Mexico" at the Interscholastic Oratorical Association on the campus of New Mexico Normal University (NMNU), now New Mexico Highlands University. With the goal of spreading her message, Spanish- and English-language newspapers across the state published (and translated) her speech in both Spanish and English (Kanellos et al. 136). Thus, presses often not only supported mexicana writers but also furthered the message of mexicana speakers by circulating their arguments to broader audiences.

Using newspapers as the basis of our archive for selection enabled us to identify a rich set of mexicana rhetors and rhetorics. In choosing texts for inclusion, we of course looked for contributions authored by women, but we were also open to articles signed with a feminine pseudonym and even anonymous pieces that forwarded women-centered concerns. As such, this selection process did at times limit our ability to offer robust biographical detail regarding the authors we chose to include. Newspaperwomen such as Juana Belén Gutiérrez de Mendoza, Hermila Galindo, and Leonor Villegas de Magnón have been well researched; thus, there is a good deal of secondary material we rely on to help readers understand these women, their rhetorical situations, and their arguments. However, for other rhetors included in this anthology, such as Catalina de Puig and Isidra T. de Cárdenas, we found little to no historical trace of them beyond their presence on the newspaper page. This issue becomes even more complex with contributors who used feminine pseudonyms, such as Paz and Ariana, as well as those who published anonymously. For these writers especially, our only option was to contextualize their words through the cues in their writings, the rhetorical situation they address, and the press that published their work. But even though the biographical information we have runs from plentiful to scarce, we are able to draw a number of overarching conclusions about the rhetors collected here. These women were literate, educated (formally or informally), and well read. They likely occupied middle- to upper-class status and had access to newspaper outlets and/or connections to editors. These women also pushed the boundaries of acceptable rhetorical action for mexicanas at the time.

Feminist scholars of rhetoric may question our decision to focus on elite or even what Barbara Biesecker might call "extraordinary" mexicanas, when the women we include in this anthology were not representative of the majority of mexicanas at this moment (145). Indeed, most Mexican women during this period did not have the "cultural capital to express themselves in writing" (Lomas, *Rebel* xiii); many were day laborers, caught in the hard grind of daily survival as field hands, factory workers, or sellers of goods.[15] We believe, however, that the recovery of the mexicana rhetors in this volume does something very important for feminist rhetorical history. It counters the dominant perception at the turn of the century—and one, we might argue, that often persists today—that mexicanas were uneducated, submissive, and silent. In stark contrast to this perception, the women in our collection were educated and outspoken, with many specifically arguing for women's rights at the local, national, transnational, and international level.

While we know or can at least assume that the rhetors in this volume likely shared similar class status and educational backgrounds, we do want to make

Introduction 9

clear the variety in their concerns, rhetorical strategies, genre enactments, and writing styles. A reading of this anthology reveals that the stances of these women range from stridently political to more conservative in their investments and arguments. The genres they adopt in their writings move too from long expository essays to short opinion pieces, and from poetry to biographic encomia of Mexican women past and present. The work of *Mestiza Rhetorics* is to show that even within the similar identity categories these women might occupy, their concerns, styles, and strategies were diverse and capacious.

LOCATION AND LANGUAGE

The map plots the various locations from which the mexicanas in this anthology wrote and published, and we hope it gives readers a deeper sense of how location plays into the writings collected here. However, while the map may not seem difficult to discern, there is an underlying complexity that bears explaining. The map identifies the sites where newspapers such as *La Crónica*, *Vésper: Justicia y Libertad*, and *El Heraldo de México* were located: in Laredo, Mexico City, and Los Angeles, respectively. The map, therefore, in some ways suggests stability in circulation, in topical concerns, in audience, and indeed in the writer's location. We want to trouble the sense of stability this map suggests, for the location and the reach of these presses were not contained, and neither in many ways was the mobility of the mexicana rhetor.

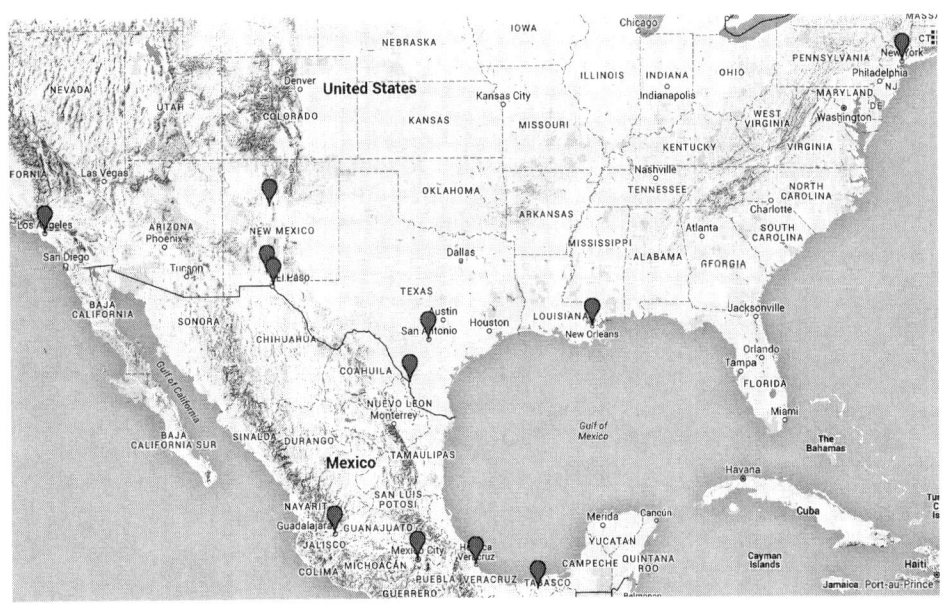

Mexicana rhetor and newspaper locations

First, as the writings in this collection make clear, even though a press might have been situated in a particular location, its concerns and those of its contributors focused not only on the issues of the paper's home city but also on national and international concerns. For instance, writing from Los Angeles, the anonymous author of "Mujeres mexicanas notables" ("Notable Mexican Women") celebrates indigenous women leaders such as Malinalxóchitl, while Mexico City writer Concepción Manresa de Pérez chronicles the accomplishments of newspaperwomen in Rome and women medical students in Bombay. Furthermore, almost all of the mexicanas writing from posts in the United States had their eyes fixed on the political strife in Mexico that generated and then fueled the Mexican Revolution. Thus, while the map may plot contributor and newspaper locations, it does not fully capture the range of topical and geographic interests of these mexicana writers.

Second, the map may also suggest that the newspapers under study had limited circulation, meaning that the readers of Veracruz, Mexico's *El Pueblo* were primarily inhabitants of that city. We want to unsettle this assumption as well. These newspapers often circulated well beyond their city's boundaries, with readers in Mexico reading U.S.-based papers and vice versa. A prime example of this fluidity is Paz's contribution to this volume. Here we see a Cuban expatriate living in New Orleans, Louisiana, lauding the writings of the newspaperwomen who contribute to Mexico City's *Violetas del Anáhuac*. Yet another indication of the wide circulation of these newspapers is the fact that many of them republished material from other presses far removed from their own physical locations. For instance, María Luisa Garza, writing under the pseudonym Loreley, was an editor and regular contributor to San Antonio's *La Época* (The Season). Her "Las mujeres que escriben" ("Women Who Write") is found within the pages of *La Época*, but as noted in her article, this piece was originally published in Guadalajara's *El Informador* (The Reporter). From these historical clues, we can deduce that although she was living in San Antonio, Garza was also reading (and publishing in) a newspaper coming out of Guadalajara.

The third point we want to make about locations in general and the map more particularly relates to this fact about Garza. The plots on the map indicate the sites of the newspapers to which mexicana rhetors contributed. Plotted too, however, are the places where rhetors indicated a piece was originally published (Guadalajara, in Garza's case) or written. For instance, while Paz's "Carta abierta" ("An Open Letter") is published in Mexico City's *Violetas del Anáhuac*, she notes she is writing from Louisiana, and readers will find this location on the map. Similarly, Catalina Zapata de Puig also contributes to *Violetas*, but a note in her article indicates she is writing from Tabasco, Mexico, so our map recognizes this location. These mappings only begin to indicate the multiple locations of these rhetors and their national and transnational mobility. Mexicanas such as Elena Arizmendi Mejía and Leonor Villegas de Magnón not only physically crossed and recrossed the border throughout the course of their lives, but they also, like Garza, read and published in U.S.- and Mexico-based presses; their interests and rhetorical interventions were not contained to a singular newspaper, city, or even nation.

The ultimate goal of providing the map and then challenging the stability it suggests is to make clear that this anthology is transnational in its selections, rhetorics, and topics. Our investment in the collected rhetors' locations and mobilities speaks directly to the arguments made by Jacqueline Jones Royster and Gesa E. Kirsch in *Feminist Rhetorical Practices: New Horizons for Rhetoric, Composition, and Literacy Studies.* Here, they celebrate scholarship that looks beyond the U.S. nation-state to explore international and transnational contexts,[16] and they invite more feminist researchers to pursue this scholarly agenda, encouraging them to investigate "within a more global context . . . the impact of patriarchy, secularism, colonialism, capitalism/global economic structures and systems, and the like" (125). *Mestiza Rhetorics* takes up this work through its transnational orientation and encourages readers to consider how location, mobility, and circulation inflect the writings of these women, as well as the ways place matters to their concerns.

Not surprisingly, the transnational quality of our collection underscores the fact that language is a significant priority for us and for many of the rhetors included here. As noted, the thirty-three collected writings were originally published in Spanish, and our prerogative is to highlight this fact. As we composed *Mestiza Rhetorics*, we strategically chose to make it bilingual and to present first the Spanish versions followed by their English translations. We offer a number of reasons for wanting our readers to encounter these writings in this way.

For the women writing in Mexico, Spanish was, of course, their primary and national language. As many scholars have made clear, language is not simply a vehicle for one's thoughts; rather, language itself holds special meaning and significance. It serves as a direct connection to a culture and perception of a people. Anzaldúa writes, for example, "ethnic identity is twin skin to linguistic identity—I am my language" (81). Thus, we present the original Spanish as a means of encouraging readers to explore the connections between language and identity and to consider how language choices informed the ways these women saw their worlds. For women writing on the U.S. side of the border, this claim regarding the significance of language gains a different nuance.

Following the 1848 Treaty of Guadalupe Hidalgo, the U.S.-Mexico border "literally migrated" over the regions in which many of these women came to live and write (Zavella 77). Furthermore, the violence of the Mexican Revolution just sixty years later spurred over eight hundred thousand Mexican people to cross the border to find refuge. Now in U.S. territory, these Spanish-speaking people were at the mercy of fierce discrimination that was especially related to their language. English-only laws dominated the public sphere, and Americanization programs infiltrated public schools (Enoch, *Refiguring* 128–29). Rhetors included in this anthology, such as Jovita Idar and Aurora Lucero-White Lea, lived in this highly charged nationalistic atmosphere. Readers will find in their articles attempts to retain and invigorate their cultural ties to Mexico as well as a desire to fight for their cultural rights within the United States. Two important ways they leveraged these claims were through writing in Spanish and arguing for its continued use.

Our concerns regarding translation reach beyond that of order and presentation, however. We also want to comment here on the act of translation itself. In *Why Translation Matters*, Edith Grossman suggests that we might read in the translation of a text into English a conferring of superiority to the English language and that such acts have the potential to compound the dominance of English as the world's *lingua franca* (14). Translation, then, could be seen as an act of violence, as Lawrence Venuti might also suggest, on a text or a culture, making differently cultured or even marginalized voices speak in the language of power (or even in the language that dispossessed or oppressed them). While we want readers to keep this perspective on translation in mind, we propose a different understanding.

In taking up our work in *Mestiza Rhetorics*, we define translation as a feminist act and method that enables us to *listen* to those who have been silenced and ignored by virtue of linguistic power and dominance. Our definition builds on the work of scholars such as Claudia de Lima Costa and Sonia E. Álvarez, who argue that, seen from a feminist perspective, translation has the potential to open up lines of communication and enable interlocutors "to engage in productive dialogue and negotiations across multiple geopolitical and theoretical borders" (557). As a mode of communication and research, translation can be seen "as politically and theoretically indispensable to forging feminist, pro–social justice and antiracist, postcolonial, and anti-imperial political alliances and epistemologies" (557–58). In terms of *Mestiza Rhetorics*, we hope our translations allow readers to hear what has been muted for them so that they might ultimately take up the specific work of *rhetorical* listening. As Krista Ratcliffe writes, rhetorical listening signifies "a stance of openness that a person may choose to assume in relation to any person, text, or culture; its purpose is to cultivate conscious identifications in ways that promote productive communication, especially, but not solely cross-culturally" (25). Seen from this feminist perspective, translation has the potential to be a key component of cross-cultural exchange in which listener-readers can begin the work of opening up toward understanding cultures, sociopolitical perspectives, languages, gendered realities, and temporal moments different from their own. We therefore agree with Ratcliffe that scholars have "been slow to imagine how listening might inform our discipline," and we posit that translation might be one critical path toward developing more robust rhetorical listening practices (19).

Such listening practices are especially critical for scholars in rhetoric and composition at this moment. As discussed above, there is a great disciplinary desire to disturb the canonical history of rhetoric that more often than not records the elite, male, Western, enfranchised experience. Yet there is a critical barrier that often stands in the way of making this disturbance happen: language. Without deep investment in translation, scholars of rhetoric, especially those who are monolingual English speakers, will continue to ignore huge swaths of rhetorical history. In reflecting on mexicana history in particular, Clara Lomas writes that these women were never silent; rather, it is scholars' "linguistic biases" that "have relegated [histories of mexicanas] to oblivion" (*Rebel* xvii). In other words, scholars' inability to read Spanish and their resistance to value it as a viable language through which rhetors leverage their interventions are major reasons for the dearth of mexicana rhetorical scholarship in the United States. *Mestiza Rhetorics* works to redress this linguistic bias. By virtue of both its bilingual formation and its dedication to translation as a method of feminist historiographic recovery, *Mestiza Rhetorics* challenges what Bruce Horner and John Trimbur have called the "tacit unidirectional monolingualism" that lies at the heart of our field (595). Not alone in their critique, Horner and Trimbur's ideas are reflected by scholars such as Suresh Canagaraja, Vershawn Ashanti Young, Hui Wu, Damián Baca, Lisa Arnold, Lahcen Elyazghi Ezzaher, and many others. Building from their arguments, this anthology overtly troubles the assumed and automatic expectation of English as *the* primary language for intellectual exchange, and it makes the point that we now live—indeed, have always lived—in a multilingual world.

With this advocacy of multilingualism and translation in mind, we want to address the way we hope readers approach the translations within this volume. As readers make their way through these selections, they may find words and phrases that sound "odd" to them, that a sentence does not read "as it should" given twenty-first century linguistic expectations and familiarity with English. We ask, however, that readers meditate upon what may seem to be the "foreignness" of these translations, because it is an important part of the project of this book. To be sure, Joel Bollinger Pouwels and Neil J. Devereaux, the two scholars who translated the readings in this volume, went to great pains to offer accurate and faithful textual representations of the primary documents collected here. In their work, Pouwels and Devereaux scrutinized sentence structure, grammar, and word choice. Theirs was an especially difficult task, because many of the mexicana rhetors whose work they translated were well educated, and their writing style in Spanish is marked by complex phrasing, extended sentence structures, and deliberate ornateness—a style popular for the educated elite of the period. The goal for Pouwels and Devereaux was not, however, to translate so that these mexicanas' writings would "sound like" what a twenty-first century reader would expect to encounter. Rather, the aim was to retain, in part, the "foreignness" in the translations as a way to remind readers that these texts were not first written in English and that the original Spanish holds intellectual, contextual, and historical value.

Placing primacy on this goal, *Mestiza Rhetorics* follows what David Bellos calls "[a]n ethics of translation"—one that "restrain[s] translators from erasing all that is foreign about works translated from a foreign tongue" (31). *Mestiza Rhetorics* therefore acknowledges that some passages in this volume might inspire discomfort in some readers, and we point to Lima Costa and Alvarez to offer guidance on how readers might negotiate their affective responses. They write, translation "is a process of opening the self to the other"; it "always involves a process of displacement of the self. Therefore, in translation there is a moral obligation to uproot ourselves, to be, even temporarily, homeless so that the other can dwell, albeit provisionally, in our home" (557). In agreement with such statements, we pronounce the point in this anthology that the act of translation is *not* an exact science; there is disturbance to and negotiation with a text when it is translated, and readers should be reminded of this linguistic, intellectual, and rhetorical complexity (and dwell within it) as they engage with the readings found here.[17]

We make these claims about the bilingual nature of *Mestiza Rhetorics*, rhetorical listening, and translation as a feminist act with one major caveat. The points we have made rest on the assumption that readers of our text are primarily English speakers. Of course, we know (and hope) this is not the case. Because we want to foreground multilingualism and purposefully reach out to readers fluent in or even familiar with Spanish, we present both the original Spanish and the translated English as an invitation to those for whom Spanish is their primary language (or one of them). We invite these readers to meditate on our translations, knowing, of course, that translation is subjective and, as noted, inexact. These readers in particular might translate some passages differently, offering ideas regarding other possibilities for translation as well as alternate meanings and messages. We hope they do. Especially for these readers, *Mestiza Rhetorics* aims to be a point of identification for and invitation to the growing population of Latinx students, teachers, and researchers within rhetorical studies. While we imagine the content and recovered figures offer nodes of connection for all readers, we purposefully offer the readings in their original Spanish as yet another important research and reflective opportunity for those who are most familiar with this language and who see it as their own.

HISTORICAL CONTEXT

To introduce each rhetor in *Mestiza Rhetorics*, we offer a brief discussion of the rhetorical context surrounding her publication(s) and any available biographical details. In this section of our introduction, we offer a more general view of the historical moment this anthology engages. Given both space and genre constraints, however, we cannot go into great depth. We encourage readers to supplement our account of the U.S. context by consulting such texts as Josue David Cisneros's *The Border Crossed Us: Rhetorics of Borders, Citizenship, and Latina/o Identity*, James Cockcroft's *Latinos in the Struggle for Equal Education: The Hispanic Experience in the Americas*, Mario T. García's *Desert Immigrants: The Mexicans of El Paso, 1880–1920*, José Limón's "El Primer Congreso Mexicanista de 1911: A Precursor to Contemporary Chicanismo," Martha Menchaca's *Recovering History, Constructing Race: The Indian, Black, and White Roots of Mexican Americans*, and David Montejano's *Anglos and Mexicans in the Making of Texas, 1836–1986*. For scholarship that delves into the Mexican historical context and especially the Mexican Revolution, relevant texts include James D. Cockcroft's *Intellectual Precursors of the Mexican Revolution: 1900–1913*, John Mason Hart's *Revolutionary Mexico: The Coming and Process of the Mexican Revolution*, and Alan Knight's *The Mexican Revolution* (volumes 1 and 2).

Mestiza Rhetorics focuses attention on the time period from 1887 to 1922—an era marked by great social upheaval due to industrialization, migration, advances in transportation, the emergence (or resurgence) of activism for women's rights, educational opportunities and constraints, as well as war and revolution, all of which served as exigencies for the mexicana rhetors in this volume. In the early years of this period, Mexico experienced a time of shifting identity due to the expulsion of the French and their Emperor Maximilian, events that led to the Restored Republic in 1867. Under the presidency of the indigenous shepherd, Benito Juárez, Mexico recognized the indigenous population as a legitimate strength in Mexico. When Porfirio Díaz later took presidential office in 1876, Mexico emerged as an international player, and its citizens began to critically reflect on their identity as mestizos. The country profited from expanded agricultural and educational opportunities, the development of industry, and the cultivation of the arts.

The Mexican press served as a discursive space for intellectual engagement and artistic expression during this period. Independent newspapers such as *El Nacional: Periódico de Política, Literatura, Ciencias, Artes, Industria, Agricultura, Minería y Comercia* (The National: Newspaper of Politics, Literature, Sciences, Arts, Industry, Agriculture, Mining and Commerce) and *La República: Periódico Político y Literario* (The Republic: Political and Literary

Newspaper) initiated and sustained vigorous conversations that worked to define an emerging Mexican identity (Benavides and McAlester 57, 67). As indicated by their titles, these newspapers published material ranging from literature and commerce to philosophy and satire, offering readers a plethora of genres and topics to suit their varied interests. Important to note is that while illiteracy rates were quite high in Mexico in this period, much of the writing included in these newspapers was cast in a tone and structure that could easily have been read aloud to an interested audience. Thus, as readers or listeners, audiences engaged with the hundreds of large and small newspapers circulating in Mexico at this time.

This moment of relative peace would not last, however. The turn of the century saw growing discontent with Díaz, as many Mexican citizens began to experience the president as more of a dictator. Increasingly, Díaz gave European and U.S. investors purchasing rights to indigenous lands rich in natural resources such as silver and copper, bought the electoral process to favor his rulings, and ignored political corruption and abuses in the areas of labor and finance. Not surprisingly, the Mexican press emerged and came to serve as a rhetorical space for social and governmental critique. Independent newspapers such as Juan Sarabia's 1900 radical liberal club newspaper *Renacimiento* (Rebirth) and Flores Magón's *Regeneración* (Regeneration), also published in 1900, challenged the legitimacy of Díaz's presidency. Additionally, others such as *El Hijo de Ahuizote* (The Son of the Gadfly), *Excélsior* (Excelsior), *La Voz de Juárez* (The Voice of Juárez), *El Porvenir* (The Future), and *Diario del Hogar* (Home Daily) emerged during this period and spurred public debate (Cockcroft, *Intellectual* 102). Díaz's government did not take this criticism lightly. As Juana Belén Gutiérrez de Mendoza and Elisa Acuña y Rossetti write in "A los mexicanos" ("To the Mexicans") in this volume, Díaz and his political henchmen responded by persecuting journalists and activists who spoke their minds through independent journals. Díaz tried to silence them by confiscating their presses, throwing the intellectual leaders in jail, and even killing some. But revolutionaries fought back. They and their newspapers helped establish the movement that would eventually oust Díaz and thereby catalyze the Mexican Revolution in 1910. Civil war continued in Mexico for the next ten years, with approximately two million sacrificed in the conflict. During this time, Mexico underwent radical sociopolitical shifts, including one critically related to gender. Women took their place as participants in the Mexican Revolution as *soldaderas*, field nurses, cooks, political leaders, and newspaperwomen.

On the other side of the border, the region was at this time still feeling the effects of the Mexican American War (1845–48) and the Treaty of Guadalupe Hidalgo (1848). The Treaty especially affected newly minted Mexican

Americans on all levels. Due to the redrawing of the border, Mexican landowners found themselves living in Texas, New Mexico, Arizona, and California, and they were often forced to give up their properties to Anglo settlers, many times becoming peasant workers on what had once been their own land. Marginalized as citizens, Mexicans now within U.S. territory had few economic opportunities and weak political influence; the majority turned to labor in the fields and emerging factories to survive. The period leading up to and including the Mexican Revolution saw still more disturbances in the region. In border cities such as Laredo and El Paso, Texas, war was waging within ear- and eye-shot. Almost one million Mexican people fled to safety on U.S. soil. Among them were political activists and revolutionaries who sought political refuge and freedom to express their discontent. Many of these revolutionaries, such as Sara Estela Ramírez and Andrea Villarreal González, became deeply involved in the Spanish-language press on the U.S. side of the border.

Building on the work of Herminio Rios and Guadalupe Castillo, Carlos Cortés records that prior to 1940 there were 372 Spanish-language newspapers published in the Southwest, the region of the United States that includes Arizona, Texas, Colorado, New Mexico, and California (248). Investigating the varied function of these publications, scholars such as Cortés, Félix Gutiérrez, Doris Meyer, and América Rodríguez conclude that while some presses simply translated Anglo news for Spanish-speaking readers, others like *La Crónica* and *La Prensa* took up a more political and activist stance. These newspapers not only overtly assessed the Mexican government and Revolution but also protested Anglo discrimination in the region. As Kanellos explains, "Besides supplying basic news of the homeland and of the Hispanic world in general," Spanish-language newspapers "[took] the lead in the effort to preserve Hispanic language and cultural identity in the face of the threat of annihilation by Anglo-Saxon culture and the English language" ("Socio-Historic Study" 107). Meyer concurs, explaining that by assuming the "unofficial role of public forum and community bulletin board," revolutionary Spanish-language newspapers often became sites "where aggrieved citizens could speak out" (406).

Presses on both sides of the border also looked beyond their particular circumstances to the international conflict of World War I and sociopolitical issues such as suffrage and women's rights that were circulating throughout both countries. The latter two concerns are, not surprisingly, of great interest to this anthology and to the newspaperwomen studied here. Commenting on the situation for women during this period and setting the stage for readers' analysis of mexicana rhetorical interventions, we want to be clear about how difficult it is to draw distinct lines between the Mexican and U.S. contexts. As discussed previously, especially due to the Mexican Revolution, women such as Sara Estela Ramírez, María Luisa Garza, and Elena Arizmendi were crossing and recrossing the border, living and writing in both countries. Thus, these women were carrying their Mexican ideals and ideologies into newly designated U.S. territory, and they were engaging in both Anglo and Mexican attitudes toward and discussions about women. Their intersectional identity as Mexicans and as women was therefore in flux as they moved back and forth between two countries. Our brief contextual summary below, then, makes distinctions between the conditions for women in Mexico and the United States when possible, but we also want to emphasize the reality that attitudes and ideas about women's roles blurred into one another throughout the borderlands.

As documented by numerous scholars, nineteenth-century Mexican gendered ideology was marked by two pervasive concepts, *machismo* (extreme male dominance) and *hembrismo* (extreme female submission) (Macías 3). This ideology guided everyday life both implicitly through daily interactions and expectations and explicitly through such institutions as the legal system and the church. Implicitly, as Carmen Ramos-Escandón writes, the Mexican woman was expected not only to embrace "submission" and "self-denial" but also to "disconnect" herself from public concerns and find only "disinterest in the world of politics" (qtd. in Lomas, *Rebel* xxxiv). Explicitly, these ideals were instantiated through laws such as the Civil Code of 1884, which freed a single woman from her paternal home at the age of twenty-one but upon marriage stripped her of rights to enter into any kind of civil contract (Macías 13). In 1891, one Mexican writer commented on the ways asymmetrical power relations were perpetuated through the legal system, stating that Mexican law "sustains an almost incredible inequality between the conditions of the husband and the wife; restricts in an exaggerated and arbitrary manner those rights due women; and . . . erases and nullifies personality" (qtd. in Tovar 38).

Anglo assessments of Mexican gender roles and women in particular were negative indeed. In his 1896 essay "The Main Streets of This City," Stephen Crane writes of the "quality lacking" in the eyes of Mexican women that "cannot regard you with sudden intelligence, comprehension, sympathy" (67). Carleton Beals seconds this point in his 1921 *North American Review* essay, "The Mexican as He Is," observing that the Mexican woman "prides herself on her submissiveness and subjection" (139). And Ruth Allen adds dimension to these derogatory assessments by linking Mexican women's submissiveness to an apathy for the emerging feminist movement. She writes that for Mexican women, "the modern Woman movement and demands for economic independence have left her untouched. . . . The supremacy of the male is seldom disputed" (qtd. in Ruíz 14–15).

These ideologies and stereotypical assessments circulated during this period, and the writings of the women collected here reveal an engagement with them. Their often-resistant writings were catalyzed and bolstered by social, political, and educational changes for women that occurred during this period. The early years of Díaz's presidency brought great opportunity, and Mexican women capitalized on this advantageous moment. Due to the growth in technology and industry, Mexican women increasingly took jobs outside the home in textile and tobacco factories (Tuñon Pablos 75). Educational change also opened new doors for women. Schools such as the *Escuela Normal para Señoritas* (Young Women's Normal School) and the *Escuela Nacional Secundaria para Niñas* (National Secondary School for Girls) not only formally educated women but also trained them to be teachers (Tuñon Pablos 75). Once women accessed these opportunities, they pushed for more. Anna Macías notes in *Against All Odds: The Feminist Movement in Mexico to 1940*, "Between 1888 and 1904 the first women were accepted, however reluctantly, in the schools of medicine, law, and commerce in Mexico City, and by 1910 a number of females began to work in commercial establishments" (12).

The dominant expectation for women's education was that it would not jeopardize their traditional positions as wives, mothers, and now teachers, since as teachers, women were often seen as simply extending their maternal duties.[18] Justo Sierra, a Mexican congressperson and director of schools and curriculum in Mexico at the turn of the twentieth century, articulates this position, stating, "The educated woman will be truly one for the home.... You are called to form souls, to sustain the soul of your husband; for this reason, we educate you.... Niña querida, do not turn feminist in our midst" (qtd. in Vaughan 138–39). Sierra is clear on the purpose of women's education. Nevertheless, as indicated by the entries in this collection, for many women, education and its ends were very much open to question and interpretation. Newspaperwomen such as Laureana Wright de Kleinhans, María Luisa Garza, Elena Arizmendi, and Hermila Galindo define and initiate debates on what education for women should be and the relationship, if any, it should have to both politics and professions.

In addition to education, the Mexican Revolution also incited in mexicanas a political consciousness and an exigency for writing. Women such as Juana Belén Gutiérrez de Mendoza, Elisa Acuña y Rosette, Leonor Villegas de Magnón, and Sara Estela Ramírez became deeply involved in the resistance movement and particularly the *Partido Liberal Mexicano* (PLM/Mexican Liberal Party). This political party touted quasi-feminist ideals, with its leader Ricardo Magón inviting women to involve themselves in his cause through his 1910 "A la mujer" (To woman). Here, Magón urges the woman reader to become a *soldadera*—the woman who "fights beside her man and cares for his needs" (qtd. in Ruíz 111). Entries by Juana Belén Gutiérrez de Mendoza and Isidra T. de Cárdenas reveal the varied ways Mexican newspaperwomen worked to participate in the Revolution and shape their readers' thinking about it.

Finally, and crucially, many of the rhetors whose writings are collected here attuned themselves to and participated in the movement toward greater rights for women. Of course, the United States passed the nineteenth amendment in 1920, which granted women full citizenship—a right Mexican women would not enjoy at the municipal level until 1947 and nationally in 1953. Given the exigency of the moment, mexicanas were thinking through the issue of suffrage while also defining other concerns relating to women's rights. The entries in *Mestiza Rhetorics* reveal mexicana writers listening to the arguments of women leaders around the world and articulating their own positions within the evolving feminist agenda. On their own, in collaboration, or in the context of a women's group such as La Liga Femenil Mexicanista, these newspaperwomen were creative in the ways they engaged in the cause for women's rights.

ARCHIVES AND METHOD

To compose *Mestiza Rhetorics*, we first conducted archival research at the Benson Latin American Collection (University of Texas, Austin), the C. L. Sonnichsen Special Collections (University of Texas, El Paso), New Mexico Highlands University Special Collection (Las Vegas, New Mexico), the Universidad Nacional Autónoma de México (Mexico City), and the newspaper archive collection at the José Ignacio Gallegos Caballero Public Library (Durango, Mexico). We culled material from digital archives such as the Latin American Women Writers database at the University of Arizona, the Arte Público Hispanic Historical Collection, and America's Historical Newspapers: Hispanic American Newspapers, 1808–1980. We drew from the microfilm collections of *Las Hijas [Violetas] del Anáhuac, Vésper: Justicia y Libertad, La Mujer Moderna, La Crónica, New Mexico Normal University Bulletin,* and *El Hogar*. After creating an extensive bank of possible texts to include in *Mestiza Rhetorics*, we asked translator and expert in Spanish language and literature Dr. Joel Bollinger Pouwels to transcribe and translate potential entries. Once Pouwels completed her work, we initiated our selection process.[19]

As discussed above, we chose texts authored by women writers, writers who used feminine pseudonyms, and anonymous writers who overtly engaged with women's issues. We included writers using pseudonyms and anonymous contributors because we believed many mexicanas may have chosen either a pseudonym or anonymity as a way to protect themselves from critique. Beyond identifying rhetors for inclusion, we also chose texts that revealed both consistency and diversity in topic, with the goal of displaying for readers the depth and breadth of mexicana writers' concerns. Finally, we looked for pieces that struck us as rhetorically interesting or complex due to the choice of argument, deployment of rhetorical appeal, engagement with audience, creation or leveraging of exigency, and so forth. Ultimately, we hope the point is clear: there was not *one* mexicana position or project. Viewing the anthology as a whole, we believe it offers much for readers to consider as they take up our invitation and contribute to the thinking and research on *mestiza* rhetorics.

ORGANIZATION

In terms of an overarching organizational strategy for the book, our partial goal is to show conversational clusters and arrange the selections to reveal how rhetors wrote together in the same publications, in similar physical locations, or about the same topics. For example, we group together Jovita Idar, Leonor Villegas de Magnón, Sara Estela Ramírez, María Rentería, and the anonymous writers who recorded the work of La Liga Femenil Mexicanista because they all published their work in the Laredo-based publication *La Crónica*. We do so because we hope that by grouping these contributions together readers will be able to assess the diverse conversations of mexicana newspaper writers in that particular border city and press. Similarly, the writings of the contributors to *Las Hijas [Violetas] del Anáhuac*—Catalina Zapata de Puig, Concepción Manresa de Pérez, and Paz—follow the selections by the newspaper's editor Laureana Wright de Kleinhans, so that readers can gain a sense of this newspaper's investments and the range of discussions its contributors engaged in. The writings of Artemisa N. Sáenz Royo and María Luisa Garza are also grouped together because the two were not only publishing in San Antonio's *La Época* but also debating one another about women's roles and duties.

However, and by contrast, we decided not to use sections to designate connections or show distinctions among rhetors and their writings. That is, we did not want to separate those women contributing to Mexican presses from those contributing to U.S. presses or those writing about feminist issues from those writing about education or Mexican politics. We believed that if we did, readers might only see particular writers in conversation and therefore *not* speaking to others. Our goal is rather for readers to identify their own affinities between and among rhetors through topic, rhetorical strategy, writing style, or political imperative. And our hope is that these affinities become heuristics for further inquiry, research, and writing.

UNA ÚLTIMA PALABRA (A FINAL WORD)

As an anthology, *Mestiza Rhetorics* continues in the genre tradition established by texts such as Bizzell and Herzberg's *The Rhetorical Tradition: Readings from Classical Times to the Present*; Ritchie and Ronald's *Available Means: An Anthology of Women's Rhetoric*; Jane Donawerth's *Rhetorical Theory by Women before 1900*; Karlyn Kohrs Campbell's *Man Cannot Speak for Her: Key Texts of the Early Feminists*; and David Houck and David Dixon's *Women and the Civil Rights Movement.* As we close our introduction, we want to acknowledge and recognize the significance of one particular text and the impact it has had on this volume. Here we refer to Shirley Wilson Logan's *With Pen and Voice: A Critical Anthology of Nineteenth-Century African American Women.* Published in 1995, Logan's anthology introduced and indeed invited rhetoricians of all stripes, but especially feminist rhetoricians, to learn about the significance of African American women's rhetorics. We hope this volume has the same effect for mexicana rhetors. Echoing Logan, our goal is that this anthology help to turn the "muffled voices" of the rhetors collected here (and others yet to be discovered) to "full volume" (*With* xi). In the spirit of Logan's text, then, we ask our readers to accept our invitation, to read and reflect on these mexicanas' writings, and to participate in the work of building a rich and diverse *mestiza* rhetorical tradition. Logan concludes her introduction with one imperative sentence: "Listen." (xvi). We do the same. *Escuchen.*

Laureana Wright de Kleinhans

Laureana Wright de Kleinhans (1845–1896) was a leading thinker and writer on Mexican women's issues and, most importantly, one of the more prolific mexicana writers of the nineteenth century. She offered a consistent message across her writing, which was that women should receive an education; that they had the intellectual capacity to take up the key issues of the time relating to science, literature, politics, law, education, and historiography, and that they should have the opportunity to obtain meaningful work. Born in 1845 in Taxco, Mexico, Laureana Wright González was the daughter of a Mexican mother and an American father, both of whom occupied an elite status. She later married a German, Sebastián Kleinhans. Wright de Kleinhans had an extensive career as a public speaker, reciting her poetry at prestigious lyceums in Mexico City. She was accepted into the scientific society El Porvenir in 1869, was admitted into Liceo Hidalgo in 1873, and received an honorary membership to Liceo Mexicano in 1885 (Murguía de Aveleyra 314). Many of these lyceums were short-lived; however, they played an important part in contributing to a consistent literary and intellectual conversation during this period. In the 1870s and 1880s, Wright de Kleinhans contributed to the Mexican literary scene by publishing such popular poems as "Dios" (God) and "Huérfana" (Orphan) and collaborating with Spanish writer and editor Concepción Gimeno de Flaquer to publish *El Álbum de la Mujer: Ilustración Hispano-Americana* (Women's Album: Hispanic-American Illustration) (Alvarado 17).

Certainly Wright de Kleinhans was well known within Mexico for her literary accomplishments and her advocacy of women, but her notoriety also extended to the United States and beyond. The 14 August 1891 edition of *The Two Republics*, a daily cross-border newspaper published in Mexico City in English and distributed throughout the United States and London during 1867–1900, made note of Wright de Kleinhans' literary work:

Mrs. Laureana Wright de Kleinhans continues to contribute her interesting and stirring articles concerning women's estate to the Diario del Hogar. Mrs. Kleinhans is doing good work in teaching her countrywomen the possibilities which the future holds for them . . . by exciting their ambition to improve their present condition. THE TWO REPUBLICS has always maintained that the women of Mexico hold their destiny in their own hands. Mrs. Kleinhans seems to fully realize this fact and she is doing much to instigate them to act for themselves regardless of traditions and customs. (2)

Along with *The Two Republics,* Mexican presses such as *El Tiempo* (*The Times*) and *La Voz de México* (*The Voice of Mexico*) as well as a French-Mexican newspaper *Le Trait d'Union* (*The Treaty of the Union*) celebrated Wright de Kleinhans' successful writing career.

A primary mode through which Wright de Kleinhans established a name for herself was by directing the literary journal, *Las Hijas del Anáhuac* (Daughters of Anáhuac). In 1887, Wright de Kleinhans worked with Ignacio Pujol and others to establish *Las Hijas del Anáhuac* out of Mexico City, and for two years she took the post of literary director. In the journal's eighth issue, dated 22 January 1888, the staff announced a title change from *Las Hijas del Anáhuac* to *Violetas del Anáhuac* (Violets of Anáhuac), because another journal from 1873 also carried the same name of *Hijas.* Collected here is "Saludo y Prospecto" ("Greeting and Prospectus"). Kleinhans published this piece in the first issue of *Las Hijas del Anáhuac,* which outlines the objectives for the woman-focused journal. As this selection demonstrates, the goal of *Las Hijas* [*Violetas*] *del Anáhuac* was to provide a venue for mexicana writers to publish their poetry, essays, opinion pieces, short stories, and biographies. Women such as Catalina Zapata de Puig, Ignacia Padilla de Piña, Dolores Correa Zapata, Concepción Manresa de Pérez, María del Alba, Albertina Puig de Borberena, Concepción Peralta, and Esther Tapia de Castellanos took advantage of this opportunity (the writings of Zapata de Puig and Manresa de Pérez follow Wright de Kleinhans's work in this volume). It is important to note that in late nineteenth-century Mexico schools for girls and women were still scarce, with the wealthy often learning to read and write through private home tutors. Thus, Wright de Kleinhans's journal served as a critical public space where educated women could submit their work.

As "Saludo y Prospecto" also indicates, Wright de Kleinhans enabled *Las Hijas* [*Violetas*] *del Anáhuac* to enter into a larger conversation that set out to establish a Mexican nationalist identity. At the time this journal appeared in 1887, there was a cultural movement to locate and celebrate a mixed indigenous and European identity through what philosophers and writers called *mestizaje*. The Mexican elite defined *mestizaje* by combining new knowledge from the modern scientific disciplines, such as anthropology and sociology, with the work of Mexican literary and journalistic writers such as Ignacio Ramírez and Ignacio Manuel Altamirano. Wright de Kleinhans contributed to these efforts through her journal; its title alone reveals this investment. *Anáhuac* is the term for the indigenous, ancestral land Wright de Kleinhans and her colleagues inhabited, known today as Mexico City. The title's claim, then, was that the authors publishing within this venue were the *Hijas* of Anáhuac: these women writers were the daughters who saw this indigenous space as their fatherland.

When Wright de Kleinhans changed the title to *Violetas del Anáhuac*, the connection to the indigenous Mexico remained, but the term *violetas* added a new rhetorical twist. Scholar Elvira Hernández Carballido notes that in nineteenth-century Mexico, the color violet carried conflicted "overtones of abnegation and reification, of doubts and certainties of what feminism stood for" (17–18). Hernández Carballido goes on to state that the color violet represented questions regarding the social changes taking place in Mexico, but it also indicated a level of criticism and irreverence to the status quo from a protofeminist perspective. The title *Violetas del Anáhuac* thus connected the journal and its mexicana contributors to the ancient Aztec kingdom, but it also added a level of disturbance to women's role in society. It signified an identity in question and in flux.[1] The articles, essays, and poems in this journal reflect this conflicted stance regarding women's place in Mexican life. Contributions by Zapata de Puig and Manresa de Pérez make clear that women were often wrestling with their dedication to the idealized space of the home and yearning toward independence.

While Wright de Kleinhans was the literary director of *Las Hijas [Violetas] del Anáhuac* and the sponsor of many other women's literary efforts, she also wrote "La lectura" ("Reading"), a chapter from a larger piece, *Educación errónea de la mujer y medios practicos para correjirla* (The erroneous education of women and practical means of correction), which was printed in Mexico City under the auspices of *La Gaceta Popular* (The Popular Gazette) in 1892. This piece reveals how Wright de Kleinhans moved beyond her own newspaper to invigorate public conversations about women and education. As an extensive treatise on women's education that also offers societal critique, *Educación* in its entirety identifies the various levels of Mexican women's development, the highest of which are women's education and literacy. Wright de Kleinhans asserts that women should have the right to an education so they can teach their children to be effective Mexican citizens. Similar to her contemporary writers in *Las Hijas [Violetas] del Anáhuac,* Wright de Kleinhans argues for women's learning and educational advancement while still assuring readers that women will continue to attend to their traditional domestic duties. In "La lectura," Wright de Kleinhans asserts that motherhood is a reason for women's education and that it is through motherhood that women could claim their civic identity.

Wright de Kleinhans extended her thinking regarding women's rights when she published "La mujer artista y artesana" ("The Woman as Artist and Artisan") in *El Tiempo* (The Times), a Spanish-language newspaper based in Las Cruces, New Mexico. In this article, Wright de Kleinhans addresses issues of women's access to work and overtly handles questions of class by identifying and reflecting on the opportunities available to women of various class backgrounds. Here, Wright de Kleinhans specifically calls attention to the very real financial needs of mexicanas who provide for their families, as well as the intellectual and agential rewards of finding work that enables women to thrive. Given the argument Wright de Kleinhans makes, readers might place this essay in conversation with another piece collected in this volume: Idar's "Debemos trabajar" ("We Must Work"). In sum, the three pieces collected here signify the variety of outlets Wright de Kleinhans contributed to as well as her cross-border interests, with the final piece indicating how she moved from writing to readers in Mexico City to those in Las Cruces.

Saludo y prospecto

Las Hijas del Anáhuac
Ciudad de México, México
4 de diciembre de 1887

SALUDO.

Con el ramo de oliva entre las manos como muestra de la regeneración intelectual de la mujer, vivificadas con las puras enseñanzas de la antigüedad, se presenta hoy al público el modesto Periódico *Las Hijas del Anáhuac* y reverentemente dirige su cordial saludo á* todas la clases de la Sociedad, á la Prensa de todos los matices políticos, y á los Hombres del Poder y del Estado; trilogía poderosa que con sus magníficos arneses ha podido evolucionar victoriosamente en beneficio de la paz, el orden, y la cultura de la Patria mexicana.

PROSPECTO

A medida que avanza la civilización de los pueblos, va produciendo nuevos elementos de engrandecimiento que crean á su vez nuevas necesidades, las cuales es preciso cubrir, si no se quiere que tales elementos se pierdan ó por lo menos permanezcan estacionarios é inútiles, como permanece la perla en el fondo de los mares, si no va á arrancarla de su escondido lecho la mano laboriosa del buzo.

Entre las necesidades de este género que el adelanto ha hecho surgir del seno de nuestro pueblo, hay una de capital interés que deseamos de preferencia atender, y que consiste en la fundación de un periódico femenil destinado á sostener los intereses, los derechos y la prerrogativas sociales de nuestras compatriotas.

La mujer mexicana, adicta por naturaleza á todo lo bello y á todo lo grande, ha llegado en su mayor parte á un grado bastante elevado de ilustración, y necesita por lo mismo un campo donde pueda ensanchar sus conocimientos y darlos á luz haciéndolos extensivos á su sexo en general, á fin de que se levante á la altura de la sociedad en que vive y de la época que representa.

México, nuestra querida patria, marcha como todos los pueblos americanos á la vanguardia del adelanto intelectual y está llamado á ocupar el lugar que

---

*In terms of the late nineteenth- and early twentieth-century Spanish-language transcriptions, we have chosen to reflect the use of the accented *á* (as a preposition and personal "a"), *é* (meaning "and"), *ó* (meaning "or"), and *ú* (meaning "or") where they appear in the original texts. Accent rules in this time period differed from contemporary ones in which these accents are no longer used.

por su ilustración le corresponde en el proscenio de la cultura moderna; pero para ello es necesario que todos y cada uno de sus hijos contribuyamos, siquiera sea con nuestro pequeño grano de arena, al edificio de su futura grandeza.

Poseyendo la conciencia de este grato cuanto sagrado deber, hemos creído que la mejor manera de cumplirlo es mejorar en cuanto nos sea posible la condición actual de la mujer, dedicándole nuestros humildes trabajos, por corta que pueda ser su utilidad; estimulado su amor al arte y á la ciencia; afirmando sus principios morales y cultivando sus bellas dotes literarias; haciéndola tomar parte en el torneo de las letras; proporcionándole el espacio que necesita para explayar sus ideas; animándola para que emprenda la noble campaña del pensamiento contra la apatía, del estudio contra la ignorancia, del progreso contra el atraso, de cuyo choque tiene que desprenderse indefectiblemente la luz.

Esta es la misión que al dar publicada á este semanario nos hemos impuesto, y el objeto que nos proponemos es el de llenar en cuanto nos sea posible esta perentoria exigencia de nuestra cultura, esta apremiante necesidad de nuestro adelanto, poniendo á disposición del bello sexo mexicano en periódico escrito y editado especialmente para fomentar por cuantos medios estén á nuestro alcance, el amplio desarrollo de su instrucción.

Nuestras compatriotas poseen brillantes disposiciones naturales que, como los tesoros vírgenes del suelo en que se ha mecido su cuna, aún no han sido explotadas; nosotras queremos ser las *obreras* que descubramos los ricos filones de su inteligencia, las *trabajadoras de la mar* que pongamos á flote las bellas perla de su talento, y muy felices no conceptuaremos si para lograrlos nos bastan á falta de mejores elementos, nuestro acendrado amor patrio, nuestra buena voluntad y nuestro ardiente entusiasmo por la educación completa de la mujer.

Con tal propósito, no sólo ponemos á las órdenes de todas la escritoras de la República las columnas de este semanario, sino que excitamos á las jóvenes que comienzan á hacer sus primeros ensayos literarios, á que nos envíen sin temor alguno sus producciones, en la seguridad de que serán, si lo necesitan, minuciosamente corregidas antes de ver la luz pública.

Ojalá que nuestros trabajos alcancen el loable fin que nos proponemos, pues en él habremos realizado uno de nuestros más bellos ideales: la representación nacional de la mujer en la prensa, con el establecimiento de un periódico femenino mexicano, que tal vez algún día llegue á figurar como uno de los primeros rudimentos de nuestra literatura patria.

La Redacción.

Greeting and Prospectus

Las Hijas del Anáhuac
Mexico City, Mexico
4 December 1887

GREETINGS.

With the olive branch in its hands as a token of women's intellectual regeneration, vivified with the pure teachings of times past, the modest Newspaper *The Daughters of Anáhuac* introduces itself today to the public and reverently directs its cordial greeting to all classes of Society, to the Press of all political shadings, and to the Men of Power and to those of the State; a powerful trilogy that with its magnificent trappings has been able to evolve victoriously for the sake of peace, order, and culture of the Mexican homeland.

PROSPECTUS

As the civilization of the common people advances, it proceeds to produce new elements of enhancement that, at the same time, create new necessities, which must be satisfied, if one does not wish for such elements to be lost or at least remain stagnant and useless, like a pearl in the depths of the seas, if the diligent hand of the diver is not going to pull it from its hidden bed.

Among the necessities of this type that progress has caused to arise from the bosom of our people, there is one of crucial interest that we desire to attend to preferentially, and that consists of the establishment of a women's periodical destined to support the interests, rights and social prerogatives of our female compatriots.

The Mexican woman, drawn by nature to everything beautiful and everything great, has for the most part reached quite a high level of culture, and therefore she needs a forum where she can broaden her knowledge and bring it to fruition, by extending it to her sex in general, so that woman may be raised to the height of the society in which she lives and the time that she represents.

Mexico, our beloved homeland, marches like all the nations of the Americas in the intellectual vanguard and is called upon to occupy her rightful place on the stage of modern culture that corresponds to her level of enlightenment; but in order to do so, it is necessary for each and every one of us, her citizens, to contribute, even if only with our own grain of sand, to the monument of her future greatness.

Possessed with the awareness of this pleasant as well as sacred duty, we have always believed that the best way to accomplish it, as much as we possibly can, is to improve the woman's current condition by dedicating to her our humble labors, no matter how small their usefulness; by stimulating her love of art and science; by affirming her moral principles and cultivating her fine literary gifts; by enabling her to participate in the arena of letters; by affording her the space she needs to expand her ideas; by encouraging her to undertake the noble campaign of thought against apathy, of education against ignorance, of progress against backwardness, so that from that clash, unfailingly, the light of greatness may be released.

This is the mission that we have shouldered as we announce this weekly publication, and the purpose that we have set ourselves is to fill as far as we are able this peremptory requirement of our culture, this urgent necessity of our advancement, by putting at the service of the fair Mexican sex a journal written and published specially to encourage by whatever means are within our reach, the extensive development of her instruction.

Our women compatriots possess brilliant natural potential that, like the untouched treasure of the land that cradled them, has yet to be exploited; we women want to be the *laborers* who discover the rich veins of their intelligence, the *workers of the sea* who bring to the surface the beautiful pearls of their talent, and we will imagine ourselves to be very fortunate if these achievements can occur, lacking better implements, by using our pure love of country, our good will and our burning enthusiasm for womankind's complete education.

With this purpose, we not only put this weekly publication's columns at the disposal of all women writers in the Republic, but we also encourage young women who are beginning to make their first literary attempts to send their works to us without any fear, secure in the knowledge that, if needed, their writings will be carefully corrected before appearing in print for all to see.

We hope that our project will reach the praiseworthy goal that we have set for ourselves, since by accomplishing it we will have achieved one of our most beautiful ideals: the national representation of the woman in the press, with the establishment of a Mexican feminine periodical that will perhaps someday earn its place as one of the first rudiments of our national literature.

The Editorial Staff.

Capítulo xxi. La lectura

Del texto *Educación errónea de la mujer y medios prácticos para correjirla*

Edición de *La Gaceta Popular*
Ciudad de México, México
1892

En una sociedad como la nuestra, que comienza apenas á entrar en la vía de la paz, del adelanto y de la prosperidad, la lectura goza aún de muy poca aceptación. La costumbre común en los jefes de familia es impedir que los jóvenes, especialmente tratándose de la mujer, conozcan las obras científicas, filosóficas, positivistas, críticas ó impugnadoras de los principios establecidos desde siglos atrás y, por lo mismo, hondamente arraigados en todas las clases de nuestro pueblo. Éste no comprende todavía, en toda la extensión de su importancia, que el alimento del alma es tan necesario como el del cuerpo, si queremos vivir moralmente y formar una sociedad culta, y no un rebaño de ilotas privados de raciocinio y de pensamiento propio.

Para que cada sujeto pueda formar un criterio particular y exacto sobre las cuestiones de vital interés que en estos momentos discute el adelanto moderno, es preciso que conozca primero el origen, naturaleza é historia de lo hoy existente, y que escuche el pro y el contra de cada asunto de los que hoy se proponen al jurado de la razón para ser reformados, sancionados ó abolidos por el gran tribunal de la verdad, la justicia y el progreso.

La mayor parte de las personas provectas consideran la instrucción variada que proporciona la lectura, como una desmoralización y un peligro para la juventud. Yo creo, á este propósito, que lo único que puede ser nocivo es el mal sistema seguido en la instrucción, y que la lectura, tomada como estudio y juiciosamente escogida y apropiada á cada una de las edades y estados del individuo es no sólo benéfica, sino precisa é indispensable para formar el corazón y el alma de la humanidad, que desea elevarse al mayor nivel que le ha sido concedido por la Inteligencia Infinita, creador de la suya.

El método y el absolutismo en la lectura son los que constituyen la verdadera ilustración, pues es evidente que si ponemos en manos de un niño la química,

---

With permissions granted by Instituto de Investigaciones sobre la Universidad y la Educación under the auspices of Universidad Nacional Autónoma de México, we used the Spanish-language transcription of this article found in Lourdes Alvarado's book, *Educación y superación femenina en el siglo xix: dos ensayos de Laureana Wright* (Feminine education and improvement in the nineteenth century: Two essays by Laureana Wright).

ó cualquiera otra ciencia experimental, comenzará por no comprenderla ó hará un uso muy torpe de lo poco que pueda comprender. Si al llegar á la pubertad le dejamos empaparse en las aventuras de capa y espada de la Edad Media ó en las exageradas tragedias del romanticismo erótico, haremos de él un héroe de novela, un Quijote y tal vez un suicida, porque hay efectivamente un inminente peligro en desarrollar la fantasía antes de cimentar el buen juicio. Esto en cuanto á las lecturas recreativas, en cuanto á las instructivas, si dejamos al adulto apegarse sin réplica ni términos de comparación divergentes á un solo sistema ó teoría, en cualquier ramo que sea, haremos de él un exclusivista obsecado, un fanático intransigente que, estacionándose en los primeros peldaños de la sabiduría, se declarará infalible á los veinte años, rechazará todo lo que no conoce y negará todo lo que se halle fuera del límite de sus escasos conocimientos.

Mientras que, si consecuentes con las exigencias y aptitudes de cada edad, damos al niño la fábula inocente y divertida, únicamente para entretener su imaginación y despertar en él la afición á la lectura; al adolescente las ciencias exactas, inductivas, abstractas y filosóficas que le den a conocer generalmente y sin subterfugios el universo físico, vital, material, espiritual, moral e intelectual en que gira y se desarrolla la existencia de la especia humana, habremos pulido su inteligencia, robustecido su razón, afirmado sus tendencias y moralizado sus sentimientos, por medio de un sólido convencimiento lógico y racional.

Entonces, justamente para completar su instrucción, debemos dejarle leer todo lo que ha producido el ingenio, la fantasía, el lirismo, la locura y aún la perversidad humana, en la seguridad de que sabrá dar á cada nuevo conocimiento que adquiera el lugar que le corresponde, separando lo útil de lo inútil, lo verosímil de lo inverosímil. No pretenderá neciamente, cualquiera que sea su sexo y condición, traer á la vida práctica las quiméricas ilusiones del idealismo, que no deben salir jamás del santuario espiritual del pensamiento. Una vez establecida en ese corazón virgen y sincero la estabilidad de principios y la rectitud de ideas, lo malo servirá sólo á su vista para formar el fondo obscuro de lo bueno, la tenebrosa lobreguez de lo inicuo, de lo infame, de lo deforme, hará resaltar en su ánimo la radiante claridad de lo noble, de lo justo, de lo bello. Y cuando ese niño ó niña llegue á la edad viril, podrá ajustar en su alma la religión á la lógica y á la verdad comprobada, la ciencia á la modestia y la virtud á la indulgencia y á la caridad cristianas, porque someterá todas sus creencias, deberes y aspiraciones al juicioso discernimiento de una conciencia bien organizada.

A vosotras, mujeres mexicanas, en quienes admiro la bondad, la nobleza y la abnegación de nuestro sexo, á la vez que deploro que hayáis carecido hasta hoy de los elementos necesarios para elevaros á la altura intelectual de que sois capaces y que de derecho os corresponde; á vosotras, á quienes amo con toda la efusión que produce la igualdad de circunstancias y la comunidad de sentimientos; á vosotras, madres de la generación presente que en el fondo santo y laborioso del hogar doméstico sacrificáis á la familia vuestro reposo, vuestra salud y vuestra vida, y á vosotras, jóvenes estudiosas, que seréis madres de las generaciones del porvenir, dedico especialmente estas ligeras consideraciones para excitaros á que, despojándoos de la injustificada costumbre de ver la ciencia y la ilustración como derechos exclusivos del hombre, y la mayor parte de las veces como peligros inminentes de la desmoralización para ambos sexos, instruyáis vuestra mente y os convirtáis en mentoras de vuestros hijos.

A vosotras me dirijo para que, desechando pueriles temores que la rutina os ha impuesto, no privéis á esos seres adorados del saber, que es el don más precioso que les ha concedido la naturaleza. No pleguéis las alas de esas nacientes inteligencias que Dios ha creado libres para volar y recorrer todos los horizontes de su grandiosa creación. No los detengáis, dirigid únicamente su vuelo, como hace el ave con sus polluelos, para enseñarlos á cruzar el espacio y, una vez enseñado por vosotras el camino, no temáis que se extravíen.

Mas para que podáis ilustrar á vuestros hijos es preciso que adoptéis para vosotras mismas la instrucción general, que hasta hoy desgraciadamente os ha faltado. Esa instrucción está en los libros, que son la historia siempre viva del mundo, la recopilación de todos los actos de la humanidad. Aprended en ellos y seréis verdaderamente sabias y útiles á vuestras familias y á la sociedad, que espera de vosotras su regeneración y su perfeccionamiento, que no ha podido alcanzar porque le ha faltado vuestra cooperación.

¡Sacerdotizas de la humanidad!, comprended vuestra verdadera misión. Sin vosotras no hay progreso posible. De vosotras esperan los siglos venideros la religión perfecta, la moral irreprochable, la virtud infalible. Y vosotras se las daréis si estudiáis y profundizáis, aplicándolas á la ciencia y á la historia, estos tres capitales principios que sólo superficialmente conocéis, y que sólo podréis encontrar, como antes he dicho, en los libros, de los cuales voy á hablaros para terminar, como de la parte más importante de la humana sabiduría.

Chapter XXI. Reading

From *The Erroneous Education of Women
and Practical Means of Correction*

Published by the *Popular Gazette*
Mexico City, Mexico
1892

In a society like ours, which is just beginning to venture onto the path to peace, progress, and prosperity, reading still enjoys very little acceptance. The usual custom among heads of families is to prevent their young people, especially in the case of women, from becoming familiar with scientific, philosophical, positivist works, which criticize or impugn principles established centuries ago and, for the same reason, are deeply rooted in all the classes of our people. Our people still do not understand, to the full extent of its importance, that nourishment of the soul is just as necessary as that of the body, if we want to live morally and form a cultured society, and not a herd of helots[2] without powers of reason or thoughts of their own.

In order for each person to form individual and exact criteria about the issues of vital interest that in these moments are being discussed by the forces of modern progress, it is crucial that this person understand first the origin, nature, and history of what exists today, and that he or she hear the pros and cons of each issue, proposed to the jury of reason in order to be reformed, sanctioned, or abolished by the great tribunal of truth, justice, and progress.

The majority of people of advanced age consider the varied education provided by reading as a corruption and danger to the young. I believe, in this matter, that the only thing that can be harmful is the bad system followed in instruction, and that reading, taken as systematic study and judiciously chosen and appropriate to each age and status of the individual, is not only beneficial, but it is necessary and indispensable to form the heart and soul of humanity, which desires to lift itself to the highest level that has been granted by the Infinite Intelligence, creator of human intelligence.

The method and absoluteness in reading are those that constitute true education, since it is evident that if we put a text of chemistry or any other experimental science in the hands of a child, he will begin by not understanding it, or he will make clumsy use of the little he may be able to understand. If upon his reaching puberty we allow him to immerse himself in cape and sword adventures from the Middle Ages or in the exaggerated tragedies of erotic romanticism, we will make him into a hero of fiction, a Quixote, and perhaps a victim of suicide, because there is in reality an imminent danger in developing the capacity for fantasy before establishing the foundations of good judgment. This applies to recreational readings, whereas with respect to educational readings, if we allow an adult to commit himself unquestionably or without divergent terms of comparison to one single system or theory, whatever the branch of knowledge, we will make him into an obsessed exclusivist, a stubborn fanatic who, by remaining positioned on the first rungs of wisdom, will declare himself infallible at twenty years of age, will reject everything he has no knowledge of, and will deny everything that is outside the limits of his scanty knowledge.

Whereas, if consistent with the requirements and aptitudes of each age, we give the innocent and enjoyable fable to the child, solely to entertain his imagination and awaken in him a love of reading; to the adolescent, the exact, inductive, abstract, and philosophical sciences, which allow him to know generally and without subterfuge the physical universe—vital, material, spiritual, moral, and intellectual—where the existence of the human species unwinds and develops; we will have polished the adolescent's intelligence, strengthened his powers of reason, affirmed his tendencies, and moralized his feelings by means of solid, logical and rational convictions.

Then, to precisely complete his education, we should let him read everything that creativity has produced: fantasy, lyricism, insanity, and even human perversity, secure in the knowledge that he will know how to give each new piece of knowledge acquired its corresponding place, by separating the useful from the useless, the probable from the improbable. This person will not attempt foolishly, whatever that person's sex and status, to apply to the practical life the chimerical illusions of idealism, which must not ever leave the spiritual sanctuary of thought. Once the stability of principles and the rectitude of ideas have been established in this sincere and pure heart, that which is evil will only serve, in his sight, to form the dark background to that which is good; the shadowy gloom of wickedness, infamy, and deformity will enhance in his spirit the radiant clarity of all things noble, just, and beautiful. And when this boy or girl reaches the age of maturity, he will be able to balance in his soul religion with logic and demonstrable truth; science with modesty, virtue with indulgence and Christian charity, because they will submit all their beliefs, duties, and aspirations to the judicious discernment of a well-organized conscience.

To you, Mexican women, in whom I admire the goodness, nobility, and self-sacrifice of our sex, while at the same time I deplore the fact that even until the present day you have lacked the necessary elements to lift yourselves to the intellectual heights of which you are capable and which by rights belong to you; to you, whom I love with all the effusion that comes from the equality of circumstances and shared feelings; to you, mothers of the present generation who in the holy background immersed in the saintly and arduous labors of the home, sacrifice to your families your repose, your health, and your lives, and to you, studious young women, who will be the mothers of generations of the future, I especially dedicate these slight deliberations, in order to encourage you to, by shedding the unjustified custom of seeing science and education as exclusive rights of men, and the majority of times as imminent dangers of corruption for both sexes, educate your minds and become mentors for your children.

To you I address myself so that, by discarding childish fears which a routine has imposed on you, you will not deprive those adored beings of knowledge, which is the most precious gift that nature has bestowed upon them. Do not fold the wings of those budding intellects that God has created to be free to fly and travel through all the horizons of his grand creation. Do not detain them, only direct their flight, like the bird does with her chicks, to teach them to traverse space and, once having been taught the path by you, do not be afraid that they will lose their way.

But, so that you may be able to educate your children, it is vital that you yourselves embrace a general education, which up until the present unfortunately you have been lacking. That education is found in books, which are the ever-living history of the world, the compendium of all the acts of humanity. Learn in them and you will be truly wise and useful to your families and to society, which expects from you its regeneration and perfection, which it has not been able to achieve because it lacked your cooperation.

Priestesses of humanity!, understand your true mission. Without you there is no progress possible. From you the future centuries expect the perfect religion, irreproachable morality, infallible virtue. And you will provide all this for them if you study and deepen your knowledge, by applying them to science and history, those three major principles that you are only superficially acquainted with, and that you will only be able to find, as I have said before, in books, about which I am going to speak to you in closing, as the most important part of human wisdom.

La mujer artista y artesana

El Tiempo
Las Cruces, New Mexico
17 de diciembre de 1891

Partidaria como soy de que la mujer, cualquiera que sea la clase á que pertenezca y las esperanzas en que pueda basar su porvenir, tenga una profesión, arte ú oficio que la ayude á salvar las dificultades prácticas de la subsistencia al hallarse sola y careciendo de la protección del hombre, única seguridad con que ha contado hasta hoy en su común impotencia, grande es mi íntima alegría, al ver que, aunque en pequeña escala, algunas jóvenes comienzan á dar cabida en su mente al arte y á tomar en su mano utensilios de trabajos que por completo desconocían hace todavía pocos años.

Voy á permitirme unir en este artículo á la mujer que trabaja ya sea por gusto, ya por necesidad, ya trate de su particular recreo, ya de buscar el medio de cubrir las apremiantes exigencias de su pobreza; á la mujer que saliendo de la inutilidad de la rutina va entrando en la vía del adelanto práctico ó manufacturero; á la mujer artista y artesana, que según los medios en que vive va tratando de utilizar en general sus aptitudes en un campo más vasto y provechoso.

El trabajo, ley imprescindible y principal del universo, tiene que ser benéfico á todos, asi como la ociosidad tiene que perjudicar tanto la parte intelectual como la parte física del sér animado que por naturaleza propende á la actividad de alma y de cuerpo inherente á la vitalidad. La mujer que carece de las múltiples distracciones callejeras del hombre; la mujer que pasa la mayor parte de su vida encerrada en la casa y que ántes empleaba y entretenía su vida solitaria y ociosa en largas ó prolijas devociones, que hoy las costumbres modernas van eliminando cada día más, necesita ocupar en algo el tiempo perdido, si es rica, y aprovecharlo en beneficio propio, si es pobre.

En los salones de las clases acomodadas comienzan á aparecer la mujer curiosa que ejecuta verdaderas preciosidades en labores de manos; que confecciona caprichos á la moda, en que la inteligencia, el ingenio y el buen gusto entran por partes iguales con el estudio minucioso que estas obras demandan, á la dibujante que se permite ya delinear lo que bosqueja su imaginación á la pintora que retrata las formas que ántes apenas le era dado contemplar; á la filarmónica que halaga su oído con las melodías de los grandes maestros; á la copiadora de la naturaleza que fabrica flores artificiales que casi llegan á competir con aquellas que dá la primera, y á la inventora de adornos y frioleras que desarrollan la iniciativa y el estudio que hasta el presente se había creído incapaz el sexo femenino.

En las pobres mansiones de las clases populares, con las máquinas de coser, aunque paulatinamente, ha comenzado á penetrar el adelanto y con él el atrevimiento que presta valor á la mujer para acercarse á demandar trabajo y pan, allí donde antes sólo se permitía la entrada franca al hombre. Verdad es que en estos tristes hogares, fuera de la pequeña industria de la costura y de los legendarios y nacionales tejidos de rebozos, no hay todavía otras industrias que atraviesen los umbrales de aquellas puertas que apenas comienzan á abrirse para que entre la civilización y el trabajo productivo; en cambio, si él no llega, la mujer va á buscarlo á las fábricas, á las casas de modas y á alguno ú otro comercio, asociando sus tareas á las del hombre.

El progreso desciende de las clases superiores á las inferiores. Los más sabios tienen que ser maestros, y á la sombra de la mujer artista tiene que irse levantando, y se ha levantado en mayor número apremiada por la necesidad, la mujer artesana, la obrera, la trabajadora libre que antes no tenía más recurso que la domesticidad si era sola ó la mendicidad, si arrastraba tras sí una infeliz familia, lo cual es no solo frecuente sino general entre las clases del pueblo, donde como es natural, los deberes conyugales y paternales son mucho menos respetados y cumplidos que en las otras clases.

La mujer huérfana y viuda ó víctima y abandonada por el hombre, la mujer que tiene que trabajar para vivir y sostener su familia y que ha comenzado á tomar algunos de los oficios y empleos monopolizados por el sexo fuerte, hallará todavía otros muchos que la auxilien en su soledad, siempre que se haga el ánimo de ver en el marido, como es en realidad, un apoyo eventual, más efímero que durable, y con el cual no debe contar como infalible.

Es seguro que ante las anomalías de nuestras costumbres, se juzgaría ridículo que una mujer se colocase como conductora en un wagón de circuito; pero no se arroja este ridículo sobre el hombre que permanece sentado tras un buzón de correos recibiendo cartas, ó tras de un mostrador de sedería despachando botones y midiendo varas de listón.

En la lucha por la vida, cuando la mujer se halla al frente de una familia y tiene que cumplir, que es de demasiada frecuencia, los mismos cargos que el hombre, creo que tiene los mismos derechos y que debe apelar á los mismos arbitrios que él para proporcionarse la subsistencia por medio de todos los trabajos que se sienta capaz de desempeñar.

Si se alega en la mujer debilidad física para ciertos oficios; debieran cedérsela aquellos en que no se necesita de la fuerza varonil; mas como en materia de concesiones pocas son las voluntades bien dispuestas, la mujer se encuentra en la necesidad de tomar lo que sin justicia se la niega, de recobrar lo que sin derecho se le usurpa, y así afortunadamente va ejecutándolo ya, á medida que va comprendiendo lo que necesita, lo que puede y lo que debe solicitar.

El paso más osado que han dado en este sentido algunas mujeres mexicanas, que atreviéndose á romper con estúpidas preocupaciones sociales, y á desplegar el valor moral de que se hallan dotadas, han seguido el camino del progreso, buscando por sí mismas su bienestar, es el haber penetrado en las oficinas telegráficas y telefónicas, donde desde hace mucho tiempo las han precedido las mujeres europeas y norte americanas, que antes que nosotros se han elevado en la escala de la instrucción que apenas comenzamos á subir.

Como decía muy bien en su periódico hace pocos días el ilustrado escritor Mr. Clareg, muchos otros oficios de este género entre ellos la escritura ejecutada por máquina, debía seguir el sexo femenino, que hoy se acoge en su pobreza al único recurso de la costura, con que se oprime, se veja y se explota su miseria.

Los que nos interesamos por el adelanto y la facilidad relativa de la parte más sufriente de la especie humana, deseamos que nuestros compatriotas, comprendiendo su propio interés, y luchando con todo el valor de que son capaces contra la amenaza constante de la indigencia y la prostitución que asechan su timidez, avancen con paso firme por estos nuevos senderos de protección que se abren ante ellas.

El trabajo es el único salvador capaz de levantaros y de consolar vuestras amarguras, pobres de la tierra, que no habéis nacido dotadas con los ricos capitales de una herencia paterna ó que no habéis recibido gratuitamente los beneficios de la fortuna. Cruelmente han obrado con vosotras, sin comprender su delito, las pasadas generaciones que os apartaron del conocimiento de vuestras aptitudes privándoos de los medios de subsistencia propia de que gozan hasta los más pequeños animales de la creación! Pero estáis á tiempo de romper los últimos grillos de estas esclavitudes, con el esfuerzo de vuestra propia voluntad. Si en otro tiempo se os exigía solo el humillante trabajo de la servidumbre, hoy incita al regenerador de la libertad!

En este campo siempre vasto siempre fructífero, podréis mejorar vuestra condición y atenuar vuestras penas. El trabajo, como ántes os he dicho, tiene que ser benéfico para todos. Mientras la opulenta dama encuentra en él, haciéndose artista, solaz para su ánimo, recreo y pulimento para su inteligencia, vosotras encontraréis haciéndoos artesanas, todo ésto y algo más noble, más eminente, más sagrado: el pan, la honradez y la tranquilidad para vosotras y vuestros hijos.

The Woman Artist and Artisan

El Tiempo
Las Cruces, New Mexico
17 December 1891

As I am a supporter of the woman, whatever social class she belongs to and the hopes upon which she may base her future, whether she has a profession, an art or a skill to help her overcome the practical difficulties of subsistence when she finds herself alone and lacking the protection of a man, even now the only security she has been able to count on in her common powerlessness, my personal happiness is great upon seeing that, albeit on a small scale, some young women are beginning to open their minds to art and to take up the tools of jobs of which they knew absolutely nothing even a few years ago.

I am going to permit myself to combine in this article the woman who works either for pleasure or out of necessity, either as her particular recreation or to find the means to cover the urgent needs of her poverty with the woman who leaving behind the futility of a routine life embarks upon the path of progress, be it of a practical or manufacturing nature; the woman artist and artisan, who according to the environment in which she lives, generally speaking attempts to utilize her talents in a broader and more profitable field.

Work, an indispensable and basic law of the universe, must be beneficial to all, just as idleness is necessarily detrimental to both the intellectual and physical aspects of a living being who by nature tends toward activity of the soul and the body, inherent in vitality. The woman who lacks the multiple distractions in the outside world of the man; the woman who spends the majority of her life shut up in the house and who always used and entertained her solitary and idle life in long or excessively meticulous devotions, which today are being eliminated more and more by modern customs, needs to occupy her free time with something, if she is rich, and take advantage of the time for her own benefit, if she is poor.

In the salons of the well-to-do classes, one is starting to see the curious woman who crafts true treasures of handiwork; who creates fashionable frills in which intelligence, ingenuity, and good taste exist in equal parts with the meticulous preparation that these works demand, the sketch-artist who frees herself to delineate what her imagination envisions; the woman painter who portrays forms that she was once scarcely allowed to contemplate; the musician who pleases her sense of hearing with melodies by the great maestros; the emulator of nature who makes artificial flowers that can almost compete with the ones made by nature, and the inventor of adornments and baubles that develops initiative and education which until recently were considered to be beyond the capabilities of the feminine sex.

In the poor residences of the working classes, progress has begun to appear, albeit slowly, with sewing machines, and with progress comes the daring that lends courage to the woman to approach a business and demand work and bread, where before only men were permitted free entry. It is true that in these women's sad homes, besides the cottage industry of sewing and the legendary and nationally emblematic weaving of shawls, there are still no other industries that cross the thresholds of those doors that are just beginning to open up so that civilization and productive work may enter; on the other hand, if work does not arrive, the woman goes to the factories in search of it, to the fashion houses and to a few other businesses, pooling her tasks with those of the man.

Progress descends from the upper to the lower classes. The wisest ones have to be the teachers, and in the shadow of the woman artist there must arise, and there have arisen, the majority of them compelled by necessity: the woman artisan, the woman factory worker, the free woman worker who previously had no other recourse than domestic servitude if she was alone or begging, if encumbered by a miserable family, which is not only frequent but ubiquitous among the masses, where, as is natural, conjugal and paternal duties are much less respected and carried out than in the other classes.

The woman who is an orphan or widow or victim of and abandoned by a man, the woman who has to work in order to live and support her family and who has begun to occupy some of the trades and jobs monopolized by the strong sex, she will still find many others to help her in her solitude, as long as she is willing to see in her husband, as he is in reality, a temporary support, more ephemeral than long-lasting, and who cannot be counted on to be infallible.

It is certain that given the anomalies of our customs, it would be judged ridiculous for a woman to be employed as the driver of public transport; but no ridicule is heaped upon the man who sits behind a post-office letter drop receiving letters, or behind the counter of a fabric shop selling buttons and measuring yards of ribbon.

In the struggle of life, when the woman finds herself at the head of a family and has to carry out, which happens all too often, the same duties as the man, I believe that she has the same rights and she should appeal to the same resources as he does in order to provide her subsistence by means of all the jobs that she feels able to perform.

If it is alleged that the woman is too weak physically for certain positions, she should be given jobs that do not require masculine strength; however, because when it comes to concessions there are few who are well disposed to grant them, the woman finds it necessary to seize what has been denied to her, to recover what is unjustly usurped from her, and so fortunately she is accomplishing that already, to the extent that she understands what she needs, what she can and should demand.

The bravest step taken in this respect by some Mexican women, who by daring to break with silly social concerns and display the gifts of moral courage which they possess have followed the path of progress, in search of their well-being by themselves, is the step of entering the telegraph and telephone offices, where for a long time they have been preceded by European and North American women, who before us have ascended the scale of education, which we are barely starting to climb.

As the enlightened Mr. Clareg[3] said in his periodical a few days ago, the feminine sex should engage in many other such jobs including typewriting, but who in their poverty these days find refuge in their only recourse which is sewing, which oppresses and harms them, and exploits their misery.

Those of us who are interested in progress and the relative comfort of the most long-suffering segment of the human species, desire that our sister Mexicans, by understanding their self-interest, and by fighting with all the courage they can muster against the constant threat of indigence and prostitution which stalk their timidity, should advance with firm steps along these new paths of protection that open before them.

Work is the only salvation capable of lifting you up and consoling your grief, you poor of the earth, you who were not born endowed with the rich capital of a paternal inheritance, nor have you received fortune's benefits freely. Past generations have treated you cruelly; without understanding their crime, they separated you from the knowledge of your talents by depriving you of the means for your own subsistence, which even the smallest animals of creation enjoy! But now is the time to break the last chains of slavery with the strength of your own willpower. If in past times only the humiliating work of servitude was required of you, the present encourages you to reclaim your liberty!

In this scenario, always vast, always fruitful, you will be able to improve your condition and attenuate your sorrows. Work, as I told you before, has to be beneficial to all. While the opulent lady finds in work, by becoming an artist, solace for her soul, recreation and refinement for her intelligence, you will discover by becoming artisans all this and something more noble, more distinguished, more sacred: bread, honor, and tranquility for you and your children.

Catalina Zapata de Puig

While biographical information on Catalina Zapata de Puig is limited, we do have some clues regarding her life and the sociopolitical context she entered when she published her essay "La mujer de este siglo" ("The Woman of This Century") in Laurena Wright de Kleinhans's *Violetas del Anáhuac* (Violets of Anáhuac)[1] in 1888. Indeed, there are just a few traces of Zapata de Puig's public activity and literary contributions from the 1860s through the 1880s. In her home state of Yucatán, the newspaper *La Libertad* (Liberty) announced in 1878 that she helped to form women's societies and gave a public talk in a local home ("Nueva sociedad" 3). Zapata de Puig is also listed as a collaborator in two newspapers: one in 1869 in the literary newspaper *Flores y Espinas* (Flowers and Thorns), and another in 1882, *Album Recreativo* (Recreational Album), published out of Mérida, Yucatán.[2] This brief, four-page journal was dedicated to the emerging progressive morals of the time, "Paz, Union y Trabajo" (Peace, Unity, and Work) and was geared toward the youth of Yucatán. There is little else indicating how Zapata de Puig contributed to these presses, but we might surmise that her early activities may have encouraged her to submit her work to Wright de Kleinhans's *Violetas*.[3]

Violetas, the weekly journal under the editorial leadership of Laureana Wright de Kleinhans, also offers insight into Zapata de Puig's background and rhetorical significance. Most journals up to this time, such as *El Semanario de la Señoritas Mejicanas: Educación Científica, Moral y Literaria del Bello Sexo* (The Weekly for Young Mexican Ladies: Education, Science, Morality and Literature for the Fair Sex) (1840–42), edited by Isidro Rafael Gondra, and *La Ilustración: Semanario de las Señoritas* (The Enlightenment: The Weekly for Young Ladies) (1869), edited by José Mariano Mota, could be seen as a combination of etiquette manual and literary journal in that they offered women both advice regarding how to conduct themselves in society and examples of superior literature, poetry, and short stories (Pouwels 17–18).[4] However, as Joel

Pouwels notes, journals such as these were mostly written by men. As Mexico became a more globally progressive and industrialized country at the turn of the twentieth century, *Violetas* took a different course. This journal positioned mexicanas like Zapata de Puig not as *receivers* but *producers* of literary, scientific, and historical writing, and *Violetas* published their work on its pages.

As Wright de Kleinhans details in the 1888 "Saludo y prospecto" ("Greetings and Prospectus"), the journal's goal was to invite women writers to contribute to the pervasive nationalist discourse that was defining a unique Mexican identity. Like Concepción Manresa de Pérez (whose writing is included here) and many other contributors such as Dolores Puig de León, Elvira Lozano Vargas, Ignacia Padilla de Piña, Emilia Rimbló, Dolores Correa Zapata, and Lucía G. Herrera, Zapata de Puig answered this call. It is important to note the creative and discursive atmosphere Wright de Kleinhans tried to establish for mexicana writers like Zapata de Puig. As Wright de Kleinhans makes clear in "Saludo y prospecto," aspiring women writers should "send their works to us without any fear." Concerns regarding error should not dissuade them, for the editors will "carefully correc[t]" their work before it goes to print. Thus, the journal was a space for women to compose with freedom and imagination.

More details on Zapata de Puig's life can also be garnered by deducing the probable class status of the contributors and readership. *Violetas* was a journal published for the Mexican female educated elite; thus, by publishing in this venue, one was likely to be a member of this class. A probable member of this cohort, Zapata de Puig wrote and published at least twice in the women's literary magazine: "La mujer de este siglo" ("The Woman of This Century"), anthologized here, and "La infancia" (Childhood). In "La mujer de este siglo," Zapata de Puig addresses the dominant discourse of religious conservatism, which functioned for centuries to keep women subjugated as silent and invisible individuals of society. Representative of the position taken by many elite and middle-class women of her day, Zapata de Puig's argument is a careful one that creates a balance between being faithful to the societal boundaries set for women and arguing for women's greater educational opportunities. Zapata de Puig does, however, seem to prefer the latter when she asserts that women should have access to an education in science, which would likely place them in a position to question tradition and religion.

Another key characteristic of Zapata de Puig's writing, as well as that of many other women of her period, is its florid language. From the time that Spanish had supplanted the indigenous languages after the conquest of Mexico, its elite written form was baroque, complex, and linguistically intricate. Stylistically, paragraphs were often marked by long sentences and connected by endless dependent clauses. Very much influenced by European modes of discourse, this approach, upheld by the learned male elite, worked to keep those less educated, such as women and the indigenous class, from entering literary circles. To the contemporary reader, the English translation may seem overly ornate, but women contributors to *Violetas* knew that by invoking this stylistic tradition, they had a greater chance of inclusion in the literary elite. So while this journal may have been directed to and about women, a tertiary audience was the elite male reader who held sway in the literary community of the time.

This tertiary male audience was certainly paying attention to *Violetas*. At this time, a regular practice in prominent journals was to publish articles celebrating the establishment of a new press. Manuel M. Romero from *El Monitor del Pueblo* published such a letter of congratulations, welcoming into the Mexican literary fold *Las Hijas del Anáhuac*—the first title of the press before it was changed to *Violetas*. He writes, "Verlas pasar, son *Las Hijas del Anáhuac* que rompen las cadenas con que en un tiempo estuvo sujeta la intelligencia de la mujer; llaman cariñosamente á sus hermanas y las convidan á tomar parte en ese noble torneo de la inteligencia" (Watch them pass, they are *The Daughters of Anáhuac* that break the chains to which at one time was subject the intelligence of women; they lovingly call to their sisters and invite them to take part in the noble tournament of intelligence) (Romero 36).

Zapata de Puig was one of the "daughters" Romero celebrated. With her complex style, Zapata de Puig's writing demonstrated that mexicanas could indeed hold their own linguistically. In "La mujer de este siglo," she deploys the stylistic register of the period to argue for woman's access to education, asserting that her newfound knowledge will assist in fulfilling her mission in the home as the educational leader of the family. Indeed, Zapata de Puig's argument may seem conservative, yet it would not be for another twenty years, during the Mexican Revolution, when women would begin in great numbers to overtly challenge their societal roles. Finally, readers might notice that at the conclusion of "La mujer de este siglo," Zapata de Puig indicates that she is writing from San Juan de Bautista, Tabasco, a city located on the southeast edge of Mexico along the Gulf of Mexico. This location suggests the far-reaching influence of *Violetas*, as its circulation extended well beyond the center of Mexican culture, Mexico City.

La mujer de este siglo

Violetas del Anáhuac
Ciudad de México, México
26 de febrero de 1888

Grato nos es consignar en estas páginas en que militan tantas plumas esclarecidas, honra de nuestro sexo, que la mujer ha logrado ocupar en nuestros días, el lugar que le corresponde, como eterna compañera que ha sido, es y será de esa mitad que con el título de hombre la tuvo bajo su tutela tantos siglos, para dejarla sumida en las sombras de la ignorancia, al no creerla digna de obtener las dotes intelectuales, sólo reservados á éste en el palenque de las letras. Pues si bien es cierto que ella ha sido el ornato de sus salones y de sus leyendas, no había merecido, (con pocas excepciones) si no es en el siglo presente, conquistar el merecido homenaje de consideración, que el sexo fuerte debe tributar al débil, ni el cariñoso respeto que su tierna y sensible compañera necesita en el hogar de la familia, para llenar completamente su misión de agradar y consolar, obteniendo el derecho legal que le asiste en la participación común á todos, de la instrucción, y que hacen de la raza humana el luminar de la ciencia, el artífice constante del progreso universal, que sólo puede efectuarse y ser un hecho, cuando esté consolidada su existencia por la unión de los sexos, que marchando unísonos, conquisten los derechos innegables de la independencia individual, otorgada al adulto emancipado por la ley natural, que sólo puede ser restringida por la civil, para castigo del vicio.

La mujer colocada en el magisterio de su poder intelectual y moral, que es lo único que la nivela al hombre, debe gozar de las prerrogativas de éste, para ayudarle en la difícil tarea de modificar las costumbres, de imprimir en la prole, el sello de la virtud, del amor al trabajo, la castidad de ideas que debe revestir á la criatura con el ropaje esplendente de espiritualidad que la acerque á su Creador. Y sin el concurso de ella, vanos serían los esfuerzos de aquel, porque no le es dable deshacer las primeras impresiones que el niño recibe en el regazo maternal.

Por eso la mujer, obteniendo en nuestros días ese precioso talismán que la preserva de necias preocupaciones, es ya el auxiliar eficaz de nuestra civilización; y empuja al hombre á sus deberes, porque iniciada en los misterios de la ciencia y la filosofía, sabe que de ella depende el hilo conductor que ha de guiar á las nuevas generaciones por el sendero de lo justo, marcando al mundo una etapa gloriosa en la ascensión sublime que lo lleva al apoteosis de todo lo noble, bello y grande.

Ella misma, conocedora del lugar que le corresponde en el sagrado recinto del hogar, no distraerá sus horas en vulgares ocupaciones, y pensará gravemente en la parte que le corresponde de responsabilidad ante el Juez Supremo, de todos los actos de su vida; y acatadora por naturaleza de los preceptos cristianos, obrará conforme á ellos y sembrará el germen fecundante de la religión verdadera, en los tiernos corazones que por ley natural Dios ha puesto bajo la salvaguardia de nuestro sexo.

La mujer ilustrada, dejando de ser una pobre ilusa descarriada, procura restaurar el tiempo perdido y hará fructíferas las lecciones obtenidas en el aprendizaje de su degradación pasada, para levantarse digna y llevar en la diestra el anillo nupcial con que su potente compañero, la asocia á sus faenas, y pulcra, y hacendosa, y económica, procurará mantener brillante esa joya preciosa, adquirida por la homogeneidad de pensamientos que la han venido haciendo acreedora de ese consorcio de almas, que hasta hace poco, sólo existía en los personajes ideales de la literatura heróica.

La mujer instruida, se hace religiosa, porque haciéndose apta para comprender al Autor del Universo, admira sus obras, y aspira á engrandecer su espíritu y ganar esa corona inmarcesible, no entrevista aún por la ignorancia, que sólo ambiciona los efímeros premios que el oro y la grandeza, conceden en el mundo.

La mujer educada, es modelo de madres y de esposas, porque sabe que todo lo debe á la sociedad que la guarda en su seno, y procura solidificar esa unión dándole corazones leales, que enaltezcan su nombre y vivifiquen su memoria.

La mujer regenerada por la ciencia, hará de sus hermanas, émulas agradecidas, porque al pisar la alfombra de flores que ella tienda á sus pies, se sentirán también regeneradas, y ya no querrán pisar los lodazales del vicio que esta les enseñará á distinguir con el prisma abrillantado de la razón y la virtud.

La mujer instruida, encontrará en el estudio y la meditación felicidades inmensas, que sólo habrá conocido después de adquirir esa instrucción, que la separarán de los triviales pasatiempos en que se anega el descreimiento de una educación descuidada.

La mujer que ha aprendido á meditar, se reconoce á sí misma, comprende su misión y se vanagloria de saberla cumplir, haciéndose solidaria voluntariamente de los decretos Divinos que la colocan en el altar de la familia, como mentora de los suyos, y de quienes tiene el deber de hacerse amar y respetar.

La mujer que dedica sus horas al desarrollo de su inteligencia, va avanzando poco á poco por el recto sendero que no conoce veredas ni encrucijadas, y hará que los que la aman dirijan también sus pasos por ese recto sendero que los lleva á la contemplación de mundos siderales, que hacen soñar al hombre con todo lo bello y esplendente de la herencia futura de las almas.

La mujer instruida, en fin, es hermana del desvalido, porque siente en su corazón esa necesidad de amar que no se sacia nunca, y ama al pobre y al rico, al criminal y al justo, á los pequeños y á los grandes y á los instruidos y á los ignorantes, porque sabe que todos son hechura del Creador, y pide á éste, eleve al chico, perdone al malo, consuele al triste, ampare al desvalido y regenere al réprobo. La oración en sus labios se hace sublime emisión de peticiones santas, formuladas en el hálito de sus pensamientos acrisolados, y la dirige con la fe poderosa que tiene de ser escuchada por el Padre misericordioso y justo.

Por último, la mujer ilustrada, no desdice nunca sus atribuciones de mujer, y si alcanza los lauros del saber, no será para enorgullecer su corazón, sino para impregnarse en la aureola de santidad que rodea á todos los mártires del trabajo; porque si sus ocupaciones la sacan momentáneamente del centro humilde del hogar, será para enjugar las lágrimas de sus hermanos, sea cualquiera la profesión que adopte, porque sus costumbres sencillas y adecuadas á su sexo, no la alejarán demasiado del núcleo de amor en que viva, si no es para ser el apoyo de los seres que ama, cuando la suerte la condena á carecer de un protector natural, en la azaroso carrera de su vida. Porque la mujer verdaderamente ilustrada, no aspirará nunca á ser igual en todo al sexo masculino, sino se contentará con poder conservar su independencia en las críticas circunstancia que la rodeen, para no ser onerosa á los extraños que quizá la exigirían un cambio de favores, que hasta hoy la han obligado á inclinar la frente ruborosa y altiva, si su corazón es digno.

Por eso hoy, la mujer llena de fe en el porvenir, se siente fuerte y feliz, porque espera dejar atrás para siempre el ominoso yugo que la ataba al poste de la indolencia forzosa, que la detenía á una distancia inconmensurable de su natural compañero, poniendo entre ambos el muro inexpugnable del desacuerdo constante en las ideas, que son los que tienden el velo purificador sobre la cabeza de los que se arrodillan ante el altar del amor, para recibir la consagración del enlace espiritual, que perpetúa en la familia la herencia inmaculada que acumula constante el genio poderoso del saber.

Y el hombre, al levantar á la mujer á la altura que ha alcanzado en nuestros días, sólo obedece al mandato imperioso de la civilización progresista, que tiende á nivelar los sexos, para completar la escuela secundaria de los principios sociales que sólo pueden llenarse cuando este reciba de las manos de la mujer, la infancia impregnada ya con el bautizo del alma, que recibe en la pila sacrosanta del seno maternal, que lo prepara para ser ungido en el altar de la patria, que lo hará tributario de su bien procomunal, al sentarlo en la cátedra de los derechos del hombre, adquiridos solamente si este lleva en sí el germen incorruptible de la moral y la religión que obtuvo inconsciente en los besos y caricias de la que al sostener sus primeros pasos, inculca en su corazón los sentimientos purísimos que le harán amar la honradez y ser el apóstol consciente de la regeneración social que espera el mundo para llegar á las verdaderas instituciones, cuyos caracteres apenas empieza á descifrar en el alfabeto de las ciencias positivas que le indican el horóscopo en que se guardan los misteriosos destinos de la humanidad, que marcha á la solución de ellos en las alas prepotentes de sus propios esfuerzos.

San Juan Bautista Tabasco, [e]nero 29 de 1888.

The Woman of This Century

Violets of Anáhuac
Mexico City, Mexico
26 February 1888

We are pleased to put in writing in these pages in which politics are discussed by so many illustrious pens, honors of our sex, in which the woman of our times has been able to occupy her rightful place as eternal companion that she has been, is and will always be of that half who with the title of man had her under his tutelage for so many centuries, only to leave her immersed in the shadows of ignorance, because he did not believe her worthy of obtaining the intellectual gifts reserved only for him in the world of letters. Then, although it is true that she has been the ornament of his salons and of his myths, she had not deserved, (with few exceptions) until the current century, to conquer the considerable homage that she merits, that the strong sex should give in tribute to the weak one, nor the loving respect that his affectionate and sensitive companion needs in the family home, so that she may completely fulfill her mission of pleasing and consoling, by obtaining the legal right which aids her in the participation shared by all, to education, and which makes the human race the luminary of science, that constant artifice of universal progress, which only can come about and be a fact, when its existence is consolidated by the union of the sexes, who by marching in step, conquer the indisputable rights of individual independence granted to the emancipated adult by natural law, and which can be restricted only by civil law, in punishment for immoral practices.

The woman placed in the teaching of her intellectual and moral power, which is the only thing that brings her to the man's level, should enjoy the prerogatives of the man, to help him in the difficult task of modifying customs, of impressing on the offspring, the mark of virtue, the love of work, the purity of ideas that ought to envelop the infant in the shining vestments of spirituality which bring it close to its Creator. And without the assistance of the woman, the efforts of the man would be in vain, because it is not possible for him to undo the first impressions that the child receives in his mother's lap.

Therefore the woman, obtaining in our day that precious talisman that preserves her from silly distractions, is now the efficient auxiliary of our civilization; and she pushes the man toward his duties, because having been initiated in the mysteries of science and philosophy, she knows that this knowledge provides the conductive thread that will guide new generations along the path of that which is just, by marking a glorious step in the sublime ascension that will bring the world to the apotheosis of everything noble, beautiful, and grand.

The woman herself, knowledgeable of her rightful place in the sacred precinct of the home, will not waste her hours on unworthy tasks, and she will think seriously about her role of responsibility before the Supreme Judge, for all the acts of her life; and obedient by nature of Christian precepts, she will work in conformance with them and she will sow the fertile seeds of true religion, in the tender hearts that by natural law God has placed under the guardianship of our sex.

The enlightened woman, ceasing to be a poor wayward dreamer, tries to restore lost time and will make fruitful the lessons learned during the apprenticeship of her past degradation, to rise up worthy and wearing on her right hand the wedding ring with which her powerful companion makes her an associate in his tasks and tidy, and hardworking, and thrifty, she will try to maintain the shine on that precious jewel, acquired through the homogeneity of thoughts that have been making her a worthy partner in this fellowship of souls, which until recently, only existed in the idealized characters of heroic literature.

The enlightened woman becomes religious, because by making herself able to understand the Author of the Universe, she admires His works, and aspires to enhance her spirit and earn that everlasting crown, hitherto unseen because of her ignorance, which only sought to attain the ephemeral prizes that gold and great status bestow in the world.

The educated woman is a model for mothers and wives, because she knows that she owes everything to the society that holds her in its bosom, and she tries to solidify this union by giving faithful hearts to society, which may exalt her name and vitalize her memory.

The woman regenerated by science will make of her sisters, grateful emulators, because when they walk on the carpet of flowers that she spreads at their feet, they will also feel regenerated, and they will no longer desire to walk in the mud-fields of vice, which she will teach them to perceive through the shining prism of reason and virtue.

The educated woman will find immense happiness in study and meditation, which she will have known only after acquiring that instruction, which will separate her from the trivial pastimes in which the unbelief of a negligent education is inundated.

The woman who has learned to reflect recognizes herself, understands her mission, and boasts of knowing how to complete it, becoming a voluntary supporter of the Divine decrees that place her at the altar of the family, as a mentor of her own family members, and from whom she has the duty to make herself be loved and respected.

The woman who dedicates her time to developing her intelligence is advancing little by little along the straight path which does not know about side-paths or crossroads, and she will ensure that those who love her will also direct their steps to follow that straight path that will lead them to the contemplation of celestial worlds, which make men dream of everything beautiful and shining of the future inheritance of souls.

In short, the educated woman is a sister to the destitute, because she feels in her heart the insatiable necessity to love, which is never fully satisfied, and she loves both poor and rich, the criminal and the just, the small and the great and the educated and the ignorant, because she knows that everyone is a creation of the Creator, and she asks Him to elevate the little ones, to pardon the bad, to console the downcast, to protect the destitute, and to regenerate the reprobate. The prayer on her lips becomes a sublime emanation of holy petitions, formulated in the calm breeze of her morally pure thoughts, and she directs her prayer with such powerful faith that it must be heard by the merciful and just Father.

Finally, the enlightened woman never denies her womanly attributes, and if she obtains the laurels of knowledge, it will not be to make her heart swell with pride, but rather she will bask in the halo of saintliness that surrounds all the martyrs of work; because if her tasks remove her momentarily from the humble center of her home, it will be to dry the tears of her brothers and sisters, whatever the profession she may adopt, because her simple customs, appropriate for her sex, will not distance her too much from the nucleus of love in which she lives, if it is not to be the support of the ones she loves, when fortune condemns her to not have a natural protector, during the hazardous course of her life. Because the truly enlightened woman will never aspire to be totally equal to the masculine sex, but she will content herself with being able to preserve her independence in the critical circumstances that surround her, so that she not be burdensome to strangers who perhaps will demand an exchange of favors, which until the present have obliged her to incline her brow, haughty and blushing, if her heart is worthy.

For that reason today, the woman who is full of faith in the future, feels strong and happy, because she hopes to leave behind forever the ominous yoke that tied her to the post of forced indolence, that detained her at an incommensurable distance from her natural companion, by putting between them the impregnable wall of constant misunderstanding of ideas, which are the ones that spread a purifying veil over the heads of those who kneel before the altar of love to receive the consecration of their spiritual union, which in the family perpetuates the immaculate inheritance that constantly accumulates the powerful genius of knowledge.

And when the man raises the woman to the height she has reached in our days, he is only obeying the imperious command of progressive civilization, which tends to bring the sexes to the same level, so they can complete the second educational level of social principles that can only be fulfilled once the man has received from woman's hands, a childhood permeated with the baptism of the soul, which he receives in the sacred font of the maternal breast, which prepares him to be anointed on the altar of the nation, that will make him a contributor to the common well-being by seating him on the teaching chair of the rights of man, acquired only if the man holds within himself the incorruptible seeds of morality and religion that he obtained subconsciously with the kisses and caresses of the woman who supporting his first steps, inculcates in his heart the very pure sentiments that will make him love honor and be the conscious apostle of the social regeneration that the world awaits, so that the regeneration will reach the authentic institutions, whose features have only just begun to be deciphered in the alphabet of positivist science, which shows the horoscope in which the mysterious destinies of humanity are kept, and which marches toward resolution of them on the domineering wings of its own efforts.

San Juan Bautista, Tabasco, 29 January 1888

Concepción Manresa de Pérez

As with Catalina Zapata de Puig and other contributors to *Las Hijas del Anáhuac* (The Daughters of Anáhuac) there is little information regarding Concepción Manresa de Pérez's life or profession outside of her contributions to this journal.[1] Señora Manresa de Pérez was married and likely a well-educated member of the elite social class in Mexico, as was the probable situation for many women contributors to *Las Hijas*. In "Mujeres de nuestra época" ("Women of Our Era"), Manresa de Pérez celebrates the progress of women in Mexico and around the globe due to their access to education.[2] She writes that women can now take part in and benefit from a full and robust education in large part because the world has changed its perspective on what education will do to and for women. "Drowned forever," Manresa de Pérez writes, "is the foolish concern harbored by Men of the past that the educated woman was harmful to society, because her education made her lose her qualities of *affectionate mother* and *priestess of the home*." Manresa de Pérez then goes on to recount the funding dedicated to education around the world in places like England, Spain, Italy, and more specifically New York, highlighting the fact that "the women of this era enjoy such benefits" and are now able to "nourish their minds by means of study and observation."

Focusing next on the specific strides women have made, Manresa de Pérez lists women in Mexico and throughout the world who have leveraged their educations to make their mark as professionals, citing women doctors, dentists, writers, and newspaperwomen. All those she lists are signs of "hope" that women such as her readers should never see themselves as "helpless" or turn to vices like prostitution as a way to sustain a living. Rather the "sciences and blessed arts will afford [them their] daily bread." The powerful message Manresa de Pérez sends and the way she sends it say much about this moment for mexicanas in general as well as her particular role as a writer and a scholar.

First, it reveals the conflicted argument women of this period often felt compelled to make regarding women's education and women's new work opportunities. To be sure, women had to assert that gaining an education and entering a profession did not signal they were losing their feminine qualities: they could still enact the work of the "affectionate mother" and "priestess of the home." But this claim is, in some way, disturbed by the lists of women professionals Manresa de Pérez offers. These women are obviously departing in some way from domestic duty to work outside the home in nonmaternal capacities. As doctors and newspaper owners, the women she cites had to have revised their work as wives and mothers. Thus, while women such as Manresa de Pérez asserted the continuance of traditional women's roles, they also could not ignore that these roles were being remade in some ways when women also pursued new professions.

Second, this article also reveals Manresa de Pérez's own education and rhetorical savvy. In this article, she hinges her argument on displaying for her readers evidence of women's progress within Mexico and outside it by citing examples of professional women from Bombay, Rome, and Chicago. To write this article, then, required a great deal of research. For a woman in the late nineteenth century, Manresa de Pérez's research skills were finely tuned, and to possess such skill was significant, since illiteracy rates for Mexican women during this period were quite high. Finally, much like the writing of Zapata de Puig, Manresa de Pérez's work is marked by a florid linguistic style that signified the elite cultural status of the writer. By invoking this style, she made clear the depth of her literate knowledge and breadth of her writing skill.

Mujeres de nuestra época

Las Hijas del Anáhuac
Ciudad de México, México
4 de diciembre de 1887

*Escrito para "Las Hijas del Anáhuac" por la
Señora Concepción Manresa de Pérez*

Cuando vemos en el horizonte de la ignorancia disiparse las nieblas y descubrimos la perspectiva de nuestro porvenir: cuando el derecho democrático lo vemos impreso en el gran libro de la humanidad, y sus leyes amoldadas en el corazón de los pueblos latinos las vemos regir con estricta justicia para gloria y regocijo de la América de Colón; nuestro espíritu se enagena de goces infinitos al considerar que la *mujer material* que ayer vivía oscura y silenciosa al pie de la cuna de sus hijos, que no podía educar porque sólo servía para *nodriza*, ha despertado hoy para la vida del progreso inspirándose en la cultura moderna y en los ejemplos de la eterna Roma, que fué grande y poderosa un tiempo, porque sus matronas supieron amamantar ciudadanos para el Derecho.

Ahogada para siempre la estulta preocupación de los hombres de antaño, de que la mujer instruida era nociva á la sociedad, porque su instrucción le hacía perder su carácter de *madre cariñosa* y de *sacerdotisa del hogar*; los hombres de la moderna edad, más prácticos y más científicos, más justos y menos egoístas, despreciando los antiguos sistemas y las enmohecidas costumbres y derribando de un golpe esas fábulas sin moraleja, condujeron á la mujer al Templo de Minerva, y la mostraron el magnífico Santuario de las Ciencias y las Artes, como el sendero más corto para la paz y el bienestar de la gran familia Universal.

Y maravilla la enorme cifra, verdaderamente gigantesca, que dedican los pueblos más civilizados para el fomento de la Instrucción Pública y para dilatar las fronteras del saber humano, y vemos con infinita satisfacción que Francia eleva actualmente á 132 millones de francos el presupuesto de la instrucción, cuando en el reinado del primer imperio no pasaba de cuatro mil francos.

En Inglaterra, el presupuesto se acerca á 136 millones de francos y el ciudadano inglés cuesta al Estado, bajo el punto de vista de la instrucción, unos 4 francos por persona.

Italia gasta hoy 52 millones de francos entre el Estado, las provincias y los municipios, cuando hace 25 años no gastaba la tercera parte.

España consagra á este servicio cerca de 30 millones de francos, cifra que se elevará en la actual Legislatura, según ha ofrecido su Ministerio al contestar la briosa defensa del eminente jurisconsulto cubano D. Rafael María de Labra, en favor de la causa del progreso y del movimiento pedagógico contemporáneo.

Y por último, New York, patria de los grandes benefactores de la humanidad y de los más serios, solícitos y eficaces promovedores de la grandeza nacional, consigna su Estado solamente, (pues no conocemos con fijeza las enormes cantidades que los particulares han legado para robustecer la enseñanza,) la suma de 70 millones de francos para su población de 5 millones de habitantes, ó sean 14 francos por cada persona.

De tales beneficios disfrutamos las mujeres de esta época, libre de las rutinarias prescripciones del enfermizo tradicionalismo y ávidas, como los hombres modernos, de nutrir su cerebro por medio del estudio y de la observación.

Ya comienzan á producir sus frutos las simientes implantadas, y México, que marcha con paso firme por la senda progresiva de la civilización, merced al orden y á la paz de que disfruta, nos ofrece como evidente muestra de sus adelantos á nuestra querida redactora, la Srita. Matilde Montoya, que ha recibido últimamente el grado de Doctora en la Escuela de Medicina, después de sustentar un brillante examen.

También la Srita. Margarita Chorné recibió en México su título de Dentista; y la inolvidable Srita. Micaela Hernández, cuya biografía daremos á conocer en breve, después de haber ejercitado la noble carrera del Magisterio, fundó una imprenta en Querétaro para enseñar á sus discípulas el arte tipográfico. Y entre la numerosa pléyade de profesoras mexicanas que con magnífico éxito han sobresalido en sus exámenes, vemos con admiración y júbilo que un cuerpo más numeroso todavía de Sritas. están matriculadas en las Escuelas profesionales para adquirir carreras facultativas.

Ya, queridas lectoras mías, se disiparon las nieblas que oscurecían nuestro hado, y en la contienda febril del *saber* con la *ignorancia*, aparece el iris de la paz definitiva anunciando el triunfo del primero para término de nuestros dolores históricos y como signo de las grandes esperanzas.

No estamos desamparadas, no. Si la desgracia nos deja en la orfandad y vemos que la costura y las labores de la mujer, *hoy en manos de los hombres*, no nos ayudan á subsistir, no por eso cubriremos de cosméticos y artificios nuestra epidermis para lanzarnos al vicio y recoger el cáncer insaciable y corrosivo de sus consecuencias, sino por el contrario, las ciencias y las artes bienaventuradas nos ofrecerán el pan cuotidiano [cotidiano], sin que por eso olvidemos los deberes de la Religión y los purísimos de la familia.

Vamos á transcribir para estímulo de las que lo necesiten y para alborozo de las que sentimos el amor devotísimo por las letras, el cuadro de las mujeres de nuestra época que no han perdido el *carácter de madre* ni de *sacerdotisas del hogar*, y sin embargo, compiten con los hombres en el mundo, cumpliendo con la ley de Dios y los preceptos morales de que el trabajo no es una pena sino una condición de la virtud.

Helas aquí:

La Sra. Fanny Dickinson, de Chicago, es la primera Doctora que será admitida como miembro del Congreso Médico Internacional.—Su especialidad es enfermedades de los ojos.

Mlle. Talbotier, una joven francesa, ha pasado con éxito sus exámenes para obtener un diploma de la lengua árabe.

Mrs. Julia Wilson, de New Haven, colaboró con su padre el Dr. E. A. Andrews en la compilación de su Diccionario Latino, y después de la muerte de éste, ha revisado la obra.

Doce Señoras naturales de Bombay, están estudiando en el Colegio de Medicina de dicha ciudad, donde son admitidas las mujeres como candidatas para los mismos exámenes que los hombres. Dos Sras. Inglesas doctoras tienen una buena clientela en esta provincia.

Ha aparecido en Roma otro periódico editado por una Señora. Publicación quincenal que se titula Galatea y cuya editora es Clelia Ber-Tini-Allilj.

Mme. Vinitski y Mme. Rostopschin han llamado la atención en Rusia con sus novelas.

El contrato por cinco años para la limpieza de las calles de Buffalo, E. U. de A., ha sido concedido á la Sra. A. M. Holoway, por $447,000.

Mme. Dowan-Lalande ha recibido un premio de 1,500 fr. de la Academia Francesa, en reconocimiento del valor y celo que desplegó durante la epidemia del cólera de 1883 y 1884 en Egipto y más tarde en Tolon. Mme. Dorvan-Lalande recibió una medalla de oro en 1885.

La joven Higinia Massarini ha obtenido un título en matemáticas en la Real Universidad de Nápoles.

El número de Doctoras que practican la medicina en la ciudad de New York pasa de 80. Media docena de ellas tienen ya una clientela que les produce $10,000 anuales.

Mme. Louise Massart, muerta recientemente, fue en un tiempo la pianista más popular de París, y la profesora de Mlle. Clotilde Kleeberg y otras eminentes artistas. Nunca ejecutó fuera de París.

(Continuará).

Women of Our Era

Las Hijas del Anáhuac
Mexico City, Mexico
4 December 1887

Written for "Las Hijas del Anáhuac" by Mrs. Concepción Manresa de Pérez

When we see the mists dissipate on the horizon of ignorance and we discover the vistas of our future: when we see democratic law printed in the great book of humanity, and its laws formed in the heart of Latin peoples, we see them govern with strict Justice for the glory and delight of the America of Columbus; our spirits become ecstatic with infinite pleasures when pondering that the *material woman* who yesterday lived obscure and silent at the foot of her children's cradle, whom she could not educate because she was only useful as a *nursemaid*, has awakened today to the life of progress by being inspired in modern culture and by the examples of eternal Rome, which was great and powerful at one time, because its matrons suckled citizens at their breast for the Law.

Drowned forever is the foolish concern harbored by Men of the past that the educated woman was harmful to society, because her instruction made her lose her qualities of *affectionate mother* and *priestess of the home*; men of the modern age, being more practical and scientific, more just and less egotistical, by scorning the old systems and the moldy customs, by demolishing at one blow those fables lacking a moral, led the woman to the Temple of Minerva,[3] and they showed her the magnificent Sanctuary of the Sciences and Arts, as the shortest path to peace and well-being of the great Universal family.

And a marvel is the enormous number, truly gigantic, that the most civilized peoples dedicate to promoting Public Instruction and expanding the frontiers of human knowledge, and we observe with infinite satisfaction that France is currently raising its educational budget to 132 million francs, when during the reign of the First Empire it was not more than four thousand francs.

In England, the budget is approaching 136 million francs[4] and the English citizen costs the State, from the instructional perspective, some 4 francs per person.

Italy today spends 52 million francs among the State, provinces and municipalities, when 25 years ago it spent less than one-third of that amount.

Spain dedicates nearly 30 million francs to this service, a figure that will rise with the current Legislature, according to what was offered up by its Ministry when he answered the energetic defense by the eminent Cuban legal expert Don Rafael María de Labra, in favor of the cause of progress and the contemporary pedagogical movement.

And finally, New York, home of the great benefactors of humanity and among the most serious, solicitous and effective promoters of national greatness, their State alone assigns, (since we do not know for certain the enormous amounts that individuals have bequeathed to strengthen education) the sum total of 70 million francs for its population of 5 million inhabitants, or in other words, 14 francs for each person.

Women of this era enjoy such benefits, free of the routine prescriptions of a sickly traditionalism and eager, as are modern men, to nourish their minds by means of study and observation.

The seeds of education that have been implanted are already starting to produce fruit, and Mexico, which marches with a firm step along the progressive path of civilization, thanks to the order and peace that it enjoys, offers us as an obvious example of its progress our beloved editor, Miss Matilde Montoya, who has recently received the degree of Doctor from the School of Medicine, after achieving brilliant examination results.

Also in Mexico, Miss Margarita Chorné received her diploma as a Dentist; and the unforgettable Miss Micaela Hernández, whose biography we will make known shortly, after having practiced the noble profession of Teaching, founded a printing press in Queretaro to teach her female pupils the art of typography. And among the numerous pleiad of Mexican women teachers who have achieved outstanding examination scores, we observe with admiration and joy the fact that an even larger number of young women are enrolled in graduate schools with the goal of pursuing medical careers.

Now, my dear readers, the mists that obscured our destiny have now dissipated, and in the feverish battle of *knowledge* against *ignorance*, there appears a rainbow of definitive peace announcing the triumph of the former, for an end to our painful histories, and as a sign of great hope.

We are not helpless, not at all. If misfortune leaves us orphaned and we see that sewing and other women's work, *today controlled by men*, do not allow us to survive, even then we will not paint our faces and adorn ourselves to throw ourselves into vice and gather in the insatiable and corrosive cancer of its consequences, but on the contrary, the sciences and the blessed arts will afford us our daily bread, without for that reason forgetting the duties of Religion and our very holy family responsibilities.

We are going to record—for the encouragement of the women who need it and for the great pleasure of those of us who feel a truly devoted love for arts and letters—the distinguished group of women of our era who have not lost the *attributes of motherhood* or of *priestesses of the home*, and who, nevertheless, compete with men in the wider world, by observing the law of God and the moral precepts according to which work is not a punishment, but rather a state of virtue.

They are as follows:

Mrs. Fanny Dickinson, from Chicago, is the first woman Doctor to be admitted as a member of the International Medical Congress.—Her specialty is disorders of the eyes.

Miss Talbotier, a young French woman, has successfully passed her examinations to obtain a diploma in the Arabic language.

Mrs. Julia Wilson, from New Haven, collaborated with her father, Dr. E. A. Andrews, on the compilation of his Latin Dictionary, and after his death, she has revised the volume.

Twelve ladies, natives of Bombay, are studying at the School of Medicine of that city, where women have been admitted as candidates with the same examinations as men. Two English lady doctors have a good clientele in this province.

In Rome, there has appeared another journal edited by a woman: a biweekly publication titled *Galatea*, whose editor is Clelia Ber-Tini-Allilj.

Mrs. Vinitski and Mrs. Rostopschin have attracted attention in Russia with their novels.

The contract for five years of street cleaning in Buffalo, in the U.S.A., has been awarded to Mrs. A. M. Holoway, for $447,000.

Mrs. Dowan-Lalande has received a prize of 1500 francs from the French Academy, in recognition for her bravery and perseverance during the cholera epidemic of 1883 and 1884 in Egypt and later in Tolon. Mrs. Dorvan-Laland received a gold medal in 1885.

The young lady Higinia Massarini earned a degree in mathematics at the Royal University of Naples.

The number of women Doctors who practice medicine in the city of New York exceeds 80. Half a dozen of them have a practice that produces $10,000 a year.

Mrs. Louise Massart, recently deceased, was at one time the most popular pianist in Paris, and was the teacher of Miss Clotilde Kleeberg and other eminent women artists. Miss Massart never performed outside Paris.

(To be continued).

Paz

In this contribution, Paz, a Cuban woman writer and teacher living in New Orleans, Louisiana, publishes in *Violetas del Anáhuac* an open letter directed to the journal's mexicana contributors—women such as Laureana Wright de Kleinhans, Catalina Zapata de Puig, and Concepción Manresa de Pérez.[1] While it is true this writer does not identify as mexicana like the other contributors to this volume, Paz's letter to *Violetas* reveals much about the transnational female readership of this press and the excitement and respect that the *Violetas* (previously *Hijas*) writers had generated.

The writer's choice of pseudonym is significant, as it offers an immediate clue to the overarching project of the open letter. The word *paz* translates to "peace," and by choosing this pseudonym, the writer foregrounds her effort to reach across the border in a spirit of good will to celebrate the journal's writers and the significance of their women-centered Spanish-language press. Through her letter, Paz works to create cross-border solidarity among women writers who are attempting to contribute to literary culture. She reinforces this effort by deploying the Spanish *vosotras* throughout her letter, a feminine plural form of *tú* and a familiar term for the word "you." Though this word was more prevalent in Spain and was not a common linguistic convention in Mexico or the rest of Latin America, writers and speakers such as Paz who invoked the informal *vosotras* used it to create a level of mutual respect or closeness with the group she addressed. Finally, Paz deploys yet another strategy to create this sense of connection and solidarity when she addresses her sister-writers as descendents of Guatimozín, another name for Cuauhtémoc, the last Aztec Emperor of Tenochtitlán (1520–21). By identifying them in this way, Paz makes clear her understanding of the goal of *Violetas* and the crafted identity of its contributors, who saw themselves as the indigenous daughters of Anáhuac, the ancient Aztec city that later became Mexico City.

The letter itself offers additional clues to Paz's life situation: it reveals that the writer emigrated from Cuba and settled in the United States to work as a teacher. She may have fled Cuba, which was still under Spanish rule, and by doing so, escaped the various slave uprisings that took place in the 1880s. While we do not know how or why she came to the United States, we do know that she was an educated woman and likely part of a privileged class. As her letter also indicates, Paz was an avid reader and had been studying the writings of Mexican women for twenty years. She tells the readers of and contributors to *Violetas* that she values the "tender and soft poems written by each one of [them], and published with so much pride in the periodicals of [their] cities." Paz goes on to assert that the contributors' prose and poetry are equal to that of women in the United States, stating that the Mexican women's writing and ideas are "undoubtedly great par excellence."

With this statement regarding Mexican women's literary abilities, Paz creates what twenty-first-century readers might read as a transnational intellectual sisterhood. Paz's letter further promotes this kind of exchange among women from different countries when she extols the women readers and writers of *Violetas* for their literary efforts and encourages them to continue the mission of writing and publishing their work. The fact that *Violetas del Anáhuac* published the letter reveals that Paz was not alone in her interest in making this cross-cultural and transnational connection. Wright de Kleinhans and her colleagues were eager to reciprocate, for the press published Paz's letter and thereby amplified and circulated the message this writer was advocating. Paz's letter, then, speaks to the intertextual, transcultural, and transnational exchange of women's ideas during this period.

Carta abierta a las damas de *Las Violetas del Anáhuac*

Violetas del Anáhuac
Ciudad de México, México
11 de marzo de 1888

Una distinguida suscritora residente en Nueva Orleans, nos favorece con el siguiente artículo.

Ante esas vehementes demostraciones de cariño nos inclinamos, y como hermana nuestra, que así consideramos á todas las hijas de la América de Colón, le devolvemos su cariñoso saludo y le ofrecemos las columnas de este insignificante semanario para que las honre con sus producciones.

Á LAS VIOLETAS DEL ANÁHUAC

¡Nobles y dignas Hijas del Anáhuac! ¡Amables descendientes de Guatimozín! Excusadme todas si en un momento de entusiasmo me tomo la libertad de dirigirme á vosotras llamándoos amigas mías, hermanas mías!

Excusadme, si no habiendo visto la luz en esa culta parte de la América, en esa tierra clásica de las grandes mujeres y de las elevadas inteligencias que se llama México, se atreve á daros tan dulces nombres una extranjera.

Con qué derecho, podéis decir vosotras, con qué derecho nos apellida hermanas una desconocida? [¿]Por ventura sabemos nosotras quién es Paz? [¿]Por ventura la vimos jamás ni sabemos en qué parte del globo está su cuna?

Pero, si es cierto que vosotras ignoráis quién es esta Paz que os habla, si es cierto que no sabéis cuál fue la patria que la vió nacer; si es verdad que nunca la visteis y que no la conocéis, ella, Paz, os conoce á todas; sí, á todas vosotras, bellas é ilustradas mexicanas. Yo os conozco porque he leído por espacio de veinte años las lindas producciones que han trazado vuestras bien cortadas plumas. Yo me he deleitado en las tiernas y suaves poesías de cada una de vosotras, que en los periódicos de esas ciudades han sido publicadas con tanto orgullo. Yo he saboreado las correspondencias epistolares, los lindos artículos de vuestros Diarios, las preciosas descripciones de vuestras fiestas, las elevadas concepciones que en prosa ó verso han dado al público los nombres de cada una de vosotras. Sí, yo os conozco, y al conoceros os admiro, y al admiraros os amo y os llamo amigas mías, hermanas mías.

Hace años, muchos años, que mi pluma no traza otras líneas que las que se forman para trasmitir á un escolar las cuestiones gramaticales de su idioma, ó las sentencias morales de un autor.

Mas, no creáis por un momento que, ni la aridez del profesorado, ni la ruda gramática, ni los embates de una existencia agitada y azarosa han embotado en mi alma el sentimiento de lo grande y lo sublime, de lo *bueno* y lo *bello*.

[¡]Cuántas veces rendido el cuerpo, fatigado el espíritu, agobiadas las fuerzas, he visto cambiar la faz de mi situación instantáneamente al recorrer las páginas de un papel cuyas dulces poesías firmadas por una mexicana, han hecho vibrar las fibras más sensibles de mi corazón!

[¡]Oh! entonces olvidando las amargas horas que acababan de pasar para mí, he gozado, he sentido, he vivido, he sido feliz. Entonces también, recordando á mi adorada patria, á mi Cuba querida, recordando mi pasada juventud, mis días de gloria y de placer, mis amadas compañeras que fueron el ornato de mi país como hoy vosotras lo sois del vuestro; entonces, he llorado; ¿por qué lloraba? Yo no lo sé.

Sumida en el silencio, mi voz no se levantaba ha largo tiempo; mas, he aquí que una mano amiga hace llegar hoy hasta mí el nuevo, lindo y bien redactado periódico que con el poético nombre de *Las Violetas del Anáhuac* encierra cual precioso joyero las firmas de tantas y tantas señoras y señoritas mexicanas. [¡]Oh! exclamé arrebatada de entusiasmo al leer y releer las preciosas composiciones y delicadas concepciones en que abunda, [¡]indudablemente la mujer mexicana es grande por excelencia!

[¡]Felices los pueblos que poseen un conjunto tan escogido de inteligencias, de instrucción y de talento! Sí, porque son ellas las que ilustran y enseñan á la juventud. Son ellas las que llevan en sí la simiente de la instrucción, para que, regándola á su paso, se arraigue y produzca los frutos del saber.

[¡]Nobles y dignas hijas del Anáhuac! Recibid mis más entusiastas felicitaciones. [¡]Desde la gran distancia que nos separa, me inclino ante cada una de vosotras y os saludo! . . .

Seguid el deber que os habéis impuesto. [¡]Seguid la senda que os habéis trazado; no desmayéis en vuestra obra porque vuestra misión es sublime, porque es grandiosa!

Miles y miles de abrojos encontraréis á vuestro paso, miles y miles de espinas punzarán vuestra existencia. [¿]Qué importa? Reíos de [é]stas, burlaos de aqu[é]llas, despreciadlas todas, y avanzad siempre, avanzad.

Nueva Orleans, [f]ebrero 15 de 1888.

An Open Letter to the Ladies of the *Violets of Anáhuac*

The Violets of Anáhuac
Mexico City, Mexico
11 March 1888

A distinguished subscriber and resident of New Orleans has favored us with the following article.

We bow before these passionate declarations of tenderness, and as a sister of ours, since that is how we consider all the daughters of the America of Columbus, we return her warm greeting and invite her to honor the columns of this insignificant weekly publication with her contributions.

TO THE VIOLETS OF ANÁHUAC

Noble and worthy Daughters of Anáhuac! Kind descendents of Guatimozín![2] I ask that you ladies all pardon me if in a moment of enthusiasm I take the liberty of addressing you as friends of mine, my neighbors!

Pardon me, not having been born in your cultured part of America, in that classical land of great women and high intellects called Mexico, if as a foreigner I dare to call you by such sweet names!

With what right, you may say, with what right does this stranger call us sisters? By any chance do we know who this Paz is? By any chance have we ever seen her or do we know in what part of the globe she was born?

But, although it is true that you do not know the identity of this Paz who is speaking to you, although it is true that you do not know what country saw her birth, although it is true that you never saw her and do not know her, Paz knows all of you; yes, all of you beautiful and erudite Mexican ladies. I know you because for about twenty years I have been reading the lovely products fashioned by your skilled pens. I have delighted in the tender and soft poems written by each one of you, and published with so much pride in the periodicals of your cities. I have savored the epistolary correspondence, the lovely articles in your daily papers, the wonderful descriptions of your parties, the elevated concepts, in prose or verse, that have made each of your names known to the public.

Yes, I know you, and because I know you I admire you, and because I admire you I love you and I call you friends and sisters of mine.

Many, many years have passed since my pen has written any lines other than advice to students about grammatical issues of their language, or about the moral maxims of an author.

However, do not believe for a moment that, either the sterility of teaching, or lowly grammar, or the upheavals of an agitated and risky life have dulled my soul to feelings of things great, sublime, *good*, and *beautiful*.

I cannot count the times that, my body exhausted, my spirit fatigued, my strength gone, I have seen the contours of my situation change instantaneously when I read the pages of a paper where sweet poetry signed by a Mexican lady has touched the most sensitive fibers of my heart.

Oh! Then forgetting the bitter hours that I had just experienced, I have enjoyed, felt, lived, I have been happy. Also then remembering my adored country, my beloved Cuba, remembering my past youth, my days of glory and pleasure, my beloved female companions who were the adornment of my native land as today you adorn your own land; then, I wept. Why did I weep? I do not know.

Immersed in silence, my voice has not been heard for a long time; but then a friendly hand sent me the new, beautiful and well-edited periodical with the poetic title *The Violets of Anáhuac*, which holds, like a precious jewel box, the signatures of so very many women, married and single. Oh! I exclaimed—carried away with enthusiasm as I read and reread the abundant and lovely compositions and exquisite ideas—The Mexican woman is undoubtedly great par excellence.

How happy are the peoples who possess such a select group of intellects, erudition and talent! Yes, because these women enlighten and teach the youth. It is they who carry the seeds of erudition, so that, scattering them as they go, the plants take root and produce the fruits of knowledge.

Noble and worthy daughters of Anáhuac! Receive my most enthusiastic congratulations. Across the great distance that separates us, I bow before each one of you and I greet you all! . . .

Follow the mission that you have taken upon yourselves. Follow the path that you have laid out; do not grow faint in your work because your mission is sublime, because it is magnificent!

You will encounter a great many prickly obstacles along the way, many thorns will torment your existence. What does it matter? Laugh the thorns away, make fun of the obstacles, and always keep advancing, ever onward.

New Orleans, 15 February 1888.

Juana Belén Gutiérrez de Mendoza and Elisa Acuña y Rossetti

At the turn of the twentieth century, militant and radical activists challenged the power of Mexican President Porfirio Díaz (1875–1910). Many of these activists were mexicana writers who claimed Díaz had turned his reign into a dictatorship and railed against his tyrannical work to bring Mexico into the industrial age. Two women who passionately engaged in this debate through radical, revolutionary rhetoric were Juana Belén Gutiérrez de Mendoza (1875–1942) and Elisa Acuña y Rossetti (1872–1946). They were among the first women to engage in this prerevolutionary political debate that hitherto had been mainly accessible only to men. Collected here is one collaboratively written piece by Gutiérrez de Mendoza and Acuña y Rossetti and two single-authored pieces by Gutiérrez de Mendoza. The two women worked together writing for *Vésper: Justicia y Libertad* (Vesper: Justice and Liberty). Whereas little can be found about Acuña y Rossetti's life, her collaborator was a well-known figure and a prolific writer who published her work consistently over her forty-year career.

JUANA BELÉN GUTIÉRREZ DE MENDOZA

Scholar Alicia Villaneda notes that before making her interventions in public discourse, Gutiérrez de Mendoza followed the cultural tradition of marrying young: at the age of seventeen, she married Cirilo Mendoza and moved to Sierra Mojada, Coahuila. There, Cirilo found a job as a miner in a mine known as "La Esmeralda," and Gutiérrez de Mendoza worked as a housekeeper (Villaneda 19). During these years, she gave birth to three children, Laura, Julia, and Santiago, witnessed and lived the degrading conditions that mining families often endured, and survived on the menial pay they earned (19). Cirilo died an early death, leaving his wife to support herself and her children by turning to journalism.

While Gutiérrez de Mendoza did attend school for a short time as a young woman, she sharpened her literacy skills largely through her own initiative as an autodidact. Mexican writer and historian Eduardo Arrieta Corral compares Gutiérrez de Mendoza's intellect and social acumen to that of Mexican writers Francisco Zarco, José Revueltas, and Sor Juana Inés de la Cruz. He comments that Gutiérrez de Mendoza

> was endowed with an early intelligence of natural intuition and artistic sensibility, and especially for this reason she was self-taught, she knew how to incorporate her education with her conflictive moment in history, emphasized in everything she learned through her indestructible civil courage, taking on the motto of don Melchor Ocampo: "I break, but I will not fold." (13)

Gutiérrez de Mendoza thus combined her education and intellect with her galvanizing experiences as a worker, a wife living in a poverty-stricken mining community, and a young widowed mother to forge her rhetorical future as an activist in the *Partido Liberal Mexicano* (PLM; Mexican Liberal Party) and as a journalist.

The first articles Gutiérrez de Mendoza wrote denounced the treatment of miners and were anonymously published in three early opposition Mexican newspapers, *Diario del Hogar* (Daily Home Journal), *Hijo de Ahuizote* (Son of the Gadfly), and *Chinaco*.[1] In 1897 authorities from the mines discovered Gutiérrez de Mendoza's connection to the antigovernment publications, and she was sent to prison in Minas Nuevas, Chihuahua (Mendieta Alatorre 63). While this was the first of many jail sentences she would endure throughout her life, this first experience solidified her resolve to speak out against Díaz's dictatorial regime. In 1900 she moved to Guanajuato, Mexico, to start the protest newspaper, *Vésper: Justicia y Libertad*. After publishing several articles leveled against the government and church, she was threatened with the seizure of her press and fled to Mexico City in January of 1901. While in Mexico City, she became more active and radical within the political scene and was appointed *primer vocal*, or first spokeswoman, for one of the prerevolutionary liberal clubs, Ponciano Arriaga (Mendieta Alatorre 64).[2] Historical accounts are unclear regarding Gutiérrez de Mendoza's time in Mexico City (1901–3), but this is likely the period when she met and began to collaborate with Elisa Acuña y Rossetti, an educator, writer, and supporter of the prerevolutionary movement.

ELISA ACUÑA Y ROSSETTI

Acuña y Rossetti was born in Mineral del Monte, Hidalgo, Mexico (1872–1946) and began her professional life as a teacher who worked against illiteracy through the Mexican Cultural Mission, Women's Council, and Pan-American League of Women. Like Gutiérrez de Mendoza, Acuña y Rossetti sympathized with the PLM and openly challenged Díaz's presidency. And like Gutiérrez de Mendoza, she was also imprisoned for her activism. With Gutiérrez de Mendoza, Acuña y Rossetti published in *Vésper: Justicia y Libertad*, and in so doing, she contributed to the growing national conversation regarding the oppressive government of Porfirio Díaz.

Newspapers such as *Vésper* and other weeklies or monthlies were key resources for public opinion at this moment. By 1888 there were 227 newspapers in Mexico, a number that rose to 385 publications in 1889 and then exploded in 1898 with a total of 531 papers (Garner 125). President Díaz was often unwilling to let these presses have the public voice they were angling for, so he shut them down, jailed many journalists, and had others killed. Given the extreme situation dedicated political leaders faced, their newspapers were often either short-lived or inconsistent in terms of publication schedules. However, as historian James Cockroft writes, "As fast as old opposition newspapers were closed down, new, more militant ones opened up" (*Intellectual* 102). The ephemeral nature of these presses garnered them the name *papeles volantes*, literally "flying papers." The life of *Vésper* could be seen as such. It would emerge and re-emerge over the course of almost forty years, being published in Guanajuato, Mexico City, and San Antonio.

AN OUTSPOKEN EDITORIAL TEAM

Gutiérrez de Mendoza and Acuña y Rossetti played critical parts in the survival of this newspaper and in the Mexican resistance movement writ large. In 1904, both women crossed the border to Laredo, Texas, joining political leaders and brothers Ricardo and Enrique Flores Magón and other revolutionaries like Sara Estela Ramírez and Camilo Arriaga. In Laredo, there was an ideological split between the more radical faction of the Magón brothers, who espoused anarchist views, and Arriaga, who at the time endorsed less radical political positions. When Arriaga left for San Antonio, Texas, Gutiérrez de Mendoza and Acuña y Rossetti followed.

The collaborative article by Gutiérrez de Mendoza and Acuña y Rossetti, "A los mexicanos" ("To the Mexican People"), is written in the tone of a public speech, as the writers directly address their *Vésper* readership and accuse them and President Díaz of wrongdoing. Unlike the tone of many of the other writings in this volume, Gutiérrez de Mendoza and

Acuña y Rossetti's work takes on a more agonistic rhetoric to overtly challenge both the president and their readers. Regarding their critiques of the president, these rhetors point to his poor financial decisions that led to both national debt and poverty, and they protest his wrongful persecution of journalists. As for the "Mexican people" to whom they address their article, the writers blame them for permitting these wrongdoings to occur, seeing anyone who does not speak out as complicit with the crimes of the government. Their aggressive rhetoric challenges their audience to make change in Mexico.

In her single-authored pieces, Gutiérrez de Mendoza continues to make use of the incisive and strident rhetorical strategy she cultivated with Acuña y Rossetti. In the 1903 editorial piece "¡Ecce homo!," which in Latin means "behold the man," she calls her readers to see the "real" Díaz. She defines him as a "thug" and challenges his masculinity by asserting that he is the "first man to be afraid of women"—women like her and Acuña y Rossetti. Here, again, she speaks directly and fearlessly to her readers: "Adulators" of Díaz, she writes, "this is your man." The final article, "Vésper siempre ocupará su puesto" ("Vesper Will Always Occupy Its Place") appeared in 1910, six months before the outbreak of the Mexican Revolution. It can be read as a declaration of Gutiérrez de Mendoza's deep investment in the power of the press and her commitment to the movement. In this piece, she identifies the press as a critical force in dismantling the corrupt Díaz government and establishing Madero as the new president of the Mexican Republic.[3]

A los mexicanos

Juana Belén Gutiérrez de Mendoza y Elisa Acuña y Rossetti

Vésper: Justicia y Libertad
Ciudad de México, México
15 de mayo de 1903

Al Gral. Díaz le hemos preguntado yá qué ha hecho de sus deberes como gobernante; á los mexicanos vamos a preguntarles hoy qué han hecho de sus deberes como ciudadanos.

Ante la República acusamos á uno y á otros porque ni el Presidente ha cumplido sus deberes, ni los ciudadanos han ejercido sus derechos.

Nuestra acusación no necesita basarse en crímenes ocultos, en la[s] sombra[s], en hecatombes sombríos, que han hecho estremecer de espanto en los pusilánimes, que no han sabido alzarse vengadores y justicieros, no; bastan para acusar, los hechos consumados á plena luz, los hechos recientes que están aún palpitantes á nuestra vista, los hechos que nadie puede negar ni dudar, los hechos que prueban que acusamos con justicia.

Demostremos. Sobre la ya legendaria é interminable deuda, nuestro gobierno, por un mero quijotismo, contrajo un compromiso con los frailes de California y sobre ese compromiso otro más ruinoso, un nuevo empréstito de 2.5 millones que no tiene más objeto que cubrir de oropel las asquerosas llagas de la administración actual.

El Gral. Díaz lo sacrifica todo á la ambición de reinar. La deuda antigua no se alcanza a cubrir, pero ni siquiera á aminorar porque el tesoro nacional se derrocha en cano[j]ías para asegurar lacayos mediante un buen salario; la deuda *piadosa* fué preciso contraerla porque el General Díaz necesita el apoyo de los mochos y de los yankees y los mochos y los yankees lo obligaron á echar sobre el tesoro nacional una deuda más, despojando al pueblo para mantener a los h[o]lgazanes de California.

El Presidente necesita prestigio en el extranjero y se lo procura como los fanfarrones de barrio, derrochando en superfluidades lo que no tienen para cubrir necesidades.

Lógico es que en el extran[j]ero se suponga bonancible á la nación que pide 2.5 millones para obras públicas.

Con ese procedimiento se entienden dos cosas: dar al pueblo una explicación del empleo de esos fondos, y hacerse pasar por unos cresos en el extran[j]ero.

A los economistas de á seis por media docena les preguntamos ¿es esto un sistema económico? A los hombres serios que se preocupan honradamente por el bienestar del país, les preguntamos: ¿Por el camino del derroche se va á la prosperidad?

Aún suponiendo que los 2.5 millones se emplearán en obras públicas, tendríamos el ridículo espectáculo de una cuidad embals[ad]a para un pueblo sin zapatos, pues es tal la miseria popular, desconocida en el extran[j]ero, pero muy visible y palpable para los hombres de nuestro país que nada hacen para evitar el derroche ni la miseria.

Si lo anterior es censurable porque conduce á la ruina, lo siguiente es monstruoso porque conduce al absoluto desprestigio, porque es el sacrificio de una nación en provecho de un solo hombre, porque es el sacrificio de principios, de instituciones y leyes en provecho de una personalidad.

Tras de la fórmula legal, esto es, tras de la ley adulterada, se comenzó á perseguir á la prensa independiente; los mexicanos toleraron aquella persecución embozada y su tolerancia envalentonó á los conculcadores del derecho que desenfrenados y rabiosos arrojaron la car[e]ta y presentaron á plena luz su monstruosa deformidad.

En el cortísimo período de dos meses se ha consumado una serie de atropellos que amenaza ser interminable, y que tendrá que ser así, interminable, porque aún en los cuerpos sociales más llagados queda algo incorruptible y con ese algo incorruptible es con lo que la tiranía estará siempre en eterna lucha.

Se toleró la persecución embozada y hoy se toleran el desenfreno y el descaro.

Ante 16 millones de habitantes, la Dictadura ha atropellado garantías, violado derechos y ultrajado ciudadanos. Con ensañamiento salvaje ha despedazado la prensa independiente, única manifestación que quedaba de libertad, ha llenado las bartolinas de ciudadanos honrados, ha arrancado talleres, ha entrado á saco en la propiedad y no ha respetado ni lo inviolable del hogar, sólo porque ese hogar pertenecía á personas que censuran tan abominable conducta.

Como prueba palpitante é innegable, están allí expuestos á morir en las inmundas bartolinas de Belem, Ricardo y Enrique Flores Magón, Alfonso Cravioto, Santiago de la Vega, Juan Sarabia, Santiago de la Hoz, Rafael Vélez y Francisco Gutiérrez.

Como comprobante del abuso desenfrenado está la persecución á dos periódicos enteramente inofensivos El Padre y el Nieto del Ahuizote, por el solo hecho de que tuvieron la humorada de ponerles un nombre que los hizo aparecer con cierto aire de familia, con cierta liga aparente con *El Hijo del Ahuizote*.

En la conciencia de todo hombre honrado, está que los periodistas citados al escribir censurando los actos punibles de un gobierno espúreo hacen uso de un derecho en nombre de su país, en nombre de su patria, en representación del pueblo que deposita su confianza en la prensa independiente y honrada; y cuando se atropella ese derecho ejercido digna y legalmente ¿no se comete un abuso incalificable y digno de castigo?

Cuando los ciudadanos que han depositado su confianza en los periodistas honrados permiten el atropello, lo toleran y lo dejan pasar ¿no se comete un acto indigno, de incalificable bajeza y cobardía? ¿No se complican en el crimen y se confunden con el criminal mismo?

Por eso ante la República acusamos al tirano que atropella y á los cobardes que se inclinan para que el atropello pase aún cuando al hacerlo sea por sobre ellos mismos.

Ante esa multitud indiferente está el grupo de periodistas ultrajados y un buen número de personas perseguidas y [a]menazadas entre las que nos contamos nosotras.

La amenaza está pendiente sobre el Sr. Soria, que ha emigrado para evitar el ultraje, está pendiente sobre el Sr. Maldonado, que ha abandonado la población para librarse de la cárcel, y esa amenaza, terrible y monstruosa, se ha desencadenado sobre nosotras, cerrando nuestras oficinas, clausurando nuestros taller[es] y lo que es más, allanando y ultrajando lo inviolable, nuestro hogar, lo sagrado, lo intocable, lo que respeta hasta el más salvaje, hasta el animal, y después de esto, la tiranía y el servilismo, tienen aún el descaro de dictar órdenes contra nosotras!

Mexicanos: ¿no os ruborizáis de que esto pase entre vosotros? [¿]Habéis degenerado tanto como vuestros enemigos que ni ellos ni vosotros sintáis vergüenza, ellos de perseguir mujeres y vosotros de permitirlo?

Por eso os acusamos y por eso hemos venido á ocupar vuestro puesto.

Porque sóis incapaces de defender á vuestros conciudadanos por eso lo hacemos nosotras, porque sóis incapaces de conservar vuestra libertad, por eso hemos venido á defenderla para nuestros hijos, para la posteridad á quien no queremos legar sólo la mancha de vuestra ignominiosa cobardía. Porque no usáis de vuestros derechos, venimos á usar de los nuestros, para que al menos conste que no todo era abyección y servilismo en nuestra época.

* * *

Hay más aún, ese grupo de incorruptibles que llevan la justificación á todos sus actos, ese grupo de inmaculados, á los que no puede hacérseles ni el más insignificante reproche, para dar la prueba más evidente de justificación más amplia de su actitud, para que esa prueba materializada, contundente, llevara el conocimiento á todos los ánimos, acusó á un criminal, y ese criminal fue absuelto, por el sólo prurito de violar la ley, por el sólo y personalísimo interés de favorecer á un hombre contra los intereses de un pueblo.

Bernardo Reyes fue acusado por la hecatombe del 2 de [a]bril en Monterrey y toda una Cámara de Diputados se inclinó ante la consigna y absolvió á Bernardo Reyes para agradar á Porfirio Díaz.

Ante el mundo entero y á plena luz los verdaderos patriotas han esgrimido todas las armas legales, y ante el mundo entero y á plena luz, la Dictadura les ha arrebatado esas armas y rotas las ha arrojado al lodazal inmundo por donde sus lacayos pasan uncidos al carro de la tiranía.

Y los 16 millones de espectadores, contemplan impasibles esa lucha descomunal y sangrienta donde se hace girones el derecho y se despedazan las garantías.

Por eso acusamos al Dictador y á los indiferentes y cobardes.

La inconcebible absolución, produjo la emigración de los principales acusadores y estos infunden terror al pensar que en México no quedará un hombre digno, porque la dignidad y la abyección son incompatibles.

* * *

Después de todo esto, hay algo más terrible aún, la conculcación suprema, la que á más de ser otro [a]tropello es una burla.

Sin respeto á nadie ni á nada, sin consideración á la patria ni á la República, sin respeto á las sagradas instituciones, sin temor al desprestigio se organiza una mascarada vergonzosa, una farsa de sufragio, en el que por fuerza se han obtenido adhesiones, en que el servilismo oficial ha agotado sus genuflexiones ridículas y sin que los tintes del rubor aparezcan en el rostro de los esclavos, esa mascarada grotesca y vergonzosa se presenta ante el mundo ataviada con el ropaje de convención nacional y como manifestación suprema de la voluntad popular.

¿A dónde se ha ido la vergüenza de los que así usurpan la representación del pueblo?

¿A dónde se ha ido el decoro del pueblo que así permite que se le exhiba en grosera caricatura?

¿A dónde está la dignidad de ciudadanos que así se dejan arrebatar sus derechos?

¡Oh, México, cuna de los heroísmos, asiento de las libertades, baluarte de los derechos!

Mexicanos, ante tan palpables errores, ante crímenes consumados en vuestra presencia, ante conculcaciones inauditas ante la muerte de las libertades y la agonía de la república, llamamos á vuestras conciencias, mostradnos el digno ejemplo de civismo que os dan vuestros conciudadanos, ese grupo incorruptible que la tiranía ha alojado en las bartolinas de Belem.

Llamamos á vuestros sentimientos de patriotismo, llamamos á vuestra dignidad de ciudadanos, no queráis que mantengamos nuestra acusación ante la posteridad para que la República al morir os maldiga y en su agonía suprema señale vuestra cobardía con el estigma bochornoso, con la marca inminente de cobardes.

Ciudadanos dignos de vuestros antepasados, dignos de vosotros mismos y en nombre del honor nacional y en nombre de vuestra propia honra, salvad á la República.

To All Mexicans

Juana Belén Gutiérrez de Mendoza and Elisa Acuña y Rossetti

Vésper: Justicia y Libertad
Mexico City, Mexico
15 May 1903

We have already asked General Díaz what he has done with his duties as government leader; today, we are going to ask Mexicans what they have done with their duties as citizens.

Before the Republic we accuse the one and the others, because neither has the President fulfilled his duties, nor have the citizens exercised their rights.

Our accusation does not need to be based on hidden crimes, in the shadows, or in gloomy hecatombs, which have made the pusillanimous shiver with fright, who have not been able to rise up as avengers and seekers of justice, no; it suffices them to accuse the deeds committed in the full light of day, recent deeds that are still vivid to our sight, deeds that nobody can deny or doubt, deeds that prove that we accuse with justice.

Let us demonstrate. On top of the already legendary and interminable debt, our government, because of a mere Quixotism, made a commitment with the friars of California and on top of that commitment, another even more ruinous, a new loan of 2.5 million pesos which has no other objective than to cover with tinsel the disgusting wounds of the current administration.

General Díaz is sacrificing all to his ambition to reign. The old debt cannot be covered, not even paid down because the national treasury is wasted on canonries that assure good salaries to his lackeys. The *pious* debt was necessary to contract because General Díaz needs the support of the sell-outs and the Yankees, and from the sell-outs and the Yankees they obliged him to burden the national treasury with another debt, by despoiling the people in order to support some do-nothings from California.

The President needs prestige abroad and he procures it like barrio show-offs do, splurging on trivialities what they don't have to cover necessities.

It is logical that abroad it is assumed that all is calm in a nation that borrows 2.5 million for public works.

Two things are understood with that method of operation: give the people an explanation of the use of those funds and give the foreigners the impression of great wealth.

We ask the conniving economists: Is this an economic system? We ask the serious men who are honorably worried about the country's well-being: Does the path of profligacy lead to prosperity?

Even supposing that the 2.5 million were used for public works, we would have the ridiculous spectacle of a paved city for a people without shoes, because the people's misery is so widespread, unknown abroad, but very visible and palpable to the men of our nation who do not act to avoid waste or extreme poverty.

If the above-stated situation is reprehensible because it leads to ruin, the following is monstrous because it leads to a total loss of prestige, because it involves the sacrifice of a nation for the benefit of a single man, because it involves the sacrifice of principles, of institutions and laws for the benefit of one personality.

Behind the legal formula, that is, behind the adulterated law, they started to persecute the independent press; Mexicans tolerated that covert persecution and their tolerance emboldened the lawbreakers, who unleashed and rabid, threw off their masks and showed their monstrous deformities in broad daylight.

In the very brief period of two months, there have been a series of outrages carried out that threaten to be endless, and that, in fact, will have to be that way, endless, because even in the most cankerous social institutions there remains something incorruptible, and with that incorruptible something is what tyranny will always be in an eternal struggle.

Covert persecution was tolerated, and today wantonness and impudence are tolerated.

Before 16 million inhabitants, the Dictatorship has trampled on guarantees, violated rights, and mistreated citizens. With savage cruelty it has broken the independent press into pieces, the only remaining manifestation of freedom; it has filled the dungeons with honorable citizens, it has dismantled shops, it has sacked property, and it has not respected even the inviolable hearth and home, only because that home belonged to people who censure such abominable conduct.

As concrete and undeniable proof, the following are exposed to death in the filthy dungeons of Belem: Ricardo and Enrique Flores Magón, Alfonso Cravioto, Santiago de la Vega, Juan Sarabia, Santiago de la Hoz, Rafael Vélez, and Francisco Gutiérrez.

As proof of the unbridled abuse there is the persecution of two newspapers entirely harmless, the Father and the Grandson of the Ahuizotes, based solely on the whim of calling them by a name that made it appear that they had a certain familial air with *El Hijo del Ahuizote*.

The conscience of every upright man holds the belief that the journalists cited, when writing to censure the punishable acts of a spurious government, make use of a right in the name of their country, in the name of their homeland, representing the people who put their trust in the independent and honorable press; and when that right—exercised honorably and legally—is trampled, is not an unspeakable and punishable abuse committed?

When the citizens who put their trust in the upright journalists permit the trampling, tolerate it and let it happen, is not an unworthy act committed, one of unspeakable baseness and cowardice? Do the citizens not become complicit in the crime and are confused with the criminal himself?

For that reason, before the Republic we accuse the tyrant who tramples and the cowards who bow down so that they enable the trampling to happen even when by doing so they themselves are crushed.

Before that indifferent multitude stands the group of violated journalists and a goodly number of persecuted and threatened individuals, among whom we also are included.

The threat hangs over Mr. Soria, who emigrated in order to avoid mistreatment, it hangs over Mr. Maldonado, who abandoned the city to avoid jail, and that threat, terrible and monstrous, has been unleashed on us, by closing our offices, shutting our printing shops and what is more, by invading and offending what is inviolable: our home, that which is sacred, untouchable, which even the most savage respect, even the animal and after all that, tyranny and servility still have the nerve to dictate orders against us [women].

Mexicans: Do you not blush to think that this should happen among you? Have you degenerated as much as your enemies, so that neither they nor you feel shame, they of persecuting women and you of permitting it?

For that reason we accuse you and for that reason we have come to take over your post.

Because you are incapable of defending your fellow citizens, for that reason we are doing it ourselves, because you are incapable of conserving your liberty, for that reason we have come to defend it for our children, for posterity, to whom we refuse to leave only the stain of your ignominious cowardice. Because you do not exercise your rights, we are here to make use of ours, to at least demonstrate that not everything in our time was abjection and servility.

* * *

There is even more, that group of incorruptible ones who bring justification to all their actions, that group of unblemished ones, to whom not even the most insignificant reproach can be directed, in order to give the clearest proof and the most well-grounded evidence of their attitude, so that that concrete and forceful proof, would carry the knowledge to every soul, it accused a criminal, and that criminal was then absolved of his crimes, due to the strong desire to violate the law, due to a very personal stake in favoring one man against the interests of the people.

Bernardo Reyes was accused of the massacre of his opponents on April 2 in Monterrey and an entire house of representatives bowed to orders and absolved Bernardo Reyes in order to please Porfirio Díaz.

Before the whole world and in full daylight the true patriots have wielded every legal weapon, and before the whole world and in full daylight, the Dictatorship has snatched those arms away, broken them, and thrown them into the filthy mud pit where its lackeys pass, harnessed to tyranny's coach.

And 16 million spectators impassively witness this enormous and bloody struggle, when the law is torn asunder and constitutional rights are shredded.

For that reason, we accuse the Dictator and the indifferent and cowardly.

The inconceivable absolution caused the emigration of the main accusers, and these men instill terror when one thinks that no honorable man will remain in Mexico, because dignity and abjection are incompatible.

* * *

After all this, there is something even more terrible, the supreme infringement, which besides being another outrage is a mockery.

Without respect for anyone or anything, without consideration for the Homeland or Republic; without respect for sacred institutions, without fear of losing prestige, they organize a shameful masquerade, a farce of suffrage, in which adherence has been obtained by force, in which official servility has exhausted its ridiculous genuflections, without any blush of shame to appear on the faces of slaves; that grotesque and shameful masquerade is presented to the world decked out in the garb of national tradition and as a supreme manifestation of the popular will.

What has become of the shame of those who thus usurp the representation of the people?

What has become of the decency of the people, who permit themselves to be exhibited in crude caricature? Where is the dignity of citizens who allow their rights to be taken in this way?

Oh, Mexico, cradle of heroism, seat of liberty, bastion of civil rights!

Mexicans, faced with such palpable errors, with crimes committed in your presence, faced with unheard of violations, faced with the death of freedoms and the agony of the Republic, we call on your consciences, show us the dignified example of civic duty which your fellow citizens give to you, that incorruptible group which tyranny has housed in the dungeons of Belem.[4]

We call on your sentiments of patriotism, we call on your dignity as citizens, do not require us to sustain our accusation in the face of your posterity, so that when the Republic dies it will curse you and, in its death throes, brand your cowardice with the stigma of shame, with the prominent mark of cowards.

Citizens worthy of your ancestors, worthy of your very selves, and in the name of national honor and in the name of your own honor, save the Republic.

¡Ecce Homo!

Juana Belén Gutiérrez de Mendoza

Vésper: Justicia y Libertad
Ciudad de México, México
15 de Mayo de 1903

En la guerra, un motinero; en la paz, un intrigante. Como hombre, un monstruo, como político, un cobarde. He aquí á Porfirio Díaz. ¡Aduladores! Hé allí á vuestro hombre.

Lo anterior está demostrado de la manera más evidente.

Todos saben de las asonadas y motines encabezados por el caudillo, todos lo conocen como un motinero afortunado y no tenemos necesidad de recordar los episodios de esa historia.

En la paz ficticia de que disfrutamos, todos lo han visto intrigar, faltando á los más rudimentarios deberes como gobernante y como amigo.

Al verse atacado, al sentir amenazada su permanencia en el poder, á todos les consta que no vacila ante los crímenes más monstruosos para deshacerse de sus enemigos.

Todo esto, no lo hace un hombre, necesariamente tiene que hacerlo un Monstruo. El motín injustificado, la intriga burda y ruín, la matanza en las sombras, tienen que ser obra del monstruo moral, desprovisto de todo sentimiento humanitario, carente en lo absoluto de conciencia humana.

Después de todo esto viene la cobardía inaudita, de la que se avergonzaría hasta el hombre primitivo, desconocedor de la dignidad humana.

La Dictadura no se detiene ya ni ante el ridículo. Ha hecho denunciar a *Vésper* y ha dictado órdenes de aprehensión para la Señorita Elisa Acuña y Rossetti y para la directora de este periódico. Si esto no es cobarde, que venga Dios y lo diga.

¡Pobre México, pobre Patria mía! Serás la primera nación donde se encarcelan mujeres por el delito de escribir en defensa del pueblo.

En cambio también será Porfirio Díaz el primer hombre que tiene miedo á las mujeres y en su espanto se olvida hasta de ocultarlo como hasta aquí había ocultado su cobardía tras de inícuos alardes de fuerza.

Que ¿se pensará el caudillo que Elisa Acuña y Rossetti ocupará la silla presidencial?

Que ¿se figurará Porfirio Díaz que su muy humilde servidora Juana B. Gutiérrez de Mendoza quiere arrebatarle la matona?

¡Pobre hombre! ¡Cómo delira!

No tenemos derechos, pero si los tuviéramos, renunciaríamos á ocupar el puesto de Porfirio Díaz. ¡Es tan triste ser como él!

He aquí una nota, una acción que pone muy alto el valor personal, civil y moral del Gral. Díaz.

¡Aduladores! Aquí está vuestro hombre tal como es.

¡ECCE HOMO! Aduladores.

Behold the Man!

Juana Belén Gutiérrez de Mendoza

Vésper: Justicia y Libertad
Mexico City, Mexico
15 May 1903

In wartime, a thug; in peacetime, a schemer. As a man, a monster; as a politician, a coward. Behold Porfirio Díaz. Adulators! Behold your man.

The above-stated is demonstrated in the most obvious way.

Everyone knows about the disturbances and riots headed by the chieftain, everyone knows him as a lucky thug and we have no need to recall the episodes of that history.

In the false peace that we enjoy, everyone has seen him scheming, by neglecting the most basic duties as a governor and as a friend.

When he sees himself under attack, when he perceives threats to his remaining in power, everyone is aware that he does not hesitate before the most monstrous crimes, in order to get rid of his enemies.

All this does not make him a man, but necessarily must make him a Monster. The unjustified tumult, the crude and ruinous intrigue, the murder in the shadows, must be works of the moral monster, deprived of all humanitarian feeling, absolutely lacking of human conscience.

After all this comes his outrageous cowardice, of which even the most primitive man, ignorant of human dignity, would be ashamed.

This transcription comes from *Mujeres y Revolución, 1900–1917,* edited by Ana Lau Jaiven and Carmen Ramos-Escandón (182–83). It is reproduced here with permission from Instituto Nacional de Estudios Históricos de la Revolución Mexicana.

The Dictatorship no longer restrains itself even when faced with ridiculousness. It has mandated the denunciation of *Vésper* and has issued arrest orders for Miss Elisa Acuña y Rossetti and for the director of this paper. If this is not cowardly, may God come and say so.

Poor Mexico, poor Fatherland of mine! You will be the first nation where women are jailed for the crime of writing in defense of the people.

On the other hand, Porfirio Díaz will also be the first man who is afraid of women and who in his fear forgets even to hide it as, until recently, he had hidden his cowardice behind perverse displays of force.

What, might the chieftain think to himself that Elisa Acuña y Rossetti will occupy the presidential seat?

What, might Porfirio Díaz imagine that his very humble servant Juana B. Gutiérrez de Mendoza wants to snatch his billy-club?

Poor man! How he raves!

We have no rights, but if we had them, we would step down from occupying the position of Porfirio Díaz. It is so sad to be like him!

Here then is a note, an act that raises on high the personal, civil, and moral valor of Gen. Díaz.

Adulators! Here you have your man just as he is.

ECCE HOMO! Adulators.

"Vésper" Siempre ocupará su puesto

Juana Belén Gutiérrez de Mendoza

Vésper: Justicia y Libertad
México, D.F.
8 de mayo de 1910

Una vez más "vésper" viene á ocupar su puesto en el campo del combate.

"vésper" no ha querido luchar sólo por un cambio de personal en la Administración Pública, eso dista mucho de sus grandes anhelos de transformación radical, de su eterna aspiración de Justicia y Libertad, de sus grandes ideales de suprema redención y si esta vez luchará exclusivamente por el triunfo de los candidatos electos y sostenidos por la Convención es porque comprende que sin quitar el primer obstáculo es imposible ir más allá.

Si el Gral. Díaz ha sido un formidable obstáculo para una simple práctica democrática, cuanto más habrá de serlo para una transformación social ante la cual están temblando los tiranos de todo el mundo.

Nosotros podríamos pasar sobre ese obstáculo y seguir la marcha hacia lo inmenso de nuestros ideales; pero, ¿podrían ir como nosotros?... Muy pocos ciertamente. Nosotros estamos en plena posesión de nuestra libertad, en pleno uso de nuestro derecho, en pleno ejercicio de nuestra soberanía; para nosotros que hemos despedazado todos los yugos, que nos hemos arrancado todas las cadenas, que hemos arrojado el peso de todas las preocupaciones y de todos los prejuicios, que desconocemos todos los temores y abominamos todas las cobardías, para nosotros no hay tiranía posible; y con ser así nos basta para ser inmensamente libres.

Pero ¿cuántos podrán ser libres como nosotros si en este pueblo horriblemente oprimido se ha perdido hasta la noción de libertad?

¿Qué idea de la soberanía de sí mismo puede tener cada uno aquí donde se desconoce la soberanía de todo un pueblo?

Es una locura creer que un pueblo atado al poste de todas las ignorancias, oprimido bajo el peso de todas las tiranías y devorado por todas las miserias, pueda seguir en su marcha á la libertad que pasa sin detenerse para arrancarle todas sus ligaduras.

No; si queremos que ese pueblo nos siga á ese más allá de la redención, es preciso ayudarlo á que rompa todas sus cadenas; esto es lo que hacemos al combatir la Dictadura del Gral. Díaz; esto es lo que hacemos al procurar el triunfo de la candidatura popular.

Por esto al dedicarse á luchar exclusivamente por los candidatos de Convención, "vésper" no abdica ni hace transacciones de sus principios; se detiene sencillamente á remover el pedrusco interpuesto en el camino.

La nación entera está interesada en esa remoción y bien pudiéramos dejar á los demás esa tarea, en la seguridad de que la llevarán á cabo; pero ni queremos ni debemos hacerlo: no es digno de nosotros esperar á que otros abran el paso para seguir adelante.

No se piense que creemos (como muchos ilusos cuyos nombres podemos citar) que para que el pueblo sea libre basta con que cualquiera sustituya al Gral. Díaz; bien se ha visto á "Vésper" ir solo contra una multitud enloquecida y apasionada, cuando los actos han sido una farza, las palabras una mentira y los hombres una amenaza para esa misma multitud que por escapar del peligro presente no advertía otro peligro mayor para el futuro; no podrá decirse que nos aturden las palabras, que nos deslumbran las personalidades, que nos hipnotiza la opinión pública, no, ya lo hemos dicho otra vez: "la caída de un tirano no es la caída de la tiranía" y si tan resuelta como espontáneamente, venimos á luchar porque el Sr. Madero ocupe la Presidencia de la República, es porque el Sr. Madero nos inspira la más completa confianza respecto á los fines que persigue; es porque tenemos la convicción de que la suerte de este desdichado país mejorará cuando el Sr. Madero esté al frente de sus destinos; y mientras algún hecho no venga á modificar nuestra opinión, "VÉSPER" siempre ocupará su puesto al lado de los que luchen por el victorioso candidato de la gran Convención.

"Vesper" Will Always Occupy Its Post

Vésper: Justicia y Libertad
Mexico City, Mexico
8 May 1910

Once again "VÉSPER" returns to occupy its post in the field of combat.

"VÉSPER" has not wanted to fight for just a change of personnel in the Public Administration; that is a long way from its great desires for radical transformation, from its eternal aspirations for Justice and Liberty, from its great ideals of supreme redemption; and if this time it will fight exclusively for the candidates elected and supported by the Convention,[5] it is because it understands that without removing the first obstacle it is impossible to go any further.

If Gen. Díaz has been a formidable obstacle to a simple democratic practice, how much more he will be for a social transformation in the face of which the tyrants of the whole world are trembling.

We could surmount that obstacle and follow the march toward the immensity of our ideals; but could you go as we do? Very few, certainly. We are in full possession of our freedom, in full use of our rights, in full exercise of our sovereignty; for us who have broken all the yokes, torn off all the chains, who have thrown off the weight of all worries and of all prejudices, who deny the acceptance of all fears and despise all cowardice, for us there is no possible tyranny; and being like that is enough for us to be monumentally free.

But how many could be free as we are if in this horribly oppressed country even the notion of liberty has been lost?

What idea of individual sovereignty can each person have here where the sovereignty of a whole people is denied?

It is crazy to believe that a people tied to the post of all ignorance, oppressed beneath the weight of all tyrannies, and devoured by all miseries might continue on its march to freedom, which passes without pausing to rip off its bonds.

No; if we want that people to follow us to that great beyond of redemption, it is necessary to help them to break their chains: this is what we do as we fight the Dictatorship of Gen. Díaz; this is what we do when we strive for the victory of the popular slate of candidates.

Therefore, upon dedicating itself to fighting exclusively on behalf of the candidates of the Convention, "vésper" is neither abdicating nor compromising its principles; it is simply pausing to remove the boulder that is blocking the road.

The entire nation has a stake in that removal, and we could well leave that task to others, assured that they would carry it out; but we neither want nor should do so: it is not worthy of us to wait for others to open the way to continue forward.

Do not let it be thought that we believe (as many dreamers whose names we can cite) that in order for the people to be free it is enough to replace Gen. Díaz with just anyone; it has been well seen that "vésper" has gone alone against a crazed and excited crowd, when actions have been a farce, words a lie, and the men a threat to that same crowd that for the sake of escaping from present danger did not perceive another greater danger for the future; it cannot be said that words bewilder us, that personalities dazzle us, that public opinion hypnotizes us; no; we have already said before: "the fall of a tyrant is not the fall of tyranny," and if we come to fight this resolutely and spontaneously so that Mr. Madero[6] will occupy the Presidency of the Republic, it is because Mr. Madero inspires our most complete confidence with respect to the objectives that he pursues; it is because we hold the conviction that the fortunes of this miserable country will improve once Mr. Madero is leading its destiny; and as long as some action doesn't come along to change our opinion, "vésper" will always occupy its post beside those who fight for the victorious candidate of the Great Convention.

Hermila Galindo

As a writer, newspaper editor, and public speaker, Hermila Galindo (1886–1954) helped introduce the concept of feminism to Mexican audiences. Galindo received what was considered a modern, progressive education in Durango and later in Chihuahua, Mexico (Orellana Trinidad 26). During a time when only 14 percent of the Mexican population could read and write, Galindo gained a formidable education, which she capitalized on by crafting a career for herself first as a college instructor and later in politics. From 1908 to 1913, Galindo worked as an instructor of typing and shorthand at various colleges in Torreón, Coahuila, such as the prestigious Miguel Lerdo de Tejada and the Colegio Zaragoza (26–28). In these positions and through involvement in various political clubs, Galindo's valuable communication skills were noticed by influencial people within the Mexican government. As a result, she made the contacts necessary to take her to the next level in public and political influence.

From 1914 to 1920, Galindo served as a spokesperson for Venustiano Carranza, a leader in the Mexican Revolution who secured power in 1915 and then was elected president from 1917 to 1920. Through this position, Galindo honed her rhetorical and leadership skills by organizing and speaking at conferences and by managing women's clubs throughout Mexico (Orellana Trinidad 26 33). More importantly, her political backing allowed her a rare level of rhetorical liberty to publicly express her ideas about women and their place in Mexican society. Galindo penned speeches for each Congreso Feminista de Yucatán, the two Feminist Congresses held in Yucatán in 1916.[1] Through these pieces, she invited audiences to consider questions of reproductive rights, among other topics.[2] Galindo was also commissioned by President Carranza's government to write *La doctrina Carranza y el acercamiento indolatino* (1919) (The Carranza Doctrine: An Indo-Latin Approach).[3] While this two-hundred-page manifesto covers numerous topics, Galindo dedicates one chapter to the women of Latin America and calls them to fight for women's suffrage (women would not receive the vote in Mexico until 1953). Galindo argued once again for women's right to suffrage at the Constitutionalist Congress of 1917 (though her demands were not met and her appeal was passed over without a vote), and she became the first woman to run for public office when she put herself on the ballot for a Deputy of 5th constituency seat of Mexico City in 1917. Historical records show that she won the majority of votes, but because of laws forbidding women to hold public office, she was passed over for the position.

One especially important way Galindo exercised her rhetorical prowess was by instituting her progressive women's magazine, *La Mujer Moderna* (*The Modern Woman*), which she published out of Mexico City starting in September 1915.[4] Collected here is Galindo's opening editorial for the first issue of her publication, "¡Laboremos!" ("Let Us Labor!"). She opens the piece noting that this first publication falls on September 16th, the anniversary of the beginning of the 1810 Mexican War of Independence. Strategically publishing her first issue on this date, Galindo was no doubt sending the message that women should fight for and enjoy similar freedoms as their historical counterparts. In the remainder of the article, Galindo sets the pace for *La Mujer Moderna*. Here, Galindo embraces what may seem to be a conservative political stance when she points to the home as the "medium and terrain" for women's prime activity and political engagement. Galindo politicizes the work of the home, however, when she repeats the tenets of what U.S. readers might recognize as a form of republican womanhood and sets out the power of the mother by citing the well-known maxim that the "hand that rocks the cradle directs the destinies of the world."[5] Even with this more traditional stance, Galindo's project is to invite women to participate in Mexican social and political life: "Come along!" she enourages her readers, "Let us labor!"

Following "¡Laboremos!" is "La mujer como colaboradora en la vida pública" ("Woman as Collaborator in Public Life"). Galindo published this article in the Spanish-language newspaper *El Pueblo* (The People), out of Veracruz, Mexico—a press established during the Mexican Revolution that focused on political events surrounding the war as well as other international news. In 1915, Galindo was asked by the editorial staff to take charge of the newspaper's weekly supplement dedicated to women. In this first installment, she approaches her readers by first deploying the humility *topos*, a rhetorical approach consistent with the period in which women downplayed or even dismissed their *ethos* as an authority on the subject at hand. Such a strategy appealed to audiences that might be suspect of women writing in public venues, seeing them as overstepping their social bounds and intellectual capabilities. Often, after women rhetors employed this *topos*, they would go on to exercise their intellectual and rhetorical prowess. Galindo follows suit. In this article, she humbles herself before her audience but then proceeds to promote women's intellectual equality to men. The writings collected here reflect Galindo's politics, but they are only a small sampling of her feminist work and indicate just a portion of her political activity and rhetorical productivity. A far more complex and involved history must be told about Galindo as a Mexican feminist rhetor.[6]

¡Laboremos!

La Mujer Moderna
Ciudad de México, México
16 de septiembre de 1915

En esta fecha grandiosa, en que la protesta imponente de un gran pueblo oprimido y befado se conmemora; en esta fecha gloriosa que marcó la primera etapa de las aspiraciones de los mexicanos por su independencia, libertad y honor; en esta fecha de nobles remembranzas, en que nuestra gratitud y nuestro amor se desbordan al recuerdo venerado de nuestros héroes; nos es grato dar comienzo a la publicación de este semanario, enviando nuestro respetuoso saludo de paz y de concordia a todas las clases y gremios del pueblo de la República, muy especialmente a la mujer mexicana, cuya reivindicación y dignificación sociales constituyen nuestros más caros ideales, y serán objeto de nuestra más entusiasta labor en la liza de la prensa.

Deseamos honrar este aniversario de redención, inaugurando nuestras tareas periodísticas, con las que deseamos coadyubar [coadyuvar] a la redención de la patria, la redención de los principios salvadores y redención de la mujer, levantando el espíritu femenino a la altura de su deber y su derecho, para que no permanezca por más tiempo impa[s]ible ante la solución de los más trascendentales problemas sociales y políticos, que afectan tanto al hombre como a la mujer, que es su compañera y su igual.

Si política es la ciencia que tiene por objeto marcar a los pueblos el derrotero que les corresponde en el concierto de las naciones cultas, por medio de leyes y preceptos adecuados a su medio y capacidad, tendentes a conquistar su bienestar por medio del progreso moral y material, no es, ciertamente, racional ni justo que la mujer se abstenga sistemáticamente de entrar en conocimiento de causa y oponer su veto.

Si la mujer es la compañera del hombre, y su igual, no hay motivo plausible para que lo abandonemos a la hora de decidir la suerte definitiva o temporal de la Patria. ¿Con qué derecho nos quejaremos de los resultados mañana, si hoy no hacemos nada de nuestra parte? Nuestras aspiraciones porque la mujer mexicana se eleve social y moralmente hasta el grado que cumple su decoro para que se compenetre de la cosa pública, y de ella participe dentro de su capacidad y circunstancias, no implica en modo alguno el propósito de usurpar o invadir los derechos del ciudadano, no concedidos aún a nuestro sexo por las leyes actuales, no, deseamos que la mujer mexicana colabore con su esfuerzo reiterado, su intuición y perseverancia, en pro de las causas nobles

---

With her permission, we use Rosa María Valles Ruiz's Spanish-language transcription of this article found in *Sol de libertad* (Sun of Freedom) (226–27).

y dignas; para ello no necesitamos de ciudadanías, y tenemos medio propicio y terreno fecundo: el hogar.

La mano que mece la cuna, dirige los destinos del mundo; ha dicho el sabio; efectivamente, es en el hogar a donde pueden forjarse los mejores ciudadanos, cuando la mujer, libre de preocupaciones y prejuicios, se identifica con la Patria y siente sus necesidades.

La noble causa constitucionalista cuya bandera simboliza la conquista de las más preciadas libertades humanas, no será la que oponga resistencia a nuestras justas aspiraciones. La honradez y prestigio de su digno Jefe, el patriota esclarecido señor Carranza, como la ilustración y altruismo de sus principales colaboradores, son prenda segura de que nuestro esfuerzo encontrará en ellos alentadora y benévola protección.

El tiempo apremia. La situación peligrosa y difícil [por la que] atraviesa el País, reclama los esfuerzos combinados de todos sus buenos hijos para salir avante.

Si el hombre pone al servicio de la Patria su brazo y su cerebro, nosotras pondremos cerebro y corazón. La grandeza de alma de la mujer mexicana le viene por abolengo, lo dice nuestra historia.

[¡]Sus! ¡A la brega!

¡Laboremos!

Let Us Labor!

La Mujer Moderna
Mexico City, Mexico
16 September 1915

On this magnificent date, in which the awe-inspiring protest of a great people, oppressed and ridiculed, is commemorated; on this glorious date that marked the first stage of the aspirations of Mexicans for their independence, liberty, and honor; on this date of noble remembrances, on which our gratitude and love are overflowing for the venerated remembrance of our heroes; we are pleased to initiate the publication of this weekly magazine, by sending our respectful greeting of peace and harmony to all the classes and trade associations of the people of the Republic, very especially to the Mexican woman, whose social vindication and dignity constitute our most cherished ideals, and they will be the objective of our most enthusiastic work on the battle of the press.[7]

We desire to honor this anniversary of redemption, by inaugurating our journalistic work with those with which we wish to contribute to the redemption of the Fatherland, the redemption of the saving principles and the redemption of the woman, by raising the feminine spirit to the heights of its duty and right, so that it will no longer remain impassive before the solution of the most transcendental social and political problems, which affect both the man and the woman, who is his companion and equal.

If politics is the science that has as its objective to mark for the people the course which corresponds to them in the community of cultured nations, by means of laws and precepts appropriate to their means and capacity, directed to conquering their well-being by means of moral and material progress, it is not, certainly, rational nor just that woman should abstain systematically from entering into full knowledge of the case and opposing their veto.

If the woman is the companion of the man, and his equal, there is no plausible motive for us to abandon him when it is time to decide the definitive or temporary destiny of the Fatherland. By what right will we complain about the results tomorrow, if today we do nothing on our behalf? Our aspirations for the Mexican woman to be lifted socially and morally to the level that fulfills her dignity so that she can have a good understanding of the *res publica*, and participate in it within her capacity and circumstances, does not imply in any way the purpose of usurping or invading the rights of the citizen, still not granted to our sex by current laws, no, we desire that the Mexican woman collaborate with her repeated efforts, her intuition and perseverance in support of noble and worthy causes; to do this, we do not need citizenry, and we have a propitious medium and fertile terrain: the home.

The hand that rocks the cradle directs the destinies of the world; the wise man has said; truly, it is in the home where the best citizens can be forged, when the woman, free from worries and prejudices, identifies herself with the Fatherland and feels its needs.

The noble constitutionalist cause, whose flag symbolizes the conquest of the most prized human liberties, will not be the one that offers resistance to our just aspirations. The honor and prestige of its worthy Leader, the illustrious patriot Mr. Carranza,[8] like the erudition and altruism of his principal collaborators, are a sure guarantee that our efforts will find in them inspiring and benevolent protection.

Time is short. The dangerous and difficult situation that the Nation is going through demands the combined efforts of all its good sons and daughters in order to be successful.

If the man puts his might and his mind at the service of the Fatherland, we women will put our minds and hearts. The greatness of soul of the Mexican woman comes from her noble ancestry, our history says so.

Come along! Into the struggle!

Let us labor!

La mujer como colaboradora en la vida pública

Crónica Dominical de *El Pueblo*
Veracruz, México
3 de marzo de 1915

Al iniciar EL PUEBLO una Sección Semanal, consagrada a la mujer, siento, aunque agradezco, que galantemente se me haya encargado de ella, pues plumas bien cortadas y razonamientos contundentes al mismo tiempo que gallardamente escritos no hubieran faltado para dar mayor lustre a esta publicación, y para mejor defender la justa y simpática causa que en esta Sección va a iniciarse.

M[a]s váyase mi p[obr]ísmo val[or] intelectual por la buena voluntad que me anima y esté la segunda presente siempre en la conciencia de quienes me conceden el honor de leer mis mal hilvanados escritos.

Dicho lo anterior, y después de presentarme respetuosamente a los ilustrados lectores de EL PUEBLO, entro en materia.

Mucho se ha escrito acerca de la capacidad intelectual de la mujer para tomar parte en la vida pública de las naciones y acerca de su igualdad e inferioridad con respecto al hombre, y después de que grandes filósofos como Stuart Mill han aducido argumentos tan contundentes como los que contiene el libro del filósofo a que acabo de hacer referencia, titulado "La Esclavitud Femenina," confieso humildemente que nada nuevo puedo agregar a este respecto.

Y en efecto, la mujer dotada de las mismas cualidades psíquicas que el hombre, como la inteligencia, la voluntad, el raciocinio, la memoria, el sentimiento, etc., etc., tiene derecho a aspirar a una vida mejor que la que actualmente tiene, y esa ley emotiva que por su misma fuerza incontrastable mejora y perfecciona, habrá de cumplirse en ella, a pesar de todas las dificultades y todos los obstáculos que se opongan a su paso, pues "aunque la predicación de Víctor Hugo—nos decía la Condesa Pardo Bazán—de que el siglo XIX emancipó al hombre, haya salido fallida, no importa, todo ha sido cuestión de mero cálculo."

Por tanto los que sostienen que la mujer debe estar siempre sujeta al predominio del hombre, han procedido juzgando a priori. ¿Cómo puede juzgarse de la inferioridad intelectual de la mujer y de su capacidad para inmiscuirse en la vida política de un pueblo, si hasta la fecha los campos de la intelectualidad y de la política le han sido vedados? A los sostenedores de esa inferioridad y de esa capacidad de la mujer, puede decírseles que se han colocado a la misma altura que aqu[é]llos que antes de la revolución de 1910 sostenían cuando decían que el pueblo mexicano no estaba apto para la democracia, siendo que los culpables de tal ineptitud eran los mismos que de ella formaban un arma en contra de la iniciación de nuestro movimiento político actual. Si el pueblo mexicano no estaba apto para la democracia, era porque sus directores de aquel entonces le vedaban el derecho de conquistar esa aptitud y para lo cual el pueblo tuvo la necesidad de rebelarse contra aqu[é]llos que le impedían su progreso; si la mujer no está apta para la vida pública, es porque no se le ha prestado facilidad para lograr tal aptitud. La mujer, cuando sus facultades intelectuales hayan sido desarrolladas cuidadosamente, llegará a constituir un elemento de primer orden en la vida social y política, pues además de sus facultades intelectuales atrofiadas hasta hoy por la esclavitud en que ha vivido, posee un espíritu intuitivo mucho más fino y desarrollado que el hombre, una sensibilidad especial, una emotividad puedo decir, que le permite adivinar por instinto el peligro, que la hace percibir por corazonadas mejor que a muchos psicólogos a los leales de los desleales, circunstancias que el hombre más ducho en el conocimiento práctico de la vida y del corazón humano, no descubre con facilidad. Allí donde un político cree haber encontrado un partidario bien intencionado, talentoso y de aptitudes técnicas, la mujer le adivina o presiente el fondo de doblez, de traición y de audacia que suple al verdadero talento.

Un elocuente ejemplo de esta verdad la encontrarán mis estimados lectores y lectoras en el caso de Madame Roland: mientras su marido, hombre de estado, meticuloso, parsimonioso, solemne, no descubría una pista o una orientación, ella sabía quiénes [e]ran los capaces de hacer triunfar las ideas revolucionarias, y supo seleccionar un grupo de ellos y dirigirlo inspirando así la admiración y el respeto de sus correligionarios, mereciendo al mismo tiempo el odio de sus enemigos, como producto del miedo que ante su penetración los sobrecogía.

Del filósofo inglés Stuart Mill, tomo la siguiente frase refiriéndose a su esposa la señora Taylor . . . "me ha sido muy útil para mis escritos largos o cortos, con sus observaciones llenas de penetración y sagacidad."

Renán se llevó a una de sus hermanas a la Siria, y allí escribieron juntos la mayor parte de las obras de este genio y cuando ella murió, hizo el escritor el gran sentimiento, repitiendo frecuentemente que "en ella había perdido su apoyo, su cariño, y su cooperación."

En nuestra patria existen ejemplos palpables de las facultades intuitivas de la mujer, pues ellas fueron las que mejor conocieron a los cómplices de Huerta, aún entre aqu[é]llos que mientras desplegaban sonrisas amistosas para la revolución, llevaban escondidas entre las ropas, las armas de la traición y el crimen. Actualmente son ellas mismas las que mejor atingencia y tacto tienen para desenmascarar y perseguir a los enemigos.

Por tanto, yo creo que en compensación de la parte activísima que la mujer mexicana ha tomado en todas las etapas de esta revolución, los revolucionarios están obligados a darle todo género de facilidades para que desarrolle sus aptitudes intelectuales para que unidas al espíritu intuitivo innato en ella, pueda colaborar en la gran obra de emancipación política y reconstrucción nacional que se está efectuando.

H. Veracruz, marzo 3 de 1915.

Woman as Collaborator in Public Life

Sunday supplement of El Pueblo
Veracruz, Mexico
3 March 1915

As EL PUEBLO begins a weekly supplement devoted to women, I regret, although I also appreciate, that I have been put in charge of it so courteously, because there is no lack of well-sharpened pens and forceful reasoning, at the same time elegantly written, that would not have failed to give greater luster to this publication, and to better defend the just and sympathetic cause that this Section is going to start up.

Furthermore, my pitiful intellectual worth is bolstered by the good will that motivates me, and that hopefully will remain uppermost in the minds of those who honor me by reading my poorly spun writings.

Having stated the above, and after introducing myself respectfully to the illustrious readers of EL PUEBLO, I now address my topic.

Much has been written about woman's intellectual capacity to take part in the public life of nations and about her equality and inferiority with respect to the man, and after great philosophers like [John] Stuart Mill have presented such forceful arguments as those that the said philosopher's book contain, to which I have just made reference, titled "The Subjection of Women," I humbly confess that I have nothing to add in this regard.

And in fact, woman, given the same psychic qualities as man, such as intelligence, willpower, reason, memory, feeling, etc., etc., has the right to aspire to a better life than the one she currently leads, and that emotive law, which by their very indisputable strength improves and perfects, must be fulfilled in her, in spite of all the difficulties and all the obstacles that obstruct her path, because "although the declaration of Victor Hugo—the Countess Pardo Bazán would tell us—about which the nineteenth-century emancipated men may have turned out to be faulty, it does not matter, everything has been a question of mere calculation."[9]

Therefore, those who maintain that woman should always be subject to man's domination, have proceeded by judging a priori. How can the intellectual inferiority of woman and her capacity for being involved in the political life of a people be judged, if up to now the fields of intellectual character and of politics have been forbidden to her? To those supporters of that inferiority and that capacity of woman, it can be said of them that they have positioned themselves at the same height as those who before the revolution of 1910 maintained saying that the Mexican people were not fit for democracy, being that the ones guilty of such ineptitude were the same ones who were making a weapon of it against the beginning of our current political movement. If the Mexican people were not fit for democracy, it was because their leaders back then prohibited their right to master that aptitude and for which end the people had to rebel against those who were blocking their progress. If the woman is not fit for public life, it is because she has not been given the means to achieve such ability. Woman, when her intellectual faculties have been carefully developed, will come to comprise a first-rank component in social and political life, because in addition to her intellectual faculties atrophied even till today by the slavery in which she has lived, she possesses an intuitive spirit much finer and developed than man's, a special sensibility, an emotivity, shall I say, that allows her to instinctively foresee danger, that makes her perceive by premonition better than many psychologists the loyal ones from the disloyal ones, situations that the man most highly skilled in practical knowledge of the life and of the human heart cannot easily discover. Where a politician believes he has found a well-intentioned partisan, talented and with technical aptitudes, the woman foresees or senses in advance the core of duplicity, treachery, and audacity, which takes the place of true talent.

An eloquent example of this truth, my dear readers, you will find in the case of Madame Roland:[10] while her husband a man of State, meticulous, parsimonious, solemn, could not find his path or an orientation, she knew who were the ones that were capable of making the revolutionary ideas triumphant, and she was able to select a group of them and direct it, thus inspiring the admiration and respect of her coreligionists, while earning at the same time the hatred of her enemies, as a result of the fear that seized them when confronted with her insight.

From the English philosopher [John] Stuart Mill I take the following phrase, referring to his wife Mrs. Taylor . . . "She has been very useful to me for my writings, long or short, with her observations full of insight and astuteness."

Renan[11] took one of his sisters to Syria, and there they wrote the greater part of the works of that genius and when she died, the writer made known his deep feelings, by repeating frequently that "in her he had lost her support, her warmth and her cooperation."

In our country there are tangible examples of women's intuitive faculties, because they were the ones who best recognized the accomplices of Huerta,[12] even among those who while they were displaying friendly smiles toward the revolution, were carrying the weapons of treachery and crime hidden in their clothing. Presently those same women are the ones who have the sharpest powers of observation and tact to unmask and pursue the enemies.

Therefore, I believe that as compensation for the highly active role that the Mexican woman has played in all the stages of this revolution, the [male] revolutionaries are obliged to give her all necessary means to develop her intellectual skills so that combined with the innate intuitive spirit within her, she may collaborate in the great undertaking of political emancipation and national reconstruction that is taking place.

H. Veracruz, 3 March 1915.[13]

Jovita Idar (A. V. Negra and Astrea)

Jovita Idar (1885–1946) was a Laredo, Texas, teacher, a key contributor to her family's Spanish-language newspaper *La Crónica* (The Chronicle), a founding member of the city's woman's group La Liga Femenil Mexicanista (The Mexican Feminine League), and a nurse who along with activist Leonor Villegas de Magnón initiated La Cruz Blanca (the Mexican White Cross) in 1913.[1] Like many of the mexicana rhetors collected here, Idar was also involved in a number of journalistic endeavors beyond *La Crónica*, taking on leadership roles as well as contributing her own writing. The article "El Estudiante" in an October 1911 issue of *La Crónica* makes clear that Idar published her own educational newspaper, *El Estudiante* (The Student). Additionally, scholar Clara Lomas has found that Idar worked for several periodicals in southern Texas: *El Eco del Golfo* (The Gulf's Echo) in Corpus Christi; *La Luz* (The Light) in San Benito; *La Prensa* (The Press) in San Antonio—and in 1916, with the assistance of her brothers, she founded the daily *Evolución* (Evolution) ("Revolutionary" xv).

Working under her father, Nicasio, and with her brothers, Clemente and Eduardo, Jovita took on both writing and editorial duties for *La Crónica*. With Jovita's help and direction, this press was a revolutionary resource for Mexican people living on the U.S.-Mexico border. Scholar Jose Limón explains that through the newspaper, the Idars launched a "campaign of journalistic resistance" in which the press and its contributors actively fought the "social conditions oppressing Texas-Mexicans" (87). One contributor to *La Crónica* confirms the newspaper's prerogatives, writing that the "objective and point of reference in [*La Crónica*'s] work" is "the INSTRUCTION, the LIBERTY, and the DIGNIFICATION of the Mexican race wherever this may be" ("El segundo año de vida de La Crónica en su segunda época"). The focus of Idar's writings supports this emphasis, but because her contributions also concern themselves specifically with women's issues, we can assume that Idar helped make the newspaper into a rhetorical space that welcomed both conversations on the topic of women's roles and mexicana writers themselves. The selections in this volume by Sara Estela Ramírez, Leonor Villegas de Magnón, and María Rentería, as well as the articles publicizing La Liga, suggest the power of Idar's editorial hand.

As a writer for *La Crónica*, Idar contributed articles under her own name, but she also published work under the psuedonyms A. V. Negra and Astrea.[2] As A. V. Negra, which phonetically translates into "Black Bird," Idar published at least two educational articles in *La Crónica*, "Por la raza: la niñez mexicana en Texas" ("For the Mexican People: Mexican Children in Texas") and "Por la raza: la conservación del nacionalismo" ("For the Mexican People: The Preservation of Nationalism"), both collected here. These articles reflect the deeply strained political and educational scene in Texas at the onset of the Mexican Revolution. Published in August 1911, just nine months after war began, the two pieces focus on the educational hardships Mexicans faced due to war and migration as well as the grave problems they encountered attempting to educate their children on U.S. soil. Idar argues that to preserve Mexican identity, schools for Mexican students must have Mexican cultural and Spanish language instruction as well as communal control. Idar is clear that Mexican children should learn the English language so they can "communicate directly with their neighbors" and "stand up for their rights," but this learning should not be at the expense of Spanish. Idar writes that Mexican students should still learn Spanish, "because it is the official stamp of the races and of the peoples." When Idar makes these claims regarding both Spanish and English language instruction, she speaks with other contributors collected here, namely Leonor Villegas de Magnón and Aurora Lucero-White Lea.

Writing under the psuedonym Astrea, Idar published at least two additional articles: "Para la mujer que lee" ("To the Woman Who Reads") and "Debemos trabajar" ("We Must Work"). In these writings, Idar specifically addresses elite women in her community and considers questions of education and work pertinent to this particular contingent. While in "Para la mujer que lee" Idar extols the benefits education grants women, in "Debemos trabajar" she takes a vigilant stance concerning women's place in the world by proposing that the educated Mexican woman should work outside the home. Such labor, of course, was traditionally reserved only for men, but with the Mexican Revolution raging just miles away across the border, Idar's world was in flux. She and her counterparts were realizing the need to work outside the home as a means of supporting their families as well as an opportunity to gain a new sense of direction and purpose in their lives.

Por la raza: la niñez mexicana en Texas

A. V. Negra

La Crónica
Laredo, Texas
10 de agosto de 1911

Nuestra Patria está demasiado ocupada en sus asuntos interiores para poder atender á sus hijos que, por los azares de la fortuna ó por cualquier otra causa de las muchas que se presentan, se han visto obligados á salvar los linderos de la Patria para internarse en terreno extranjero; por lo tanto, si queremos que no se estanque el desenvolvimiento mental de nuestros compatriotas, no nos queda otro recurso que el de velar nosotros mismos por el bien de nuestros coterráneos.

Gran parte del desprecio con que nos ven los extranjeros que nos rodean, es debido á la falta de instrucción, y más aún, á la ignorancia crasa de una inmensa mayoría de nuestros compatriotas y puesto que ya no es fácil instruir á esas grandes masas de obreros, cuando menos podemos esforzarnos y hasta llegar al sacrificio, si fuere necesario, para ilustrar á nuestros hijos, para que cuando menos conjuremos el mal en el futuro.

Con profunda pena hemos visto á maestros mexicanos enseñando inglés á niños de su raza, sin tomar para nada en cuenta el idioma materno, que cada día se va olvidando más y cada día va sufriendo adulteraciones y cambios que hieren materialmente el oído de cualquier mexicano, por poco versado que esté en [el] idioma de Cervantes.

Y este problema no tiene más que una solución: dado que nuestro gobierno no puede enviar profesores aptos, que á expensas de él ilustren á sus hijos expatriados, y puesto que en las Escuelas americanas ni aún los maestros mexicanos (con muy honrosas excepciones) quieren enseñar la lengua nacional á nuestra niñez, de allí se impone que nosotros, los padres de niños mexicanos en Texas, debemos unirnos para sufragar los gastos que una escuela requiere.

Casi no hay pueblo en la parte sur del Estado de Texas y aún en toda la línea divisoria en que no habiten suficientes mexicanos aptos para sufragar las expensas que una Escuela requiere y solo falta que, unidos todos en los distintos lugares comprendamos la enorme trascendencia del asunto de que nos ocupamos.

De las Escuelas Normales de Monterrey, Saltillo y muchos otros lugares salen cada año jóvenes profesores, viriles, llenos de energías y de profundos conocimientos y con pocas presunciones respecto de la parte pecuniaria, jóvenes que, estoy seguro, vendrían gustosos á desempeñar entre nosotros los servicios de su profesión á nuestro primer llamado.

La niñez mexicana en Texas necesita instruirse. Ni nuestro gobierno ni el de EE. UU. pueden hacer nada por ella, y no queda otro recurso que el de hacerlo por nuestro propio impulso á trueque da no seguir despreciados y vejados por los extranjeros que nos rodean.

For the Mexican People: Mexican Children in Texas

A. V. Negra

La Crónica
Laredo, Texas
10 August 1911

Our Nation is too busy with her internal affairs to be able to attend to her sons and daughters who, due to accidents of fortune or for any other reason of the many which present themselves, have been obliged to cross the borders of the Nation to enter into foreign terrain; therefore, if we desire that the mental development of our compatriots not become stagnant, we have no other recourse than to watch over the welfare of our countrymen ourselves.

Much of the disdain that the foreigners who surround us feel toward us is due to the lack of education, and even more, the crass ignorance of the great majority of our compatriots, and since it is no longer easy to instruct those great masses of workers, we can at least make an effort even to the point of sacrifice, if it were necessary, to educate our children, so that we at least avert harm in the future.

With deep sorrow we have seen our Mexican teachers teaching English to children of their race, without taking into account at all their mother tongue, which daily is being forgotten more and is suffering adulterations and changes that absolutely wound the ears of any Mexican, no matter how little he is versed in the language of Cervantes.

And this problem has no more than one solution: given that our government cannot send skilled instructors, which at its own expense can educate its expatriate sons and daughters, and since in the American schools not even the Mexican teachers (with very honorable exceptions) want to teach the national language to our children, therefore it is imperative that we, the parents of Mexican children in Texas, should unite in order to finance the expenses that a school requires.

There is virtually no town in the southern part of the State of Texas or even all along the entire border where there are not enough Mexicans who live there equipped to support the expenses that a School requires, and the only remaining task is that everyone together in the different places understand the huge transcendence of the issue that we are undertaking.

From the Normal Schools of Monterrey, Saltillo, and many other places are graduating each year young teachers, strong, full of energy and deep knowledge, and with few presumptions about pecuniary matters, young people who, I am sure, would gladly come at our first call to carry out the services of their profession among us.

The Mexican children in Texas need to be educated. Neither our government nor that of the U.S.A. can do anything for them, and there remains no other recourse than to undertake it through our own efforts, in exchange for not continuing to be despised and humiliated by the foreigners who surround us.

Por la raza: la conservación del nacionalismo

A. V. Negra

La Crónica
Laredo, Texas
17 de agosto de 1911

En nuestro articulo anterior dijimos que "con profunda pena hemos visto á maestros mexicanos enseñando inglés á niños de su raza, sin tomar para nada en cuenta el idioma materno," con lo cual no quisimos significar, ni mucho menos, que no deba enseñárseles la lengua de la tierra que habitan, puesto que es el medio que los ha de poner en comunicación directa con sus vecinos, y el que los habilitará para que hagan valer sus derechos; lo que quisimos significar simplemente, es que no debe desatenderse el idioma nacional, porque es el sello característico de las razas y de los pueblos. Las naciones desaparecen y las castas se hunden cuando se olvida la lengua nacional; por eso no existen ya como nación los Aztecas. Por su idioma influyó tanto Roma en las naciones que había conquistado y si no constituyen una nación los judíos del día, es porque cada uno habla el idioma de la tierra que habita.

No decimos que no se enseñe el inglés á la niñez méxico-texana, sea en hora buena, decimos que no se olviden de enseñarles el castellano, pues así como les es útil la aritmética y la gramática así les es útil el inglés á los que viven entre los que hablan ese idioma.

Todos somos la hechura del medio ambiente: amamos las cosas que hemos visto desde nuestra infancia y creemos en lo que se infiltró en nuestra alma desde los primeros años de nuestra vida, por lo tanto, si en la escuela americana á que concurren nuestros niños se les enseña la biografía de Washington y no la de Hidalgo y en vez de los hechos gloriosos de Juárez se le refieren las hazañas de Lincoln, por más que éstas sean nobles y justas, no conocerá ese niño las glorias de su Patria, no la amará y hasta verá con indiferencia á los coterráneos de sus padres.

No faltó algún México-Texano que, con la más sana intención del mundo engalanara la solapa de su saco con el retrato del heróico Juárez, el 16 de [s]eptiembre de 1910. Eso subleva a cualquiera qua ama á su raza. Mexicanos tan buenos y honrados, tan patriotas y dignos ¿Por qué han de ignorar las acciones sublimes de los que se sacrificaron por darnos libertad?

Cierto es que estamos en el país del negocio, y que "time is money" pero, aunque no son indispensables la historia ni la geografía para ganar el sustento, sí lo son buenos para la conservación del patriotismo.

La niñez México-Texana necesita de instrucción para granjearse el aprecio y simpatía de los que le rodean, para obtener con mayor facilidad el sustento y para ser más influyente.

For the Mexican People: The Preservation of Nationalism

A. V. Negra

La Crónica
Laredo, Texas
17 August 1911

In our last article we said that "with deep sorrow we had seen Mexican teachers teaching English to the children of their race, without taking into account at all their mother tongue," by this we did not mean, far from it, that our children should not be taught the language of the land that they live in, since it is the means that will enable them to communicate directly with their neighbors, and that will equip them to stand up for their rights; what we simply meant to say is that the national language must not be disregarded, because it is the official stamp of the races and of the peoples. Nations disappear and lineage sinks into oblivion once the national language is forgotten; that is why the Aztecs do not exist anymore as a nation. Rome had so much influence in all the nations that it had conquered because of its language, and if the Jews are not a nation today it is because each one of them speaks the language of the land they inhabit.

We do not say that English should not be taught to Mexican-Texan children, it is very fortunate, we do say that it should not be forgotten to teach them Spanish, just as arithmetic and grammar is useful to them, English is useful to those who live among those who speak that language.

We are all shaped by our surroundings: we love the things that we have seen since our childhood and we believe in what was infused into our spirit since the first years of our lives; therefore, if in the American schools that our children attend they are taught the biography of Washington and not that of Hidalgo and if instead of the glorious acts of Juárez they are told of the accomplishments of Lincoln, no matter how noble and just they might be, that child will never know the glories of his country, he will not love it, and will even look with indifference at the countrymen of his parents.

Even some Mexican-Texan, with the best intentions in the world, decorated the lapel of his suit coat with the portrait of the hero Juárez on the 16th of September of 1910.[3] This stirs up anyone who loves his people. Such good and honorable Mexicans, patriotic and dignified, why must they ignore the sublime actions of those that sacrificed themselves to give us liberty?

It is certain that we are in the country of business and that "time is money," but although history and geography are not indispensable to earn a living, they are good for the preservation of our patriotism.

The Mexican-Texan children need education to gain the appreciation and sympathy of those around them, to obtain their living more easily, and to be more influential.

Para la mujer que lee

Astrea

La Crónica

Laredo, Texas

26 de octubre de 1911

No cabe duda que la instrucción eleva á la mujer. La mujer que posee algunos conocimientos trata siempre de conservarse á cierto nivel moral que mucho le ayuda en la lucha por la vida, haciéndola más buena, más pura y guiando sus pasos por la senda de la virtud.

La mujer educada, que ha recibido en el hogar y en la escuela los principios fundamentales de una buena enseñanza moral y que los sigue, se ve respetada, exaltada y atendida en todas partes donde se presenta, notándose la influencia de su educación en todos sus actos. Si va por la calle, va con recato y honestidad, no buscando el piropo callejero ni la admiración pasajera que todos los hombres están dispuestos á rendir á aquella que sale á la calle con deseos de "hacer conquistas," faltando aún al respeto que a sí misma se deben.

La influencia de la educación se extiende aún hasta á las relaciones sociales, pues la mujer pura y honesta gana sus amigos (no admiradores) en buena lid; no conquistará muchos pero los que llegan á comprender las cualidades de su corazón, fraternizan con ella, rindiéndole siempre el incienso de un cariño leal y perdurable que la mujer coqueta nunca puede llegar á conquistar.

La mujer, instruida, tendrá más oportunidades para hacerse valer, hacerse respetar y para obtener trabajos con mejores salarios que la ignorante que solo puede dedicarse á las faenas más duras y pesadas cuando llega el momento en que afrontar el problema de buscar su propio sustento.

La mujer, instruida, las más de las veces es buena, y siendo buena esparce un ambiente de pureza que eleva al hombre, pues ante su presencia, ante la rectitud de su porte, ante la nobleza y lo exaltado de sus pensamientos y sentimientos, ante la naturalidad de sus acciones y la sencillez de sus modales, el hombre rinde respetuoso las nobles cualidades y los más inmaculados sentimientos de que es susceptible.

Los hombres halagan la vanidad de las que van buscando alabanzas, de las que desean verse siempre agasajadas y entronizadas, pues conocen su lado débil, pero la mujer que es pura, con su misma castidad se ve defendida, pues los hombres por incultos que sean siempre respetan á la mujer que se da á respetar.

La mujer debe procurar siempre adquirir conocimientos útiles y benéficos pues en los tiempos modernos tiene amplios horizontes; las ciencias, las industrias, el taller, y aún el mismo hogar, exigen sus mejores aptitudes, su perseverancia y constancia en el trabajo y su influencia y ayuda para todo lo que sea progreso y adelanto para la humanidad.

To the Woman Who Reads

Astrea

La Crónica
Laredo, Texas
26 October 1911

There is no doubt that education elevates the woman. The woman who possesses some knowledge always tries to keep herself at a certain moral level that helps her greatly in the fight for life, by making her better, more pure, and by guiding her steps along the path of virtue.

The educated woman, who has received at home and in school the fundamental principles of a good moral education, and follows it, is respected, exalted, and received well wherever she goes, by the influence of her education being visible in all her acts. If she walks along the street, she walks with circumspection and honesty, not searching for flirtatious remarks nor the fleeting admiration that every man is willing to give to that woman who goes out in public with desires "to make conquests," by offending even the respect that she owes to herself.

The influence of education extends even to social relations, because the pure and honest woman wins her friends (not admirers) fair and square; she will not conquer many but those who come to understand the qualities of her heart will befriend her, by always burning the incense of a loyal and lasting affection to her, that the flirtatious woman can never come to conquer.

The educated woman will have more opportunities to make herself valued, to make herself respected, and to obtain jobs with better salaries than the ignorant woman who can only dedicate herself to the most difficult and tiring tasks when the moment arrives to face the problem of finding her own sustenance.

The educated woman is good most of the time, and since she is good, she exudes an atmosphere of purity that elevates the man, because in her presence, in the presence of the righteousness of her behavior, in the presence of the loftiness and the exalted nature of her thoughts and feelings, in the presence of the unaffectedness of her actions, and the simplicity of her manners, the man respectfully gives back the noble qualities and the most pure feelings he is sensitive to.

Men flatter the vanity of those women who seek praise, who always want to be complimented and enthroned because they know their weak side, but the woman who is pure, with her own chastity she is protected, because men, no matter how uneducated they are, always respect the woman who shows herself to be worthy of respect.

The woman should always try to acquire useful and beneficial knowledge, because in these modern times she has wide horizons; the sciences, industries, workshops, and even her very home demand her better abilities, her perseverance and consistency in her work, and her influence and aid for everything that is progress and advancement for humanity.

Debemos trabajar

Astrea

La Crónica
Laredo, Texas
23 de noviembre de 1911

La mujer moderna, enterada de y reconociendo la necesidad de aportar su contingente para ayudar al desarrollo á ilustración de los pueblos, se apresta valerosa, é invade los campos de la industria en todas sus fases sin temor y sin pereza. Abandona la holganza y la inacción, puesto que en la época actual, tan llena de oportunidades de vida; tan repleta de energía y de esperanzas, no hay lugar para los zánganos sociales.

La inacción, indolencia, se ven hoy en día como indignas, y como tal, se desechan por todos aquellos que se consideren factores en el desenvolvimiento y progreso de los pueblos.

La mujer moderna no pasa sus días arrell[a]nada en cómoda butaca, ni la rica lo hace, puesto que también las halagadas de la fortuna se dedican á la práctica de la caridad, ú obras filantrópicas, á la organización de clubs benéficos, ó recreativos, pues lo que se desea es hace[r] algo útil pa[r]a sí ó para sus semejantes.

La mujer obrera reconociendo sus derechos, alza la frente orgullosa y se apronta a la lucha; la época de su degradación ha pasado, ya no es la esclava vendida por unas cuantas monedas, ya no es la sierva, sino la igual del hombre, su compañera, [siendo] [é]ste su protector natural y no su amo y señor.

Mucho se ha tratado y escrito contra el movimiento fem[i]nista, pero á pesar de los oposicionistas ya en California las mujeres pueden dar su voto como jurados y pueden desempeñar oficinas públicas.

Yerran y mucho, esos espíritus descontentadizos, superficiales é indignos de una buena obra, críticos de aquella mujer, que haciendo á un lado los convencionalismos sociales dedica sus energías á trabajar por algo provechoso ó benéfico; los que, desconociendo la influencia moral que esto acarrea, puesto que una persona dedicada á ciertas labores ó tareas, no tiene tiempo para ocuparse de cosas fútiles ó perjudiciales. Más hace la constante obrera, tras las tablas de un mostrador sentada ante su máquina de coser, ó ya de oficinista, que la señorita holgada de tiempo que se ocupa de ir á visitas diarias, ó de recorrer uno por uno los establecimientos comerciales, viviente embudo de chismes ó cuentos vulgares.

La mujer soltera, digna y trabajadora, no exige vida á expensas del jefe de la familia, sea [é]ste padre, hermano, ó pariente, no; una mujer saludable, valerosa y fuerte, dedica sus energías, su talento á ayudar á su familia, ó cuando menos proveer su propia manutención.

Así como los hombres dignos y trabajadores ven con desprecio á los vagos y desocupados, así las obreras no aprecian á las inútiles y desocupadas.

We Must Work

Astrea

La Crónica
Laredo, Texas
23 November 1911

The modern woman, aware of and recognizing the need to contribute her part to the people in the educational development of nations, prepares herself bravely and invades the fields of industry, in all its phases, without fear and without laziness. She abandons all idleness and inactivity because in current times, so full of life opportunities; so replete with energy and hope, there is no place for social loafers.

Inaction, indolence are today seen as contemptible, and, as such, they are rejected by all those who may consider themselves to be factors in the development and progress of nations.

The modern woman does not spend her days lounging on her comfortable armchair; not even a rich woman does this, since also those who have been flattered by fortune dedicate themselves to the practice of charity or to philanthropic works, to the organization of charitable or recreational clubs, because what is wanted is to do something useful for themselves or for their fellow men.

The working woman, by recognizing her rights, raises her head in pride and gets ready for the struggle. The time of her degradation has passed, she is no longer the slave sold for a few coins, she is no longer the servant of, but the equal to man, his partner, by his being her natural protector, and not her lord and master.

Much has been dealt with and written against the feminist movement, but despite the oppositionists already in California, women can now cast their vote as members of a jury and can hold public office.[4]

How wrong they are, those disdainful souls, superficial, and unworthy of a good deed, critical of that woman who, pushing aside social conventions, dedicates her energies to work for something profitable or beneficial; those who, refusing to accept the moral influence which this brings about, since a person dedicated to certain jobs or tasks has no time to busy herself with futile or harmful things. The constant worker does more, behind the boards of a counter, seated in front of her sewing machine, or even as an office clerk, than the lazy young lady who busies herself with going on daily visits or going through business establishments, a living funnel of gossip or vulgar stories.

A single woman, both dignified and hardworking, does not demand a life at the expense of the head of the family, whether he be a father, brother, or relative, no; a healthy woman, brave and strong, dedicates her energy, her talent to helping her family, or at the very least to provide for her own support.

Just as dignified and hardworking men look with contempt on deadbeats and unemployed men, so also working women do not esteem useless and unemployed women.

Leonor Villegas de Magnón

Leonor Villegas de Magnón (1876–1955) was an activist in the Mexican Revolution, a nurse who, with Jovita Idar, started La Cruz Blanca (the Mexican White Cross), and a Laredo teacher who opened one of the first bilingual kindergartens in the city (Lomas, "Revolutionary" xxiv). Villegas de Magnón spent her life crossing and recrossing the border. Born in Nuevo Laredo, Mexico, she was educated at the Academy of Mount St. Ursula in New York. After earning her teaching certificate, she returned to Mexico, married Adolpho Magnón, and taught kindergarten. Deeply involved in the Mexican Revolution, Villegas de Magnón fled Mexico for Laredo, Texas, to find political refuge. There, she not only began her work with Idar for La Cruz Blanca but also contributed to the Idar family newspaper, *La Crónica* (The Chronicle), joining mexicana writers collected here such as Sara Estela Ramírez and María Rentería. During this period, Villegas de Magnón also composed her autobiography *The Rebel*, which chronicles her experiences during the Revolution and with La Cruz Blanca in particular.[1]

On 12 September 1911 the pages of *La Crónica* announced Villegas de Magnón and her work to its readers in this way:

> The columns of our newspaper are adorned with articles written by the distinguished and reputable woman from Laredo whose name [Villegas de Magnón] serves as an epigraph to these lines. I hope that other women of our cultured Laredo will come to know her ideas and imitate this honorable woman, this is why we offer to her the humble columns of this newspaper. ("Sra. Leonor Villegas de Mag[n]ón" 1)

While such an announcement may seem to define Villegas de Magnón as a demure Mexican woman, her articles challenge this perception. The two pieces collected here reveal Villegas de Magnón to be an outspoken activist who was eager to stake her claims regarding politics, education, and women's roles. In "Evolución mexicana" ("Mexican Evolution"), Villegas de Magnón praises Mexican revolutionary Francisco Madero, persuading her readers to see the exemplary qualities she identifies in him such as his "elevated understanding" and "heroic virtues." Importantly, though, Villegas de Magnón focuses on Madero's rhetorical acumen: she respects him because he does not attempt to rule by force but instead he leads people by "reasoning and logical argument." This quality is one she especially wants *La Crónica* readers to note, for it is through reasoned discourse, Villegas de Magnón explains, that citizens will gain trust in their leaders. Furthermore, she highlights the significance of Madero's leadership skills because by governing through reasoned discourse rather than the threat or violence Mexico will be equal to all other "civilized nations."

In "Adelanto de los mexicanos de Texas" ("Progress of Mexicans in Texas"), Villegas de Magnón turns her attention to everyday life for Mexican people living within the U.S. borderlands. She begins by citing the important work of El Congreso Mexicanista (Mexican Congress). This was the first of two congresses held in Laredo from 14 to 22 September 1911 and supported by *La Crónica*. As Villegas de Magnón notes in her opening, Mexican women were invited to participate. Recent scholars such as Sonia Salvídar-Hull and José Limón have discussed how this congress not only provided a space for Mexican people to discuss issues such as discrimination and education but also "offered a forum" for "an emergent feminist consciousness" (Salvídar-Hull 17–18).[2] Mexicana speakers at El Congreso such as Soledad Flores de Peña and Hortencia Moncayo used this moment to argue that women's rights should play a major part in the success of the Mexican community in Texas.

In "Adelanto de los Mexicanos de Texas," Villegas de Magnón considers a number of issues beyond the congress, focusing particularly on the preservation of the Spanish language and the role women, and especially mothers, should play in children's education. It is important to reflect critically on her position regarding Mexicans speaking what she calls "a jumble of English and Spanish words." From a twenty-first-century perspective, one might read in her argument a sense of elitism and even a precursor to an "English-only" or, in this case, "Spanish-only" claim. Remember, though, the context in which Villegas de Magnón was writing. Mexican people were at war and attempting to define their nation and their culture. Her words may thus illustrate a call for her people to hold tight to their Mexican identity.

Evolución mexicana

La Crónica
Laredo, Texas
7 de septiembre de 1911

(COLABORACIÓN.)

¿Qué mexicano puede leer el magnífico discurso de Francisco I. Madero, pronunciado últimamente en Cuautla, sin conmoverse, y sin rendirle espontáneo homenaje? Las justas razones que expone, serán las dominadoras del país y sus maravillosas acciones son solamente gérmenes de grandes virtudes.

Tenemos que reconocer en él, un entendimiento elevado, un entusiasmo sincero y desinteresado. Él trata de convencer por medio de la razón y el argumento, poniendo así al pueblo Mexicano á la altura de cualquier nación civilizada.

Ya no necesitamos el machete y el fusil, para enseñarnos nuestros deberes de ciudadanos, esos tiempos ya pasaron.

Madero domina al pueblo demostrándole que las virtudes heroicas no han muerto en el corazón mexicano, y aclama á los más nobles sentimientos que encierra el alma; nos recuerda que estamos á la altura de los héroes más magnánimos que ha tenido nuestra Patria.

Madero nos trata como seres racionales, como lo requiere una nación civilizada, pues la idea del honor y el patriotismo infundida por medio del machete y el fusil, solo ocasionará venganzas traidoras y horribles asesinatos, pero la idea de lealtad y respeto al gobierno infundida por la razón y guiada por nuestra conciencia, nos hará cumplir bien nuestro deber como buenos ciudadanos, pues las ideas deben ser soberanamente decididas por la razón.

Para mejorar y desarrollar La Constitución le fue menester ponerse en lucha abierta por medio de las armas; y habiendo triunfado, ahora nos predica el civismo que es, y será, causa y ocasión de progreso.

Deja el campo libre para todos. Todos podemos seguir las ideas políticas que más nos convengan sin temer de lucha injusta que se nos oponga.

La religión mezclada en asuntos interiores de Estado impide el progreso de la humanidad, y es monstruoso, falso é imposible que nuestro gran héroe tenga compromisos secretos con ningún partido ó secta.

También necesitamos en nuestra patria el militarismo, el ejército, pero no para combatirnos á nosotros mismos, no queremos que llene de terror á sus mismos hermanos pero sí, que nos proteja del enemigo extranjero, que sea una nota brillante en nuestras solemnizaciones, en nuestros [p]arques y lugares públicos, una protección en sus cuarteles; dóciles y héroes en el campo de batalla, que predomine el sentimiento moral. Ahora se cometen crímenes por los que siguen la causa de la revolución, crímenes que deben reportarse, pero estos crímenes no deben ni pueden denigrar la causa de la revolución en cuyo nombre se cometen.

Un "leader" no puede ser culpable por todos los desórdenes ni las intrigas de los enemigos y si la causa es buena tiene que triunfar.

Mexican Evolution

La Crónica
Laredo, Texas
7 September 1911

(COLLABORATION.)

What Mexican can read the magnificent speech of Francisco I. Madero,[3] delivered recently in Cuautla, without being moved, and without rendering spontaneous homage to him? The just reasoning that he expounds will be that which dominates the country, and his marvelous actions are only the seedlings of great virtues.

We have to recognize in him an elevated understanding, and a sincere and altruistic enthusiasm. He tries to persuade by means of reasoning and logical argument, in this way putting the Mexican people at the height of any civilized nation.

We no longer need the machete and the rifle to teach us our duties as citizens, those times have already passed.

Madero commands the people by demonstrating to them that the heroic virtues have not died in the Mexican heart, and he acclaims the noblest sentiments held by the soul; he reminds us that we are at the height of the most magnanimous heroes that our Fatherland has had.

Madero treats us like rational beings, as a civilized nation requires, because the idea of honor and patriotism instilled by the machete and rifle will only result in treacherous revenge and horrible assassinations, but the idea of loyalty and respect for the government inspired by reason and guided by our conscience will make us fulfill our duty well as good citizens, because ideas must be decided supremely by reason.

In order to improve and develop The Constitution, he had to engage in an open struggle by means of weapons; and having triumphed, now he preaches good citizenship that is, and will be, the cause and opportunity of progress.

He leaves the field free for all. We can follow the political ideas that most suit our purposes without fear that an unjust fight will oppose us.

Religion mixed in internal affairs of State impedes the progress of humanity, and it is monstrous, false, and impossible for our great hero to have secret commitments with any party or sect.

We also need militarism in our fatherland, the army, but not for fighting each other, we do not want them to fill their own brothers with fear but yes, to protect us from foreign enemies, let it be a brilliant note in our solemn occasions, in our parks and public places, a protection in their barracks; docile and heroes on the battlefield, and let moral sentiment predominate. Now crimes are committed by those who support the cause of the revolution, crimes that must be reported, but these crimes cannot and must not denigrate the cause of the revolution in whose name they are committed.

A "leader" cannot be culpable for all the disorder or intrigues of his enemies, and if the cause is good it has to triumph.

Adelanto de los mexicanos de Texas

La Crónica
Laredo, Texas
21 de septiembre de 1911

(COLABORACIÓN.)

Con profundo agradecimiento habrán leído todas las mujeres mexicanas la atenta invitación que se les hace por medio de "La Crónica," para concurrir á las reuniones del Congreso Mexicanista.

"La realización de tan bello ideal es ya un hecho" y la cortesía que se tiene para con las mujeres demuestra el grado de civilización de un país.

Es verdad que nuestra Patria ha tenido últimamente un sacudimiento espantoso, pues al llegar la verdadera hora de la democracia se ha descubierto que es necesario no s[o]lamente conquistar el poder, sino que es aún más necesaria la inteligencia para conservarlo.

El artículo escrito por el Señor Mercado es muy loable pues en [é]l expone ciertas condiciones que realmente existen en el Estado de Texas.

El vocabulario del mexicano en la frontera es pésimo y la tendencia de mezclar nuestro lindo y bello idioma con el [i]nglés está muy arraigado.

Con frecuencia, se escuchan conversaciones principiadas en español sostenidas en inglés y terminadas en [e]spañol haciendo un horroroso "pot pourri," ó usando las palabras salteadas, unas en inglés y otras en español.

Esta tendencia parece ser enfermedad crónica de los fronterizos.

¿Qué no es bastante rico nuestro propio idioma para sostener una conversación satisfactoriamente?

¡Y con cu[á]nto orgullo cometemos estos errores, como si eso nos hiciera valer más!

Debemos evitar [e]ste abuso de lenguaje que predomina ahora.

Los países tienen sus cambios pausadamente y lo que contribuye más al progreso de una nación, es la educación de las masas.

La voz del pueblo es la autoridad infalible, que se debe de oír, así como hacerse sentir clara y distintamente.

Si damos una mirada retrospectiva veremos que las mujeres no ocupaban el lugar que hoy se nos da, y hoy, más que nunca[,] debemos hacernos dignas de ese lugar que se nos proporciona.

Debemos marchar con los tiempos, debemos revestirnos de energías y voluntad para alcanzar, percibir y comprender los pasos gigantezcos de progreso que está dando nuestro país.

"La mano que mece la cuna es la que gobierna el mundo," de nosotras depende la inteligencia, el saber y la riqueza que proporcionarán más tarde á la patria, los pequeños ciudadanos que Dios nos confía desde el momento que llegan al mundo.

¡Con cu[á]nto anhelo, debemos vigilar la educación *moral* y *física* de tan preciosa carga! Pero el mal entendido amor maternal nos hace á veces perjudicar á nuestros hijos, esclavizándonos al prepararlos para lo que nos parece un porvenir brillante.

Más tarde sufrimos amargas decepciones, pues nuestros hijos resultan holgazanes, por haberles evitado que hicieran trabajo alguno, ya porque no había necesidad ó porque lo consideramos degradante, sin comprender ¡pobres madres! cegadas por el cariño, que el trabajo físico desarrolla la salud y la fuerza y que el trabajo moral é intelectual es el que más dignifica y enaltece al hombre.

Y en cuanto al sexo femenino, es falso el amor propio de nuestra raza que evita á las mujeres que aprendan á trabajar.

Si en nuestra juventud se nos enseñara toda clase de labores como un lujo, como un adorno, evitaríamos mas tarde amargos sufrimientos.

Nuestros connacionales caminan hacia una época más venturosa, todo demuestra el adelanto y el progreso del elemento mexicano en Texas; como se ha evidenciado por las concurridas reuniones que ha verificado el Congreso Mexicanista, á cuyos miembros felicitamos muy cordialmente, rogando á Dios los ilumine en esta grandiosa obra que han principiado y colme de bendiciones al joven que tuvo la feliz idea de convocar esta asamblea.

The Progress of the Mexicans in Texas

La Crónica
Laredo, Texas
21 September 1911

(COLLABORATION.)

With profound gratitude all Mexican women will have read the courteous invitation which was extended to them by means of "La Crónica" to attend the meetings of the Mexican Congress.

"The realization of such a beautiful ideal is now a fact," and the courtesy that is shown toward the women demonstrates the degree of civilization of a country.

It is true that our Nation has recently had a frightful shock, because when the true hour of democracy arrived, it has been discovered that it is necessary not only to conquer power, but the intelligence to preserve it is even more necessary.

The article written by Mr. Mercado is very praiseworthy, because in it he exposes certain conditions that really exist in the State of Texas.[4]

The vocabulary of the Mexican at the border is terrible, and the tendency to mix our beautiful, lovely language with English is deeply rooted.

Frequently, one hears conversations begun in Spanish, continued in English, and ended in Spanish, making a horrible "potpourri," or by using stolen words, some in English and others in Spanish.

This tendency seems to be a chronic disease of borderland inhabitants.

Isn't our own language rich enough to carry on a satisfactory conversation?

And with how much pride do we commit these errors, as if that made us worth more!

We should avoid this abuse of language, which is predominant now.

Countries have their changes unhurriedly, and what contributes most to the progress of a nation is the education of the masses.

The voice of the people is the infallible authority, which must be heard, just as it must be perceived clearly and distinctly.

If we look back in time we will see that women did not use to occupy the place that we are now given, and today, more than ever, we should make ourselves worthy of that place that is afforded to us.

We should march with the times, we should arm ourselves with energies and willpower in order to reach, perceive, and understand the gigantic steps of progress that our country is taking.

"The hand that rocks the cradle is the one that governs the world." It depends on us, the intelligence, knowledge, and richness that they will later provide to the nation, the little citizens who God entrusts to us from the moment that they arrive on earth.

With how much yearning we must watch over the moral and physical education of such a precious cargo! But the misunderstood maternal love at times leads us to harm our children, by enslaving ourselves when preparing them for what appears to us a brilliant future.

Later we suffer bitter disappointments, since our children turn out to be lazybones, by having prevented them from doing any work, perhaps because there was no need or because we thought it was degrading, without understanding, poor mothers, blinded by love that physical work develops health and strength, and that intellectual and moral labor is what most dignifies and ennobles mankind.

And with regard to the feminine sex, the self-esteem of our people that prevents women from learning to work is false.

If in our youth we were taught all kinds of labor as a sort of luxury, as an adornment, then later we would avoid bitter suffering.

Our countrymen are walking toward a happier age, everything demonstrates the advancement and progress of the Mexican population in Texas; as has been shown by the well-attended meetings that the Mexican Congress has carried out, whose members we very cordially congratulate, praying that God may inspire them in the magnificent work that they have begun and that He may shower blessings upon the young man who had the felicitous idea of convoking this assembly.

Sara Estela Ramírez

Sara Estela Ramírez (1881–1910) was born in Coahuila, Mexico, where she was also educated and earned her teacher's certificate. In 1898 she crossed the border to Laredo, Texas, and worked as a teacher in the Seminario Laredo. Although Ramírez died at twenty-nine, she lived a full, active life. In addition to her work as a teacher, she was a poet, labor organizer, and political activist who steadfastly supported Mexico's Partido Liberal Mexicano (PLM; Mexican Liberal Party), an activist group that challenged the rule of Mexican president Porfirio Díaz. Ramírez also worked extensively for Spanish-language presses along the Texas-Mexico border: she contributed to newspapers such as *La Crónica* (The Chronicle) and *El Democrata Fronterizo* (The Democratic Frontier); began two publications of her own, *La Corregidora*[1] and *Aurora*; and collaborated with Juana Gutiérrez B. de Mendoza and Elisa Acuña y Rossetti to work on *Vésper: Justicia y Libertad* (Vesper: Justice and Liberty). Through her active presence in these newspapers and her involvement in women's groups like Regeneración y Concordia (Regeneration and Unity), Ramírez embodied her own belief that women could and should "rise up" to change their worlds.

In 1910, Ramírez published her poem "¡Surge! A la mujer" ("Rise Up! To Womankind") in *La Crónica*, a poem originally printed in Ramírez's *Aurora*.[2] At this time, poetry was often published in both U.S. and Mexican newspapers, so while this genre may seem out of place to twenty-first-century newspaper readers, those encountering "¡Surge! A la mujer" in 1910 would not have found it unusual. In this poem, Ramírez offers a new vision for the educated middle- and upper-class mexicana by arguing that she should see herself neither as distanced and reclusive from public life nor as servile to her husband. Rather, women should be actively involved in their communities. It is also important to note that this poem was published right before the commencement of the Mexican Revolution on 20 November 1910. Given Ramírez's activism, it is likely that she intended this poem to incite women to see themselves as key contributors to the political movement.

¡Surge! A la mujer

La Crónica
Laredo, Texas
9 de abril de 1910

¡Surge! surge á la vida, á la actividad, á la belleza de vivir realmente: pero surge radiante y poderosa, bella de cualidades, esplendente de virtudes, fuerte de energías.

Tú, la reina del mundo; Diosa de la adoración universal; tú, la soberana á quien se rinde vasallaje, no te encierres así en tu templo de Dios, ni en tu camarín de cortesana triunfadora.

Eso es indigno de ti, antes que Diosa y Reina, sé madre, sé mujer.

Una mujer que lo es verdaderamente, es más que diosa y que reina. No te embriague el incienso en el altar, ni el aplauso en el escenario, hay algo más noble y más grande que todo eso.

Los dioses son arrojados de los templos; los reyes son echados de sus tronos, la mujer es siempre la mujer.

Los Dioses viven lo que sus creyentes quieren. Los reyes viven mientras no son destronados; la mujer vive siempre y [é]ste es el secreto de su dicha, vivir.

Sólo la acción es vida; sentir que se vive, es la más hermosa sensación.

Surge, pues, á las bellezas de la vida; pero surge así, bella de cualidades, esplendente de virtudes, fuerte de energías.

(Tomado de "AURORA")

Rise Up! To Womankind

La Crónica
Laredo, Texas
9 April 1910

Rise up! rise up to life, to activity, to the beauty of truly living; but rise up radiant and powerful, beautiful with qualities, resplendent with virtues, strong with energies.

You, the queen of the world, Goddess of universal adoration; you, the sovereign to whom homage is given, do not confine yourself so in your temple of God, nor to your triumphant courtesan's chamber.

In other versions and printings of this poem, the line breaks vary. In our transcription and translation, we maintain the poem's original format in *La Crónica*.

That is unworthy of you, before Goddess or Queen, be a mother, be a woman.

One who is truly a woman is more than a goddess and one who reigns. Do not let the incense on the altar intoxicate you, nor the applause on the stage, there is something more noble and grand than all of that.

The gods are thrown out of temples; kings are driven from their thrones, woman is always woman.

The Gods live what their believers want. Kings live as long as they are not dethroned; woman always lives and this is the secret of her happiness, to live.

Only action is life; to feel that one lives is the most beautiful sensation.

But rise up, then, to the beauties of life; but rise up so, beautiful with qualities, resplendent with virtues, strong with energies.

(Taken from "AURORA")

Anonymous Writings on La Liga Femenil Mexicanista (The Mexicanist Feminine League)

As noted in the introductory material dedicated to Jovita Idar, at the onset of the Mexican Revolution in 1910, there was also in Laredo, Texas, the emergence of La Liga Femenil Mexicanista (The Mexicanist Feminine League). Founded on 15 October 1911, this Mexican women's league was led by Idar. Due to her professional and familial relationship to Laredo's Spanish-language newspaper *La Crónica*, it is no surprise that the women's group was publicized in the pages of the press on numerous occasions, two of which are collected here (Cotera 227).

The 19 October 1911 article displays a listing of La Liga's board members, a rhetorical move that legitimized the group's activities and advanced the *ethos* of women coming together on the community's behalf. This article underscores a central function of the group: as the writer notes, women who were previously "isolated and scattered" are now by virtue of their collaborative work "allies" who are "strong and respected." The second article on 30 November 1911 makes clear that another purpose of La Liga was philanthropic and educational. These women cared for and instructed poor children in their city. But La Liga also offered a space for mexicana members to cultivate their own educational and rhetorical prowess. For instance, when debating a new name for La Liga, members such as María de Jesús de León and María Rentería composed biographies of Mexican heroines and delivered them at their meetings with the goal of persuading their peers to name the group after one of these women. Rentería's presentation was published in *La Crónica* and is collected here.

Liga Femenil Mexicanista

La Crónica
Laredo, Texas
19 de octubre de 1911

Para dar esta noticia el cronista quisiera tener palabras que fueran música y pensamientos sublimes, llenos de expresión y de sublime poesía.

Un grupo de damas que forman sociedad. Esto dicho así, tan á secas, parece algo sin importancia, algo insignificante, sin embargo, es de alta trascendencia y de mucha significación. Muchos huérfanos tendrán pan y muchas mujeres que aisladas y dispersas eran partes tan solo del sexo débil, aliadas serán fuertes y respetadas.

Entremos en materia. Un grupo de damas tan respetables como bellas se reunieron el domingo como á las diez de la mañana en el Salón de la Respetable Sociedad de Obreros "Igualdad y Progreso" y bajo los auspicios del Congreso Mexicanista organizaron la primera Liga Femenil Mexicanista con el ardiente anhelo de luchar ellas también POR LA RAZA Y PARA LA RAZA.

Como en su personal está lo más selecto y granado de la intelectualidad femenina, los debates que se presentaron para escoger el nombre de la heroína mexicana que habría de darse á la Liga, fueron instructivos y animados. La Srita. Profa. María de Jesús de León opinaba que debiera llamarse Liga Femenil Mexicanista "Josefa Ortiz de Domínguez" y para apoyar su tésis presentó la biografía de esa heroína, que es quizás la más grande que registran los anales de la Historia de México.

Alguien propuso llevar el nombre de alguna poeti[s]a mexicana y la Srita. Rentería presentó las biografías de Doña Leona Vicario y de Doña Manuela Aguado de Abasolo por ser ella de opinión que la Liga llevara alguno de esos dos nombres.

Nuestros lectores encontrarán esas biografías en otro lugar de LA CR[Ó]NICA.

En las elecciones que hicieron para señalar qui[é]nes debían formar la Mesa Directiva resultaron electas por mayoría las siguientes señoras y señoritas:

Para Presidenta, Jovita Idar.
Para Vice-Presidenta, Profa. M. de J. de León.
Para Secretaria, Profa. Soledad F. de Peña.
Para Tesorera, Profa. María Rentería.
Para Consejera [Generala], Profa. María Villarreal.
Vocales: Sritas Profas. Luisa Cabrera, Rita Tarvin y Sra. de Silva.
Comisión de Hacienda: Sra. de Jiménez y Srita. Silva.
Comisión de Propaganda: Sritas. Dolores Lawson y Herlinda Villarreal.

Es para nosotros un verdadero placer consignar noticias tan gratas y halagüeñas, pues la Sdad. de Sras. y Sritas. era una necesidad apremiante en Laredo.

Vaya nuestro parabién á la agrupación, por todos títulos honorable, de las damas Laredenses.

Mexicanist Feminine League

La Crónica
Laredo, Texas
19 October 1911

To impart this news, the reporter would like to have words that would be like music and sublime thoughts, full of expression and sublime poetry.

A group of ladies who form a society. Expressed this way, so bluntly, it seems like something without importance, something insignificant; nevertheless, it is highly transcendent and very significant. Many orphans will have bread and many women who, isolated and scattered, were part of only the weak sex, as allies will be strong and respected.

Let us get into the subject. A group of ladies, who are as respectable as they are beautiful, met on Sunday at about 10:00 in the morning in the salon of the Respectable Society of Workers "Equality and Progress" and under the auspices of the Mexicanist Conference they organized the first Liga Femenil Mexicanista [Mexicanist Feminine League] with the women's passionate desire to fight also ON BEHALF OF THE RACE AND FOR THE BENEFIT OF THE PEOPLE.

Since its membership includes the most select and eminent of the female intelligentsia, the debates that took place to choose the name of the Mexican heroine that would be given to the League were instructive and lively. The señorita Profesora María de Jesús de León was of the opinion that the club should be called the Mexicanist Feminine League "Josefa Ortiz de Domínguez," and to support her opinion she presented the heroine's biography, which is perhaps the greatest that has been recorded in the annals of the History of Mexico.

Someone proposed to take on the name of some Mexican poetess, and Miss Rentería presented the biographies of Doña Leona Vicario and Doña Manuela Aguado de Abasolo, because she was of the opinion that the League should carry one of these two names.

Our readers will find these biographies in another section of LA CRÓNICA.

In the elections that they held to indicate who should be the members of the Board of Directors, the following ladies were elected by majority vote:

For President, Jovita Idar.
For Vice-President, Prof. M. de J. de León.
For Secretary, Prof. Soledad F. de Peña.
For Treasurer, Prof. María Rentería.
For General Advisor, Prof. María Villarreal.
Members of the Board of Directors: The señoritas Prof. Luisa Cabrera, Prof. Rita Tarvin, and Mrs. De Silva.

Finance Committee: Mrs. Jiménez and Miss Silva.

Publicity Committee: Miss Dolores Lawson and Miss Herlinda Villarreal.

It is for us a true pleasure to report such agreeable and promising news, because the Society of señoras and señoritas was an urgent necessity in Laredo.

We send our congratulations to this group, honorable by all measures, of the ladies from Laredo.

La Liga Femenil Mexicanista

La Crónica
Laredo, Texas
30 de noviembre de 1911

La Liga Femenil Mexicanista No. 1. de Laredo, Texas, integrada por numerosas y muy respetables señoritas de Laredo, acaba de hacer su primera obra de beneficencia.

Los altos ideales y las altruistas miras que guía á este respetable cuerpo, organizado apenas hace dos meses, empiezan á realizarse.

Esta "Liga" en su sesión general, verificada el domingo pasado, acordó encargarse de la educación de dos niños pobres y para este efecto, las honorables señoritas Profesoras María Rentería y Berta Cantú ofrecieron espontáneamente y generosamente dar la enseñanza gratuita en sus establecimientos respectivos, comprometiéndose la asociación á encargarse del vestuario, compra de útiles, etc. etc. por contribución de l[o]s mismos miembros.

Uno de los fines porque trabajará esta sociedad, será también por ayudar algo á los pobres de Laredo. Se han visitado algunos que se encuentran en la más completa miseria y abandono, á quienes se ha proveído de ropa por algunas de las señoritas y alimentos por la muy respetable señora Doña Tomasita de Mendoza.

Esta asociación, que trabaja activamente por el adelanto general de sus co-asociados, que verifica sesiones donde se estudia y se aprende, donde se adquiere cultura y se desarrolla el talento sin orgías y sin ambiciones malsanas, que se dedica á realizar nobles y generosos fines, no cuenta con elementos pecuniarios, puesto que sus miembros todos pertenecen á la noble clase obrera; acaba de solicitar un beneficio de "El Teatro Solórzano" el cual se dará el viernes en la noche. Hacemos un llamamiento al pueblo mexicano en general para que asista á la función que se dará esa noche, y que en algo beneficiar[i]a á esta nueva y activa organización.

The Mexicanist Feminine League

La Crónica
Laredo, Texas
30 November 1911

The First Mexicanist Feminine League of Laredo, Texas, made up of numerous and highly respectable young women from Laredo, has just completed its first charity work.

The high ideals and altruistic goals that serve as a guide for this distinguished body, organized just two months ago, are beginning to be realized.

This "League" in its general session, which took place last Sunday, agreed to take charge of the education of two poor children and to this end, the honorable young ladies, Professors María Rentería and Berta Cantú, generously and spontaneously offered to give free instruction in their respective establishments, with the Association committing to take charge of clothing, purchasing supplies, etc. etc., by means of contributions from the members themselves.

One of the objectives for which this Society will work, will also be to help the poor people of Laredo a little. Some have been visited and are found living in the most extreme poverty and abandonment, to whom some of the ladies have provided clothing, and food by the distinguished lady, Doña Tomasita de Mendoza.

This Association, which works actively for the general progress of its co-associates, which holds sessions where one studies and learns, where culture is acquired and talent is developed without orgies and without unhealthy ambitions, which dedicates itself to carry out noble and generous ends, has no pecuniary resources, since its members all belong to the noble working class; it has just requested a benefit at "El Teatro Solórzano," which will take place Friday evening. We call upon the Mexican population in general to attend the function that will take place that night, and which will provide some support for this new and active organization.

María Rentería

María Rentería was a teacher and member of La Liga Femenil Mexicanista (The Mexicanist Feminine League), the woman's league that Jovita Idar helped to establish in Laredo, Texas. Like Idar, Rentería was likely an educated member of the Laredo elite and one of the city's teachers. Rentería published her work in *La Crónica* (The Chronicle), the newspaper that was owned and operated by Idar and her family, and by doing so, Rentería helped to extend the political goals of the press: to contribute to "the INSTRUCTION, the LIBERTY, and the DIGNIFICATION of the Mexican race wherever this may be" ("El segundo año"). Further, the growing pressures of the suffrage movement for women in the United States likely resonated among mexicanas, as women like Rentería explored concerns relating to women's rights and achievements. Through her participation in La Liga, Rentería worked towards the objectives identified by and for this collective of Laredo women and engaged with larger questions regarding women's civic engagement.

As noted by Chicana scholar Martha Cotera, La Liga's "goals were to struggle on behalf of the Mexican-American and to educate and develop women" (227).[1] The description of La Liga in a November 1911 issue of *La Crónica* (anthologized here) makes this point clear when the anonymous writer explains that this group aimed to achieve the "general progress" of its members by carrying out sessions where a woman "studies and learns, where culture is acquired and talent developed without . . . unhealthy ambitions" ("La Liga" 4). The overarching priority of La Liga, however, was to bring together women who might otherwise see themselves as "isolated and scattered" so that they could become "strong and respected" as "allies" ("Liga" 1).

Rentería's essay, "Leona Vicario y Rafaela López," which was a reprinted speech first given at a Liga meeting, reinforces the work of the collective. By speaking to her peers and then by writing to the readership of *La Crónica*, Rentería offers two biographies of exemplary, heroic women with whom her mexicana audience could identify. Moreover, Rentería's writing also reveals what might be read as a feminist impulse to challenge masculine forms of heroism when she sets out what heroism looks like from a woman's perspective. Finally, as the 19 October 1911 *La Crónica* entry dedicated to La Liga Feminil Mexicanista makes clear, while Rentería's speech is certainly an encomium to celebrate exemplary Mexican women, it was also part of a contest. At least three Liga members were proposing heroines after whom the league could be named, and the members of the group were tasked to decide which heroine to choose. Therefore, while La Liga was indeed a space for philanthropy and women's education, it was also a site for women such as Rentería to engage in rhetorical debate.

Leona Vicario y Rafaela López

La Crónica
Laredo, Texas
19 de octubre de 1911

Biografías leídas por la Srita. Profesora M. Rentería, en la Sesión la "Liga Femenil Mexicanista," verificada el [d]omingo 15 del mes en curso.

En nuestra Patria, en esta tierra querida que á veces ha sido desgraciada; han aparecido mujeres heróicas, dignas de que su nombre se perpetúe entre nosotros; al estudiar la Historia encontramos hermosos ejemplos de madres que se sacrificaron por sus hijas, de esposas que arrostraron mil peligros por salvar á sus esposos y engrandecer su patria, y de hijas que nada temieron y desafiaron todo por alcanzar la dicha de sus padres y Honor y Gloria para su Patria[.]

El amor a la Patria es uno de los más sublimes sentimientos del alma; tanto los hombres como las mujeres han sentido siempre intenso amor por el lugar en donde recibieron el primer beso maternal; por el sacrosanto lugar que guarda los despojos de los seres que les fueron queridos; tanto el sexo femenino como el masculino han sentido el amor patrio y unos y otras lo han manifestado de mil distintas maneras. Los hombres han humedecido el suelo patrio con la sangre que derramaron sus heridas en las luchas que sostuvieron contra el enemigo que pretendía mancillar este suelo, y las mujeres, unas han peleado directamente en el campo de batalla y otras auxiliando á sus compatriotas, haciéndolos fuertes contra el enemigo; ya proporcionándoles recursos pecuniarios ó enviando oportunas noticias, pero principalmente animándoles con su resignación y su fé, pues son una de las principales armas de la mujer.

En nuestro hermoso país han existido mujeres de alma grande y noble, que se han sacrificado en aras del patriotismo, es decir; mujeres que han sido unas verdaderas Heroínas.

Hoy, con el mayor placer; sintiendo altamente la falta de aptitud que tengo para ello, cumplo los deseos de esta Respetable Sociedad, poniendo á su alcance las biografías de algunas de las principales heroínas, empezando por Doña Leona Vicario. Esta era hija de padres muy ricos y vivía en la ciudad de México.

Desde la edad de 19 años comenzó á manifestar profundas simpatías por la libertad de su patria, cuando supo que en Dolores estalló la revolución, pretendió establecer correspondencia con Hidalgo y Allende con objeto de ayudarles de alguna manera pero no pudo conseguirlo y la entabló con algunos de los jefes insurgentes, á los que mandaba noticias importantes del movimiento del enemigo y los auxiliaba también con dinero.

Para que sus noticias llegaran oportunamente, había establecido varios correos. En una ocasión, fue interceptado uno de ellos y Doña Leona Vicario temiendo ser aprehendida, se fugó y logró llegar hasta un pueblo algo distante de la ciudad de México, hasta allí la alcanzaron unos parientes y la disuadieron de su intento animándola á que regresase.

Así lo hizo aquella dama y fué hecha prisionera y llevada en calidad de tal al Colegio de Belén; allí le formaron juicio y por mil medios quisieron obligarla á qu[e] dijera los nombres de los insurgentes que le escribían con nombres supuestos, pero nada lograron, ni los halagos primero ni las terribles amenazas después, hicieron que Doña Leona Vicario descubriera el nombre de aquellos con los cuales se comunicaba por escrito.

Cada vez que sus jueces la hicieron comparecer ante ellos, con objeto de arrancarle su secreto, aquella esforzada joven contestaba; "estoy resuelta á morir antes de entregar á nadie."

Doña Leona Vicario logró evadirse de su prisión gracias á la ayuda que para ello le prestaron algunos amigos, y permaneció oculta por mucho tiempo en México. Luego marchó á Oaxaca, tan pronto como pudo llegó á dicha ciudad, precisamente cuando estaba ocupada por Morelos.

En Tlalpujahua (estado de Michoacán) se casó con un joven yucateco D. Andrés Quintana Roo, hombre de excelente educación, de gran instrucción, eminente abogado é insigne poeta, que prestó también servicios á la causa de la independencia nacional, por esto la nación ha honrado su memoria dando su nombre al territorio que del estado de Yucatán, acaba de formarse y toma el nombre de Territorio "Quintana Roo."

En el año de 1812 se estableció en Tlalpujahua una fábrica de armas; y los maestros que la dirigieron fueron enviados por ella misma quien además sostenía á las familias de tales individuos, viéndose obligada á vender sus alhajas, pues sus fondos ya estaban escasos y sólo pudo sostener los gastos para fabricar las primeras armas.

Además de esta heroína, hubo en la época de la independencia otras mujeres acreedoras al hermoso título de heroínas como nos lo prueban los siguientes relatos.

Un jefe español hizo prisionero á un hermano de Don Ignacio Rayón, el defensor de Cóporo, y ofreció a este valiente la vida del prisionero D. Francisco si en cambio le entregaba la fortaleza. Rayón, cediendo a un impulso de amor filial, consultó el caso con su madre y esta digna mujer en cuyo sér ardía inextinguible y vivísima la llama de amor patrio, pronunció como contestación estas palabras: "El deber del militar y del patriota es morir en defensa de su patria, y todo sentimiento contrario á este deber, debe sofocarse." Pocos días después el rostro de Doña Rafaela López Aguado de Rayón, que éste era el nombre de la heroína que en este momento llama nuestra atención; se veía surcado por el llanto; era que el cuerpo de su hijo D. Francisco yacía destrozado por las balas enemigas y sin embargo del intenso dolor que torturaba el alma de aquella señora, la entereza y el ánimo no abandonaron ni por un momento á la noble heroína.

DIJE.

Leona Vicario and Rafaela López

La Crónica
Laredo, Texas
19 October 1911

Biographies read by Professor Miss M. Rentería, at the meeting of La Liga Femenil Mexicanista on Sunday, the 15th of the current month.

In our fatherland, in this beloved land that has sometimes been unfortunate, there have appeared heroic women, deserving that their names be perpetuated among us. When we study History, we find beautiful examples of mothers who sacrificed for their children, of wives who confronted thousands of risks to save their husbands and to exalt their country, and of daughters who feared nothing and defied everything to reach the happiness for their parents and Honor and Glory for their homeland.

Love for the homeland is one of the most sublime feelings of the soul; both men and women have always felt immense love for the place where they received their first maternal kiss; for the sacrosanct place that keeps the remains of the beings that were dear to them; both the feminine and masculine sex have felt patriotic love and all of them have expressed it in a thousand different ways. Men have wetted their native land with the blood that their injuries shed in the battles they held against enemies that wanted to defile this land, and the women, some have directly fought in the battlefield and others by helping their compatriots, by making them strong in the face of the enemy; either by providing them with economical resources or by sending timely news, but mainly by encouraging them with their resignation and their faith, because they are two of the main weapons of the woman.

In our beautiful country there have existed women with a big and noble soul, who sacrificed themselves for the sake of patriotism, that is to say, women who have been true heroines.

Today, and with greatest pleasure; feeling the lack of aptitude I have for that, I fulfill the wish of this respectable society, by making accessible to you the biographies of some of the main heroines, starting with Mrs. Leona Vicario. She was the daughter of very rich parents and lived in Mexico City.

From the age of nineteen she began to show deep sympathies for the liberty of her country; when she found out that the Revolution had exploded in Dolores, she sought to establish correspondence with Hidalgo and Allende in order to help them somehow, but she was not able to do this and so she established it with some of the insurgent leaders, to whom she would send important news about the movement of the enemy and she also helped them with money.

So that her news would arrive in a timely manner, she had established several messengers. On one occasion, one of them was intercepted and Mrs. Leona Vicario, fearing to be apprehended, fled away and she was able to reach a town that was somewhat distant from Mexico City, from there some relatives caught up with her and she was dissuaded from her attempt by encouraging her to go back.

That lady did that and she was taken prisoner and taken as such to the Colegio de Belén; there she was put on trial, and in a thousand ways they attempted to make her tell the names of the insurgents that wrote to her with false names, but they did not succeed in anything, neither the compliments first nor the terrible threats later made Doña Leona Vicario expose the names of those with whom she communicated in writing.

Every time her judges made her to appear before them, with the purpose of dragging her secret out of her, that brave young woman would answer, "I am resolved to die before giving anybody up."

Mrs. Leona Vicario was able to escape from her prison thanks to the help that some friends gave to her, and she stayed hidden in Mexico for a long time. Then she left for Oaxaca, as soon as she was able she arrived in that city, precisely when it was occupied by Morelos.[2]

In Tlalpujahua [state of Michoacán] she married a young Yucatecan man, Mr. Andrés Quintana Roo, a man of excellent manners, great education, an eminent lawyer and celebrated poet, who also rendered service to the cause of national independence; for this reason the nation has honored his memory by giving his name to the territory that from the state of Yucatán has just been formed and it takes the name of "Quintana Roo."

In the year of 1812 a weapons factory was established in Tlapujahua; and the masters who directed it were sent by the very person who also supported the families of such individuals; she had to sell her jewelry because her funds were already scarce and she was only able to cover the expenses to produce the first weapons.

Besides this heroine, there were in the period of independence more women that deserved the beautiful title of heroines, as the following stories prove.

A Spanish chief took a brother of Mr. Ignacio Rayón, the defender of Cóporo, prisoner, and he offered this brave man the life of the prisoner Francisco if in exchange he would give up the fortress. Rayón, by yielding to an impulse of filial love, consulted with his mother about the situation and this worthy lady in whose being there burnt the inexhaustible and lively fire of love for her homeland, uttered as an answer these words: "The obligation of a military man or of a patriot is to die in defense of his country, and any feeling in contrary of this duty must be suffocated." A few days later the face of Mrs. Rafaela López Aguado de Rayón, which was the name of the heroine who in this moment we are calling attention to; her face was furrowed with tears; it was because the corpse of her son Francisco lay ravaged by the bullets of the enemy, and, notwithstanding the intense pain that was torturing the soul of that lady, her integrity and her spirit never abandoned the noble heroine, not even for one minute.

I SAID.

Andrea Villarreal González

Born in Lampazas, Nuevo León, Mexico (1881–1963), Andrea Villarreal was part of a family of outspoken writers and politically minded activists who wrote about the Mexican government and its failings and, consequently, contributed to the movement that led to the Mexican Revolution in 1910. During the war, the Villarreal family's activism became a dangerous and risky practice. For example, Andrea's brother Antonio I. Villarreal, member of the Partido Liberal Mexicano (PLM; Mexican Liberal Party), openly spoke out against Porfirio Díaz in newspapers and magazines and was imprisoned in Mexico (Lomas, "Revolutionary" xv). Antonio and members of his family, including Andrea and their sister Teresa, eventually fled to San Antonio, Texas, to escape persecution from the Mexican government. There, Andrea and Teresa supported captured PLM members and condemned the government's prosecution of the revolutionaries (xxi–xxiii). In 1909 Andrea met with Mother Jones in San Antonio to present the case of the PLM refugees. Andrea was known as a talented speaker, and because of her rhetorical and militant work, she gained the name of the Mexican Joan of Arc (Melero, "Sara" 192).

Like many of the women in this anthology, Villarreal was an active newspaperwoman who used the press to voice political concerns. With Ariana, whose writings are collected here, Villarreal contributed to *La Prensa* (The Press), a San Antonio, Texas-based, Spanish-language press, but it was the newspaper work she accomplished with her sister Teresa that set Andrea apart as an early Mexican feminist writer. In 1909 the sisters started two political presses, *El Obrero* (The Worker) and *La Mujer Moderna* (The Modern Woman) in San Antonio.[1] Andrea's most well-known work within these publications is "A qué venimos" ("What We Have Come For"), which served as a mission statement for *La Mujer Moderna*'s inaugural issue and set the agenda for the press.

In "A qué venimos," Villarreal identifies the work of *La Mujer Moderna* and makes clear that it is dedicated to "facilitat[ing] the evolution of women" and "female liberation." But even as she establishes "women's rights" as a prime concern, this concern is couched in the context of the burgeoning revolutionary moment. Composing this piece less than a year before the Mexican Revolution started in November 1910, Villarreal writes that the liberated woman she hopes her press cultivates is one who "make[s] rebels." One might read this recommendation as a traditional and maternal one: the woman, as mother, should give birth to rebels. Villarreal establishes, however, that this is not the vision she has for her readers. To Villareal, *this* woman "makes rebels" through persuasion: she must generate "the spirit of freedom and justice" and "dig into the hearts of those who are resigned." It is important to note too that stylistically Villarreal combines this language of revolution with the register of traditional Mexican oratory, which played a major role in literary writing at this time. In the final lines of "A qué venimos," she invokes a grand rhetorical style, writing: "We have come to find freedom for us women and also for you our men. Oh! You serfs who moan like cowards, when the sword of tyranny writes in insulting grooves its hateful orders on the pliable surface of your bent backs!" Through these highly charged stylistic choices, Villarreal encourages her women readers to become activists and to persuade their male counterparts to foment social movement and change.

A qué venimos

La Mujer Moderna
San Antonio, Texas
diciembre de 1909

Si algunos periódicos de la prensa mexicana de Texas dedican de tiempo en tiempo este o aquel artículo a la mujer, no por ello puede considerárseles como devotos al desenvolvimiento y emancipación de la personalidad femenina, todavía hoy postergada a preocupaciones añejas, "parasitadas" al corazón de las sociedades.

No existe en la región fronteriza de ambas naciones un periódico dedicado por entero a la propaganda de ideas que faciliten la evolución de la mujer; y muy raro es el que obrando con sincera honradez indica el camino recto de la liberación femenina, despreciando los torpes egoísmos de ciertos hombres que prefieren la sierva humilde, ignara y sometida, a la compañera digna, inteligente y libre, capaz de dar con su amor la felicidad que de otra manera sería tan sólo un placer morboso, y la fuerza y el valor que al hombre muchas veces faltan en las horas tormentosas de la vida.

Y conociendo y deplorando la falta de esta clase de prensa, venimos a tomar un modestísimo puesto a la vanguardia de la que más tarde será vigorosa luchadora por los derechos de la mujer.

Iniciamos el movimiento; otras más competentes vendrán después a levantar sobre la piedra de nuestros esfuerzos la futura liberación de nuestras hermanas, y con ella, la dicha de la humanidad.

Pero no solamente por nosotras venimos a combatir; tarea más grande acometemos: Tanto como al oído de la mujer hablaremos al de los hombres; desgranaremos en su alma la gama doliente de las inmensas amarguras patrias, junta con la rebelde nota despertadora de heroísmos.

Gritaremos si es preciso para que los hombres recuerden lo que deben ser, sientan vergüenza de su infamia actual y despedacen sus yugos. Si es necesario nuestras manos serán rudas para sacudir los desmayados brazos de los tímidos.

La mujer moderna tiene, más allá de los viejos límites marcados, por el capricho masculino, una misión nobilísima que cumplir:

La de hacer rebeldes.

Porque en estos momentos la rebeldía es la salvadora del mundo que se pudre en el pacifismo abyecto.

The transcription of "A qué venimos" appears in this anthology with permissions from Instituto Nacional de Estudios Históricos de la Revolución Mexicana. This version can be found on pp. 192–93 of *Mujeres y Revolución, 1900–1917*.

Hay que hacer, de la carne de explotación y servidumbre, espíritu de libertad y de justicia. Hay que hurgar en el pecho de los resignados hasta hacer aparecer los descontentos.

El mundo tiene congestión de esclavos y anemia de luchadores y un estado así tan miserable no debe prolongarse más.

Y, ya que muchos hombres permanecen de rodillas, nosotras nos levantaremos y haremos que ellos se pongan también de pie.

Venimos a buscar libertad para nosotras y también para vosotros. ¡Oh! Siervos que gemís cobardes, cuando el sable de la tiranía escribe en surcos insultantes sus mandatos odiosos sobre la dúctil página de vuestras espaldas combas.

—La redacción

What We Have Come For

La Mujer Moderna
San Antonio, Texas
December 1909

If some periodicals of the Mexican press in Texas dedicate this or that article to women once in a while, that is no reason to consider them as committed to the development and liberation of the female personality, which still today is postponed by other, stale preoccupations, which are "parasitic" at the heart of society.

In the border region between the two countries, there does not exist a single periodical dedicated completely to the propagation of ideas that might facilitate the evolution of women, and it is very rare to find one that, operating with sincere honesty, shows the straight path to female liberation, by disparaging the crude egotism of certain men who prefer the humble servant, ignorant and submissive, to a worthy companion, intelligent and free, capable of giving happiness with her love, which otherwise would only be a morbid pleasure, and the strength and courage that men often lack during life's tortured times.

And by being acquainted with and deploring the lack of this type of publication, we have come to take a very modest place at the vanguard of what will later become a vigorous fighter for women's rights.

We are starting the movement; other more competent women will come later to erect on the rock of our efforts the future liberation of our sisters, and with that the joy of humanity.

But we are here to fight not only for us women; we undertake a greater task. As much to the ear of women we will speak to that of men; we will extract from their souls the painful variety of the immense national sorrow, together with the rebellious wake-up call to heroism.

We will shout if necessary so that men remember what they must be, and so they feel ashamed of their present infamy and shatter their yokes. If it is necessary, our hands will be rough in order to shake up the fainted arms of the timid.

The modern woman has, beyond the old boundaries established by a male whim, an extremely noble mission to fulfill:

She must make rebels.

Because in these times rebellion is the savior of a world that is rotting in abject pacifism.

We must make, from the flesh of exploitation and servitude, the spirit of freedom and justice. We must dig into the hearts of those who are resigned, until we can make to appear those who are discontented.

The world is crowded with slaves and an anemia of warriors, and such a miserable state must not linger on longer.

And, since so many men remain on their knees, we women will stand up and make them get on their feet too.

We have come to find freedom for us women and also for you men.

Oh! You serfs who moan like cowards, when the sword of tyranny writes in insulting grooves its hateful orders on the pliable surface of your bent backs!

—The editorial staff

Isidra T. de Cárdenas

Little is known about Isidra T. de Cárdenas outside of her work as director of *La Voz de la Mujer* (The Voice of Women), which was founded in El Paso, Texas, in 1907. Much like *La Crónica* (The Chronicle) and *La Prensa* (The Press) (selections from which are anthologized here), *La Voz de la Mujer* was a Spanish-language newspaper that emerged on the U.S. side of the border to address the political questions of the Mexican Revolution. This newspaper focused on women's interest and involvement in the Revolution, attending specifically to the concerns of the insurgent Partido Liberal Mexicano (PLM; Mexican Liberal Party). *La Voz de la Mujer* alerted women readers to wartime developments and identified particular roles they could play within the war and PLM's cause.

As director of the press, Cárdenas worked with two other women, María Sánchez, the editor in chief, and María P. García, the manager. While these women oversaw the newspaper's publication, they were also likely consistent contributors. Many of the articles or editorials were written in the collective voice of first person plural—*las hermanas* (the sisters), *nosotras* (feminine form of "we"), *las madres* (the mothers), *las esposas* (the wives), *las hijas* (the daughters)—and were not signed (Lomas, "Transborder" 56). While the number of articles that Cárdenas actually penned is unclear, the next selection, "¡Unifiquémonos!" ("Let Us Unite"), reveals her vision for *La Voz de la Mujer*. Here she outlines, in descriptive and provocative detail, the crimes of Mexican president Porfirio Díaz and calls her readers to action. Railing against women's indifference to the movement, Cárdenas prompts them to act with courage and stand in unity alongside their "brothers-in-ideals" to defend those who have been martyred for their cause.

Cárdenas's words in "¡Unifiquémonos!" and the title of the newspaper itself suggest that *La Voz de la Mujer* would articulate a broad-minded vision for women's place in society. Yet the focus of the press was on more conservative interests, calling women to support their husbands and brothers during the war, to raise funds for families of soldiers, and to organize mutualistic societies (Lomas, "Transborder" 59). There was, then, no great focus on changing women's actual sociopolitical condition. Indeed, as Clara Lomas states, "extant issues of *La Voz de la Mujer* do not address the specific condition of women" (58). Furthermore, the discourse within *La Voz de la Mujer* kept women mainly within their traditional domestic roles, and when the press did advocate for women's presence in the public sphere it was "ultimately intended for the benefit of the state, and, therefore, limited within the constraints of nationalism" (59). From this perspective, it would seem the press was prompting women to fight for the nation, not advocate for themselves.[1]

It is also important to note that in the first lines of "¡Unifiquémonos!" Cárdenas encourages her female readership to support the PLM committee in St. Louis, Missouri. While it is unclear why Cárdenas would see this particular need at this moment, her reference to this PLM sect reveals the reach of Mexican politics and the Revolution. Deep into what twenty-first-century readers recognize as the U.S. Midwest, champions of the PLM cause were at work. Additionally and importantly, newspaper editors and readers in El Paso were alert to the party's actions in Missouri and supportive of their efforts.

¡Unifiquémonos!

La Voz de la Mujer
El Paso, Texas
6 de septiembre de 1907

Trabajemos en Fa[v]or de la Junta de San Louis, Mo.

Somos deudoras de grandes compromisos á la causa de libertad; un deber de convicciones esclavisa nuestros principios; y en estos momentos en que la Dictadura ha segregado al martirol[o]gio de sus víctimas nuevas energías, toca á nuestro deber mostrar nuestros pechos, descubrir el antif[a]z para ungirnos con la inquina con que nuestros innobles adversarios saben acometer á sus leales y francos enemigos.

No seremos nosotras las que permane[z]camos indiferentes ante la desgracia que apostrofa a nuestros hermanos de ideales; como no será el oro ni las inquisitoriales persecusiones de la tiranía de Porfirio Díaz, quienes acallen nuestras protestas reb[e]ldes, "La Voz de la Mujer," surguió [surgió] al estadío de la prensa independiente, como cauterio de protervos, como flagelo de burgueses; enarboló su pendón de combate en defensa de un principio, y ese principio es, la libertad de la Patria de Hidalgo; la dignificación de sus asesinadas instituciones; el respeto y e[s]tricto apego á las leyes que, escritas con sangre de martirio, supieron legarnos nuestros inmortales héroes.

El parangón entre aquellos invictos paladines y nuestros pro-hombres de cetro en la actualidad, forman un contraste rayando en absurdo: los primeros, respetuosos se apegaban á la ley, tributando pleito homenaje a los preceptos que de ella emanaban. Los segundos, altaneros é impúdicos tienen la vanidad de con[s]iderarse sobre toda ley pactada, en virtud de creerse imbulnerables [invulnerables] y con poderes omnímodos sobre sus gobernados, y la ley que debería normar sus actos, si sus elásticas conciencias, acariciaran siquiera, por rubor la potentada idea de ser representantes de un pueblo a quién se le ha engañado mi[s]erablemente, a quién se le han arrebatado, sable en mano y horca en práctica, sus caras libertades, y para quién sólo se tiene la fusta del feudal que le destroza sus carnes cuando osa reclamar su jornal robado ó suele exasperarse [porque] algún potentado innoculó la deshonra en los seres femeninos que albergan en esas humildes chozas donde anida la miseria con todo el te[c]nicismo del [vocablo].

¡Triste condición la de una nación des[c]endiente de bravos luchadores, convertida, por un proditorio Czar, en una ergástula de esclavos!

Un felino decrépito, agitado en el cubil de su impura senectud; manchado con la sangre de sus víctimas; ese remedo de Ludovico y de Estrada Cabrera, desde la guarida del crimen se levanta galvanizado é insa[c]iable de sangre, ordenando a sus esbirros los fu[s]ilamientos, los tormentos, y persecuciones de sus enemigos políticos, de esos ciudadanos viriles y activos que desafiando enconos saben apostrofar tiranos sin inclinar sus frentes erguidas, ante la [b]acanal inmunda de ese maldito rey de hotentotes, de ese tártaro salvaje sin entrañas.

No termina a[ú]n la impresión causada con el nefando crimen del secuestro de Sarabia, cuando tenemos que consignar en nuestro semanario nuevas víctimas inmoladas en aras del sacrificio por consigna del Dictador Porfirio Díaz.

Fieles perros de presa a quienes el autócrata remunera con un mesquino mendrugo que satisfaga sus vacíos abdómen[es]. Son bellacos de nota y su oficio es morder a los enemigos del Czar.

El viejo histrión, el [b]andolero de Tuxtepec debe estar satisfecho de la aprehensión verificada en los miembros de la Junta del Partido Liberal; aprehensiones acae[c]idas en Los Angeles, California, el día 23 del mes próximo pasado, por la jauría de cachorros en funciones de det[e]ctives, autorizados por los bandidos de antesala para sangrar al pueblo.

En la guarida de la bestia inmunda, en los castillos de la inmunidad, ahí se traman las celadas que deben inhabilitar de su libertad a los hombres que se sonrrojan [sonrojan] de ser esclavos y que con entereza apostrofan a los bandidos [investidos] de autoridad en las esferas Porfiristas.

Convencidos, deberían estar la horda de bandoleros laborantes en la obra de oprobio, tan generalizada bajo el sistema implant[ado] por el llorón de Icamole; convencidos deberían estar de lo est[é]ril de sus labores en las persecuciones a sus enemigos políticos, persecuciones que les han ser[v]ido para exhibirlos en la picota del ridículo, hasta quedar palmariamente justificados sus fines macabros en contubernio con sus manejos turbios.

Para la preponderancia en que sueña el Estrada Cabrera mexicano, que abriga la vanidad de disponer de la libertad de los leaders del Partido Liberal, nada favorable han obtenido, que no sean anatemas execrantes, maldiciones candentes como justa recompensa de la maldad con que se ha caracterizado el chicanero de Tuxtepec, que derrama lágrimas de histeria, cuando fracasan sus maldades que [per]sonifican su escamosa cuanto maldecida existencia[.]

El pueblo mexicano como una sola voluntad, debe aprestarse enérgicamente a la defensa de nuestros [cerreligioarios] privados de su libertad; no debemos ser criminales de tal indiferencia, sino al contrario, alejando temores, desafiemos la inquina del bandidaje oficial. Es el momento de demostrar que somos unidos y que a la caída de algún hermano, todos nos encaramos con nuestros tiranos, y sin temores de ninguna especie los apostrofamos denunciando los hechos autoritarios que con toda impunidad cometen los lémures de gabinetes.

Al pueblo por quien se están sacrificando grandes energías, toca coadyuvar a la defensa de sus mártires. ¡Así lo esperamos!

Let Us Unite!

La Voz de la Mujer
El Paso, Texas
6 September 1907

Let us work in Favor of the Junta of St. Louis, Mo.

We women owe a debt of great commitment to the cause of liberty; a duty of conviction enslaves our principles; and in these moments in which the Dictatorship has set aside new energy for the martyrology of its victims, it is up to our duty to show our courage, to remove the mask in order to anoint ourselves with the aversion with which our ignoble adversaries know how to attack their loyal and forthright enemies.

We will not be the women who remain indifferent in the presence of the misfortunes that accost our brothers-in-ideals; since it will not be gold nor the inquisitorial persecutions of Porfirio Díaz's tyranny that will mute our rebellious protests. "La Voz de la Mujer" appeared in the arena of the independent press, as a cautery of the perverted men, as a scourge of the bourgeoisie, and raised its banner of combat in defense of a principle, and this principle is, the liberty of the Homeland of Hidalgo[2]; the dignification of its slain institutions; the respect and strict adherence to the laws that, written with the blood of martyrs, our immortal heroes were able to bequeath us.

A comparison between these unconquered champions and our present domineering leaders forms a contrast bordering on the absurd; the former followed the law respectfully, by paying tribute and homage to the precepts that emanated from it. The latter, haughty and shameless, have the vanity to consider themselves above all established laws, by virtue of believing themselves invulnerable and with absolute power over their subjects, and the law that ought to regulate their actions, if their flexible conscience could at least harbor, out of shame, the sovereign idea of being representatives of a people who have been miserably deceived, from whom have been wrested, sword in hand and gallows in practice, their beloved freedoms, and for whom there is only the whip of the feudal lord that destroys their flesh when they try to demand their stolen wages, or often feels frustrated because some potentate inoculated dishonor in the female beings who harbor in those primitive huts where misery abides in the profoundest sense of the word.

What a sad condition for a nation descended from brave fighters, converted, by a treacherous Tsar, into a dungeon for slaves!

A decrepit feline, restless in the den of its lustful senility; stained with the blood of his victims; this parody of Ludovico and Estrada Cabrera,[3] arises from his den of crime, galvanized and with an insatiable thirst for blood, by ordering his henchmen to conduct firing squads, the torture, and persecution of his political enemies, of those virile and dynamic citizens who defying his rancor, know how to declaim tyrants without bowing their heads held high, against the filthy bacchanal of that cursed king of Hottentots, that savage Tartar[4] without guts.

The shock caused by the nefarious crime of the kidnapping of Sarabia[5] has not yet subsided, and we must record in our weekly paper that new victims were immolated for the sake of sacrifice by order of Dictator Porfirio Diaz.

The faithful hunting hounds whom the autocrat remunerates with a wretched crust of stale bread to fill their empty bellies. They are infamous villains and their job is to bite the enemies of the Tsar.

The old histrion, the bandit of Tuxtepec[6] must be satisfied with the confirmed capture of members of the Committee of the Liberal Party; captures that occurred in Los Angeles, California, on the 23rd of last month, by the pack of whelps acting as detectives, authorized by the antechamber bandits to bleed the people dry.

In the den of the filthy beast, in his castles of immunity, they plot the ambushes meant to disable the liberty of men who blush at being slaves and who with integrity declaim the bandits who are endowed with authority in the Porfirian realm.

The horde of thieves laboring on this ignominious project should be convinced, so widespread under the system imposed by the cry-baby of Icamole[7]; they should be convinced of the sterility of their labors in the persecutions of their political enemies, persecutions that have only served to show them in the pillory of ridicule, until such time as their macabre goals in collusion with their shady tactics may be clearly justified.

About the preponderance of which the Mexican Estrada Cabrera[8] dreams, who harbors the vanity of determining the freedom of the leaders of the Liberal Party, nothing favorable has been achieved, except loathsome anathemas, red-hot curses in just recompense for the evil that has characterized the trickster of Tuxtepec, who spills tears of hysteria, when his evil acts fail that personify his squamate and accursed existence?

The Mexican people, in a single act of willpower, must energetically prepare themselves for the defense of our compatriots who are deprived of their freedom; we should not be criminals of such indifference, but rather by putting aside fears, let us challenge the aversion of official banditry. It is the moment to demonstrate that we are united and that when one brother falls, we will all confront our tyrants, and without any kind of fear we will declaim them by denouncing the authoritarian deeds which with all impunity the lemur-like ministers of the cabinet commit.

It is time for the people on behalf of whom great energy is being sacrificed, to contribute to the defense of their martyrs. This is what we expect!

Artemisa N. Sáenz Royo (Xóchitl)

Artemisa Sáenz Royo worked as a journalist and social activist in Veracruz, Mexico, during the first half of the twentieth century. She identified with a prehispanic indigeneity by choosing to use the pseudonym Xóchitl, after the Aztec princess who is said to have created pulque[1] (Ramos-Escandón 133). Early in her writing career, Sáenz Royo published political pieces such as "México para los mexicanos" (Mexico for Mexicans) in *El Pueblo* (1915), and the article anthologized here, "La mujer en el pasado, el presente y en el porvenir" ("Women in the Past, Present, and Future") in *La Época* (The Epoch). In the latter piece, Sáenz Royo promotes a progressive vision for women, first by citing what women have accomplished and the strides they have made to break from their traditional roles, and then by pointing to the future and prompting her readers to press on in their struggles for a fuller, more active, and even independent life. She writes, "The feminine sex reclaims its rights; today's woman aspires to more, and to obtain it, she educates and teaches herself, and enters completely, serenely, and in a manner more extensive and intensive into all of society's realms."

Appearing in the Sunday edition of *La Época* in the section "Para el Hogar" (For the Home), the essay "La mujer en el pasado, el presente y en el porvenir" may have been too progressive for the conservative editor of the newspaper, María Luisa Garza. On the same page as Sáenz Royo's article is an excerpt from Garza's book, published under the pseudonym Loreley.[2] In the piece, "La verdadera misión de la mujer" (Woman's True Mission), Garza articulates a familiar argument for Mexican women: that their true calling is in the home. Through the pages of *La Época*, then, Sáenz Royo and Garza offered readers two competing visions for women—one progressive and one conservative. Garza would later respond more directly to Sáenz Royo's claims by publishing "Las mujeres que escriben" ("Women Who Write") in *La Época* in February 1921 (included here). This public exchange represents the ongoing conversation and even debate regarding Mexican women's roles at the onset of the twentieth century.

The context surrounding these publications is especially important. While both women's pieces were published in San Antonio's *La Época*, the note at the end of Sáenz Royo's article reveals that she wrote it in Veracruz, Mexico. Adding even more complexity to the rhetorical situation, at the conclusion of Garza's "Las mujeres que escriben" is the information that the piece was originally published in *El Informador* (The Reporter), a newspaper out of Guadalajara. This publication history only deepens the overarching point of this volume: newspaperwomen were writing for venues in both the United States and Mexico, and their work was being published and republished for readers of various presses.

Throughout her life, Sáenz Royo would continue writing and working on behalf of mexicanas by specifically arguing for women's suffrage rights (Lau 103). Her historical writings also made significant contributions to the preservation of a mexicana past. In 1955, she published *Historia político-social-cultural del movimiento femenino en México, 1914–1950* (Political, Social, and Cultural History of the Feminine Movement in Mexico, 1914–1950), which is still frequently cited in present-day scholarship. Her other works include *Historia de una vida: del caos a la luz* (History of a Life: From Chaos to the Light) (1945); *El Venustiano Carranza que yo conocí* (The Venustiano Carranza That I Knew) (1959); and *Semblanzas: mujeres mexicanas revolucionarias y guerras revolucionarias ideológicas* (Portraits: Mexican Women Revolutionaries and Ideological Revolutionary Wars) (1960).

La mujer en el pasado, en el presente y en el porvenir

La Época
San Antonio, Texas
31 de octubre de 1920

Especial para "La [É]poca"
"Bienaventurados los que tienen hambre y sed de Justicia: porque ellos serán hartos."

Por mucho tiempo han sido las mujeres víctimas de un funesto error de los hombres; se les ha considerado, como seres inferiores por su naturaleza, se les ha galanteado mucho, llenando su cabeza de efímer[a]s ilusiones y... nada más. El hombre en su egoísmo y en medio de él, se ha rendido ante una cabecita de tentadores y negros bucles, o ante unos ojos de pestañas y rizadas, pero... nada más... Ha declarado a la mujer reina del hogar, ama de su casa, para convertirla en minúscula hormiguita que trabaja cotidianamente; y deja de ser hormiguita, para convertirse en objeto de lujo y de placer. El hogar, he ahí el único lugar que corresponde a la mujer. Fuera de los muros de ese hogar, las puertas han permanecido cerradas para libre paso a sus ideas, a sus deseos de libertad y de emancipación, y cuando se habla de esto hay quien diga "el rigor de la ley" "el poder de las costumbres" "el ridículo." La mujer ha sido colocada siempre en el más bajo nivel, se la ha sometido a tutela como a un incapacitado, poniéndole mil trabas a la libre expansión de sus ideas, sus costumbres y sus aspiraciones.

Desde que Stuar[t] Mill, inició y dio carácter de solidez científica (juzguémoslo así) al problema de la emancipación femenina, un espíritu nuevo fíltrase en la opinión de los países civilizados, que ven siempre en "algo nuevo" un nuevo bienestar para la patria y para el completo desenvolvimiento de las evoluciones que en distintas formas se presentan para ser adaptadas.

El sexo femenino reivindica sus derechos, la mujer actual aspira a más, y para obtenerlo, se educa, se instruye, y entra de llen[o], serena, y de un modo más amplio y más intenso en todas las manifestaciones sociales. Ella sabe que "solo un ingenio cultivado hace agradable el trato" y con él, el de la mujer que aspira a más, y ante esta nueva verdad, descubre nuevos y amplios horizontes, que la animan y que poco a poco la hacen ensanchar su esfera de acción y va triunfando en las conciencias ilustradas, en las conciencias NO [A]TROFIADAS por el "ridículo poder de las costumbres[.]"

¿Podéis negar que la mujer es cada vez más la compañera de la vida...? Ella despierta la alegría y el dolor del hombre, y también sabe compartir con él esas dos sensaciones humanas...

La mujer en el pasado (Women in the Past)   149

Hemos tenido ejemplos de mujeres abnegadas y virtuosas; la guerra europea dió márgen a infinidad de heroísmos y acciones sublimes donde la mujer tenía el principal papel.

Y aún hay quien se atreva a decir esa frase vulgar, pero muy adecuada al momento, de que la mujer debe ser "sana y tonta." Sin profundizar, se ve desde luego, la malignidad de la frase.

En la guerra europea, cuando los hombres poseídos de espíritu de demonio, sólo inventaban armas mortíferas para despedazarse y aniquilarse unos a otros, la mujer restañaba heridas, cultivaba campos, manejaba a conciencia los tractores, las máquinas que conducían los carros llenos de comestibles, conducía a los hospitales de sangre a los heridos, y ante aquel vértigo de destrucción permanecía serena, siempre dispuesta a llevar el consuelo al necesitado, a los heridos que caían en el campo de la lucha fratricida y cruel. Allí donde Marte era glorificado, y afluía a torrentes la sangre de Caín . . . allí, repito, supo cumplir la mujer con su dolorosa misión, impuesta por ella misma, y no solo fué la hija del pueblo la que acudió al llamado de la patria adolorida; ahí estuvieron también la Reina de Ruman[i]a, la Reina Mary de Inglaterra, la Srita. Margaret Wilson, la heroica Reina de los Belgas, ejemplos sublimes de mujeres abnegadas y heroicas. Sus manos blancas y aterciopeladas restañaban heridas, levantaban apósitos, su voz cariñosa y rituálica curaba los dolores morales, las heridas del alma, más grandes que los dolores físicos.

Así como se les vió en el campo de la lucha, se les vió desempeñando múltiples oficios y cargos que antes hallábanse reservados a la exclusiva actividad masculina; la mujer adquirió conocimientos técnicos y perfecta habilidad para entablar después competencia, para luchar con buen éxito, para crearse una posición definitiva, independiente, que la desligue de las rancias teorías de sus antepasados, para que vaya serena y firme hacia el porvenir.

En México desde los albores de la Revolución de 191[0], se vió el papel importante que desempeñó la mujer; más tarde, el gobierno que presidió el señor Carranza, no desconociendo la superioridad de la mujer, y los trabajos que en pro de la revolución, triunfante había desarrollado, le abrió amplios horizontes que constituyeron un factor importante para el trabajo y el progreso; y la evolución femenina se inició. Brotaron una falange de mujeres antes ignaras para el campo de la lucha intelectual.

Patrocinada por el Gobierno de Don Venustiano Carranza, bajo un cielo azul y diáfano, Mérida, la culta y floreciente capital del Estado de Yucatán, dio la primera clarinada de libertad: Salvador Alvarado, hombre de grandes dotes, culto y luchador incansable del bienestar de un pueblo, acogió la idea de emancipación, y dándole su apoyo, se llevó a cabo el primer Congreso Feminista, y Mérida, la culta Mérida, acogió en su seno a todas las representantes de los Estados que iban a contribuír con su granito de arena en pro de la idea de la emancipación social de la mujer Mexicana; México se resistía y se resiste aún a aceptar esta novedad (pudiéramos llamarla así) contraria a sus tradiciones que alteraría[n] las costumbres legadas por la Madre España; y si aún existe la indecisión en aceptar la nueva doctrina y hay obstáculos para que la nueva simiente fructifique, es porque desde luego notamos el sentimiento egoísta, mal entendido y un cúmulo de falsos prejuicios difíciles de desarraigar.

Hoy la mujer, ya acostumbrada a nuevos trabajos, (de seis años a esta parte) desarrolladas sus facultades extraordinarias, rotos, un poco, los estrechos moldes en que se hallaba encerrada, ha adquirido el gusto de la laboriosidad y de la energía, y solo tiene que luchar por alcanzar la correspondiente retribución, su igualdad con la del hombre a iguales formas de trabajo: pero la mujer no desmaya ante el fracaso; luchará, vencerá, y se habrá redimido, mediante su propio esfuerzo. La mujer soltera es la que tiene delante de sí esta perspectiva. La mujer casada tendrá en su salario un nuevo ingreso para la familia en unión del proporcionado por el esposo.

La mujer soltera además de que con el producto de su trabajo puede asegurarse una posición independiente, dejará de ser una carga pesada para su familia; y podrá constituirse en el sostén de sus ancianos padres.

Trabajará para que no tenga que adoptar el matrimonio, como el único recurso, como la tabla de salvación; y en fin, las pobres huérfanas que tanto abundan, las madres solteras, las abandonadas, no caerán en esa angustiosa situación de recurrir al vicio y aumentar los males, las infamias que provoca el amor libre, recurso este siempre el supremo para la mujer ignorante y torpe, criada en una atmósfera de malsana frivolidad y de misticismo crónico, y cuyo epílogo es casi siempre el hospital o la plancha infamante de un manicomio.

En Europa ha pasado ya el huracán de fuego que devastara poblaciones florecientes y ricas, formando además legiones interminables de huérfanos y viudas, ya empieza a reconstruirse y reorganizarse y fuerza será recordar a esos seres que contribuyeron por el bienestar de la patria con su propio esfuerzo y que mantuvieron la dignidad del buen nombre una generación que ha dejado bárbaras huellas de su paso en el suelo ensangrentado de la vieja Europa.

Artemisa N. SAENZ ROYO.
"Xóchitl"
Veracruz, octubre de 1920.

Women in the Past, Present, and Future

La Época
San Antonio, Texas
31 October 1920

Special to "La Época"
"Blessed are those who hunger and thirst for Justice: for they shall be filled."

For a long time women have been victims of a disastrous error made by men; they have been considered to be inferior beings by nature, they have been flattered a great deal, by filling their heads with ephemeral illusions and ... nothing else. The man in his egotism, in the midst of it, has surrendered to a little head of tempting and jet-black curls, or in the presence of some eyes with curled lashes, but ... nothing more. He has declared woman to be the queen of the home, mistress of his house, only to change her into a tiny little ant that labors daily; then she stops being an ant, to become an object of lust and pleasure. The home, lo and behold the only place that belongs to the woman. Outside the walls of that home, the doors have remained closed to the free flow of her ideas, to her desires of freedom and emancipation, and when anyone speaks of this there is always someone who says "the rigor of the law" "the power of customs" "absurdity." The woman has always been situated at the lowest level, being subjected to the custody afforded an invalid, by placing a thousand obstacles to the free expansion of her ideas, her customs, and her aspirations.

Since [John] Stuart Mill initiated and gave the moral strength of scientific soundness (let us judge it that way) to the problem of feminine emancipation, a new spirit is filtering into the conviction in civilized countries, which always sees in "something new" a new well-being for the nation and for the complete development of the evolutions which in various forms present themselves to be adapted.[3]

The feminine sex reclaims its rights; today's woman aspires to more, and to obtain it, she educates herself, she teaches herself, and enters completely, serenely, and in a manner more extensive and intensive into all of society's realms. She knows that "only a cultured intelligence makes a pleasant companion" and with it, the treatment of the woman who aspires to more, and in view of this new truth, she discovers new and broader horizons, which encourage her and little by little they make her enlarge her sphere of action, and she gradually wins over enlightened minds, minds NOT ATROPHIED by the "ridiculous power of customs."

Can you deny that the woman is increasingly a life companion ... ? She awakens the joys and sorrows of the man, and she also knows how to share with him these two human sensations.

We have had examples of self-sacrificing virtuous women; the European war gave opportunities for an infinite number of acts of heroism and sublime actions where the woman played the leading role.

And still there are people who dare to say that ignorant phrase, but appropriate to the moment, that the woman should be both "sound of body and foolish of mind." Without going into details, the malignity of the phrase is of course obvious.

In the European war, when men, possessed by the spirit of the devil, only invented deadly weapons to maim and annihilate each other, women staunched wounds, cultivated fields, conscientiously drove tractors, the machines that carried wagons full of food, drove the wounded to the field hospitals, and in the face of that vortex of destruction they remained serene, always ready to take comfort to the needy, to the wounded that fell on the fratricidal and cruel field of battle. There, where Mars was glorified, and the blood of Cain was flowing in torrents . . . there, I repeat, the woman knew how to fulfill her painful and self-imposed mission, and it was not only the daughter of the masses who answered the wounded nations' call; there also were the Queen of Romania,[4] Queen Mary of England,[5] Miss Margaret Wilson,[6] the heroic Queen of the Belgians,[7] sublime examples of self-sacrificing and heroic women. Their white, velvety hands staunched wounds, changed bandages, and their tender and reassuring voices cured moral pains, the wounds of the soul, greater than physical wounds.

Just as women were seen on the battlefields, they were seen carrying out many functions and tasks that had previously been reserved exclusively as masculine activity; the woman acquired technical knowledge and total expertise to later establish her competence, to fight with good success, to create for herself a definitive position, independent, that would unbind her from the antiquated theories of her ancestors, so that she may proceed serenely and firmly toward the future.

In Mexico since the dawn of the Revolution of 1910, the important role that women played was noted; later, the government that Mr. Carranza[8] presided over, by not ignoring the superiority of women, and the efforts that they had developed in support of the triumphant revolution, opened broad horizons to them, which constituted an important factor for work and progress; and the feminine evolution began. There sprang up a phalanx of women who were previously ignorant of the intellectual field of battle.

Supported by the Government of Don Venustiano Carranza, under a blue and diaphanous sky, Mérida, the cultured and flower-filled capital of the State of Yucatán, sounded the first clarion call to liberty: Salvador Alvarado,[9] a man of great gifts, cultured and tireless fighter for the well-being of a people, accepted the idea of emancipation, and by giving it his support, the First Feminist Congress was carried out, and Mérida, the cultured Mérida, gathered to her breast all the representatives of the States that were going to contribute with their little grain of sand in favor of the idea of the social emancipation of Mexican women; Mexico resisted, and continues resisting, this novelty (as we could call it) contrary to its traditions which would alter the customs bequeathed by Mother Spain; and if there still exists indecision in accepting the new doctrine and there are obstacles to the new seed giving fruit, it is because we naturally take due notice of the egocentric feeling, poorly understood and an accumulation of false prejudices that are difficult to uproot.

Today the woman, now accustomed to new occupations (for the past six years), having developed her extraordinary faculties, broken, a little, the narrow molds in which she found herself enclosed, has acquired a taste for industry and energy, and she only has to fight to achieve the corresponding reward, her equality with that of the man in equal kinds of jobs: but the woman does not lose heart in the face of failure; she will fight, she will win, and she will have redeemed herself through her own effort. The single woman is the one who has this perspective before her. The married woman will have in her salary a new income for the family, along with that provided by the husband.

The single woman, besides the fact that with the product of her work she can assure herself an independent position, will no longer be a heavy burden for her family; and she will be able to establish herself as the support of her parents in their old age.

She will work so that she does not have to resort to marriage, as the only choice, as the last hope; and, finally, the poor orphaned girls that are so abundant, the single mothers, the abandoned women, will not fall into that wretched situation of turning to vice and increasing their afflictions, the infamies which free love provokes, this option always the primary one for the ignorant or awkward woman, raised in an atmosphere of unhealthy frivolity and chronic mysticism, and whose epilogue is almost always the hospital or the shameful embarrassment of a mental asylum.

In Europe the fiery hurricane has now passed which devastated rich and flourishing populations, besides producing interminable legions of orphans and widows, already reconstruction and reorganization are beginning and it will be a struggle to remember those people who contributed their own effort for the welfare of the nation and who maintained the dignity of the good name, a generation that has left barbarous tracks of its passing on the bloody soil of the old Europe.

Artemisa N. SAENZ ROYO
"Xóchitl"
Veracruz, October 1920

María Luisa Garza (Loreley)

María Luisa Garza (1887–1980) was a Texas-based journalist and novelist who wrote under the pseudonym Loreley. Her early work as a journalist was influential in re-asserting conservative roles for Mexican women during a progressive moment in history. Garza's writings included here were published respectively in 1920 and 1921; on 18 August 1920, women won the right to vote in the United States. Thus, when Garza calls for her mexicana readers to be feminine but not feminist, she is writing in contrast to the transnational feminist ideals circulating at this moment. Her conservative position, which on several occasions was called out as hypocritical in the press, stirred a great deal of controversy and response from her readers. On one significant occasion, Garza was not accepted into the May 1923 Congreso de Mujeres in Mexico. An article in *Feminismo Internacional* notes that Garza was the chosen delegate from her state of Nuevo León but was not accepted by the other delegates "porque es católica y además, porque sabe manifestar sus propias opiniones" (because she is Catholic and also because she knows how to manifest her own opinions) (E. A. 11). These rejections and criticisms did not stop her from writing, however. Her articles appeared in San Antonio–based Spanish-language newspapers *La Prensa* (The Press), *La Época* (The Epoch), and *El Imparcial de Texas* (The Impartial of Texas) as well as in Trinidad, Colorado's *El Anunciador* (The Announcer) (Baeza Ventura 62). Her extensive work with these presses led her to take on her own weekly column "Crónicas Femeninas" (Women's Chronicles) in *El Imparcial de Texas* and to become the editor of *La Época*, headed by José Quiroga. Later in her life and working on her own, she founded the journal, *Alma Femenina* (Feminine Spirit) (Luna Lawhn 83).

Born in Cadereyta de Jiménez, Nuevo Léon, Garza was a member of the elite class of Mexicans who immigrated to Texas in the aftermath of the Mexican Revolution and then participated in the turn-of-the-century conservative Mexican intellectual movement in the United

States coined by Rodolfo Uranga as El México de Afuera (Mexico on the outside) (Luna Lawhn 85). Those involved in El México de Afuera looked to their homeland's values and beliefs to stave off the virulent Americanization of Mexican people in the U.S. and to reject what they saw as the commercialization of society. In both pieces included here "[¿]Feministas . . . ? [¡]No! Femeninas" ("Feminists . . . ? No! Feminine Women") and "Las mujeres que escriben" ("Women Who Write"), Garza comes to terms with the clash of cultures and gendered ideologies. In the first article, she first considers the importance of the newly won vote for U.S. women, prompting *La Época* readers to respond to the questions she poses about the vote's efficacy and value in their lives. She then moves to reflect more broadly on what the consequences of feminism may yield, asserting that feminist gains may bring about more substantial losses for Mexican women.

In "Las mujeres que escriben," Garza explicitly engages the feminist writings of Artemisa Sáenz Royo, writing under the pseudonym Xóchitl, whose article "La mujer en el pasado, el presente y en el porvenir" ("Women in the Past, Present, and Future") appeared in *La Época* in 1920 and is collected here. As editor of *La Época*, Garza published Sáenz Royo's article, but alongside it she also placed an excerpt from her own book, titled *La verdadera de la mujer* (The True Mission of Women) as a conservative corrective to Sáenz Royo's liberal stance on women. In "Las mujeres que escriben" Garza continues to respond to Sáenz Royo's claims. Here, Garza discusses her own experiences with education and work, indicating that due to financial difficulties, she was forced to enter the world of work and especially journalism. She powerfully asserts her vision for herself and indeed her expectation for other women writers. She writes, "I will never forget that I am above all a woman rather than a WRITER." In "The Politics of Border Crossing: A Transnational Encounter in the Work of María Luisa Garza," Maria Napiorski assesses Garza's writing, noting "Garza urges to maintain tradition within modernization" (46). Garza's "coercive nationalism" put the progressive and ever-increasing number of educated Mexican women at odds with the traditional Mexican women relegated to the home space. Taking stock of Garza's writings, Napiorski's contends, "Garza eliminates the border experience to protect Mexican women of the Diaspora from being seduced by the plural belonging that transnational mobility brings" (46).

Garza's unconventional questioning and dialogic approach in both pieces illustrate a rhetorical style that creates a tone of familiarity with her audience. This style was not typically seen in Mexican newspaper writing, which was often highly formalized. But these rhetorical elements did not mean that Garza took on a less serious tone regarding the mexicana's identity within the context of the United States. On the contrary, the tone of her pieces is serious and at times even stern. Scholar Gabriela Baeza Ventura notes that Garza was primarily interested in "moralizing the public" (63–64). In her articles, Garza warns mexicana readers against losing their femininity, culture, language, and religion, and she argues that women should sustain their home through participating in education and the arts. Evaluating Garza's rhetorical and stylistic choices, readers may find her aggressive stance inconsistent with her argument that women adopt a feminine submissive lifestyle, for as she calls women to take on a conservative role, Garza's own arguments are confrontational and agonistic.

A similar contradiction emerges when considering the message of Garza's writings and her biography. While she advised mexicanas to remain true to their traditional heritage, Garza wrote and published her work weekly, even taking on leadership roles as editor and founder of presses. In 1922, she served as the president of La Cruz Azul Mexicana (Mexican Blue Cross), an organization that served the medical needs of Mexican nationals (De León 168). She also published two novels, *La novia de Nervo* (Nervo's Girlfriend) (1922) and *Los amores de Gaona: Apuntes realistas de Loreley* (The Many Loves of Gaona: Realistic Reflections from Loreley) (1922) as well as two other books, *Escucha* (Listen) (1928), and *Tentáculos de fuego* (Tentacles of Fire) (1930). Upon her return to Mexico in 1922, she worked as educator and continued to write, contributing to two newspapers, *El Universal Gráfico* (The Universal Graphic) and *Renacimiento* (Revival). Thus, even though she professed a preference to stay in the home and take on traditional women's roles, Garza found great success as a writer, editor, and educator.

[¿]Feministas . . . ? [¡]No! Femeninas

La Época
San Antonio, Texas
12 de septiembre de 1920

No es mi objeto criticar a las distinguidas damas que van tras la luz y el progreso ¡allá ellas! Y cada quien que haga de su capa un sayo.

Al dar mi humilde opinión, no creo atacar personalidades; quien quiera, que me tome en cuenta; quien no, bien hará en dejarme en paz ¡soy tan poca cosa!

Veamos: ¿qué le importa a la mujer que el Gobernador de su Estado sea X o H? Podrá su candidato impartirle ayuda en el difícil problema de la carencia cada vez más absoluta de domésticos?

¿Logrará con el triunfo de su elegido que el sueldo de su futuro amante reali[c]e pronto sus promesas de amor?

¿Podrá con nombrar un gobernante a su albedrío conseguir que el hijo venga al mundo con menos dolores, que su lactancia sea sana y su desarrollo físico y moral, inmejorable?

¿Modernismo? ¿Así lo entienden ustedes?

[¿]Se llama modernismo el dejar de ser mujer, para no ser hombre y convertirnos en ridículos marimachos?

¿Se preocupa el sexo fuerte por fundar clubs para discutir sobre si la cocina resulta mejor con gas o con carbón, si la falda es más bella corta que de toda cola?

Si ellos no nos imitan ¿por qué hacerles el honor de ocuparnos de sus asuntos?

¿Votar? ¿Tener derechos?

Sé de un pueblo cuyos habitantes iban casi desnudos, hambrientos, famélicos sin tener casas donde morar, pero eso sí: elegantemente calzados.

¿Qué pasa? Inquiere el rey a sus vasallos.

Pues nada . . . ¡que todos son zapateros!

¿No estamos hoy en el caso?

Abundaremos en médicos, en abogados, hasta en Generales: llegaráse el día en que todos seamos hombres: más acaso, hayamos de concurrir al Senado o a la consulta en traje paradisíaco, ostentando la simbólica hojita de higuera; aún más, con macábricos semblantes a fuerza de alimentación artificial pues las cocineras se van con las modistas, siguiendo a la mujer que se pierde allá en las brumas lejanas de un pasado que no volverá más. [¿]No estamos satisfechas con abandonar a nuestros pequeñuelos en manos mercenarias por no perder fiesta ni sarao, exponiéndonos a que las criadas maten en esos niños el sentimiento divino que sólo el alma maternal puede sostener?

¿No nos basta con internar en un colegio a nuestras hijas hasta los veinte años, para entregarlas luego al marido, ayunas en lo absoluto de moral y buenas costumbres pero ahítas de latinajos?

"Luz, más luz," dijo Goethe al expirar, mas él se refería a esa luz infinita y eterna, a esa luz del alma que nunca se alcanza en toda su intensidad.

—Pero jamás,—podéis creerlo—él pensó que la luz estaba en ese modernismo que hoy se nos echa encima con toda su sombra, no con su fulgor.

¿Feministas?

Conozco algunas señoritas (casi siempre conservadas) que se ufanan en presidir tal o cual sociedad progresista. Que me perdone Dios, pero cuando el diablo se mete a fraile ¿por qué será?

Adivínalo lector . . .

Yo sé que si alguna escritora de altos vuelos me lee, una sonrisa de desprecio rizará en su boca . . . [¡]Ay! acaso esa boca no ha sentido jamás el beso amante del esposo idolatrado, ni el ósculo inefable del niño que la llama Madre.

¿La grandeza de la mujer existe. En la abnegación, en el deber cumplido, en la ternura indecible para el que llora.

Alcestea tímida y dulce sacrificándose por el amado de su corazón, es cien veces más grande que Atalante, la atrevida cazadora, asombro de los griegos y que daba muerte a sus contrarios después de haberlos vencido.

¿Dominio? ¿Poderío?

¿Y quién, siendo mujer joven y bella no lo tiene?

¿Cuál mayor soberanía?

La de la pedante y risible conferencista que desde la tribuna pregona ideas de libertad e independencia o la de la pura y angelical mujer cuya alma de artista, noble y soñadora como nueva Beatriz guía a su Dante por el temible infierno de la vida?

¿Que Safo venció con su astro a un poeta? No lo dudo, pero . . . ¿no quería el poeta ser vencido para lograr ser amado?

¿Que existen mujeres cuyo talento supera al de algunos varones hijos de las Musas? Tampoco lo dudo, pero el talento de la mujer es relativo . . . muy relativo . . . y no quiero con ello denigrar a las de mi sexo; mas, que se me diga: ¿ha existido una Homera o una Huga?

Mujer de vasta ilustración y de modernas ideas, ¿te causó lástima, verdad?

No importa: Si tengo hijas, prefiero para ellas la corona de azahares que la de las victorias y el himno entonado a sus oídos, sonará mejor si es la trova galante del poeta enamorado, que la voz estridente del triunfo mundano. Ansío contemplarlas en las veladas invernales arrullando al Nene que "vino de Europa," mientras saborean baladas de Heine, antes que ensalzadas por la prensa, distinguiéndolas como "modernas progresistas."

Triunfos, aplausos, lauros, ¡todo es humo! ¡mentira todo!

Sólo es verdad el amor.

El amor al esposo, al hijo; a esos pobres viejos que nos dieron el ser.

¿Soberanía? ¡La Femenina!

Pues el artista que labra, el genio que crea, el poeta que canta, el guerrero que lucha, todos van a la conquista de la gloria por traer lauros a las plantas de la mujer querida.

Fundemos clubs . . . muchos clubs.

Ayudemos a nuestros gobernantes enalteciendo su pueblo. ¡Hagamos caridad!

Instalemos casas de socorro, arrancando al obrero de las garras alcohólicas que le aprisionan. Tendamos la mano a esas inocentes vírgenes que la miseria arroja en el lodo de la prostitución y la infamia.

Calmemos el hambre de esos niños irredentos que cual hojas de otoño arrastra el viento de la fatalidad por el suelo de la existencia sin conocer, ¡ay! . . . míseros, la sonrisa de la alegría.

Fundemos clubs ya que queremos ayudar a nuestra patria enferma y dolorida.

Seamos mujeres sin aspirar a ser hombres, tengamos alma antes que elocuencia, abundemos en sentimientos más que en retórica.

¿Que la senda de la mujer está sembrada de abrojos?

Es verdad, m[a]s cuando la dura prosa de la vida nos azote, al[c]emos al Cielo los ojos y perdámonos en el ensueño; que la idealidad hace olvidar el sufrimiento. Cultivemos el espíritu con libros sanos, tomemos alguna vez la pluma, no con la pretensión de alcanzar fama y renombre, sino con la esperanza de que nuestras ideas aunque pequeñas, puedan penetrar a las almas femeninas.

Y sobre todo, no olvidemos la distancia que del hombre nos separa, prefiramos siempre ser admiradas, enaltecidas, como mujeres, no trocando nuestro cetro femenino, por el problemático derecho de "ciudadanía."

Feminist Women . . . ? No! Feminine Women

La Época
San Antonio, Texas
12 September 1920

It is not my objective to criticize the distinguished ladies who pursue light and progress, that's their affair! Each one should do whatever she wants.

While giving my humble opinion, I do not believe in attacking personalities; whoever wants to should heed me; those who do not, will you please leave me in peace, I am such a little thing!

Let us see: What does it matter to a woman if the Governor of her State be X or H? Will her candidate be able to give her aid in the difficult problem of the shortage, ever more absolute, of domestic help?

Will she achieve with the victory of her chosen one that the salary of her future lover will quickly bring about his promises of love?

Will she be able, by naming a ruler of her own free will, to find a way so that her child will come into the world with fewer labor pains, that her lactation will be healthy, and the child's physical and moral development will be unimprovable?

Modernism? Is that what you understand it to be?

Does the term *modernism* mean to stop being a woman, in order not to be a man, and so we become ridiculous manly females?

Does the strong sex worry about establishing clubs to discuss whether the kitchen is better with gas or with coal, or whether a short skirt is prettier than one with a train?

If they do not imitate us, why should we do them the honor of taking on their issues?

Voting? Having rights?

I know of a town whose inhabitants went around almost naked, hungry, starving, without houses to live in, but, oh yes, they all wore elegant shoes.

What is going on? Asks the king of his vassals.

Nothing much . . . They are all shoemakers!

Are we not in the same situation at the present time?

We will have an abundance of doctors, lawyers, even Generals. The day will come when we may all be men. Perhaps more, we may have to appear at the Senate or at the doctor's office in our birthday suits, showing off the symbolic little fig leaf. Even more, with macabre faces due to artificial food, because the cooks run off with the seamstresses, following after the woman who is lost in the distant fogs of a past that will not return again. Are we not satisfied with leaving our little ones in mercenary hands so as not to miss a party or soiree, exposing ourselves to [the possibility] that the nannies might kill in those children the divine feeling that only the maternal soul can sustain?

Is it not enough for us to put our daughters in boarding schools until they are twenty years old, in order to hand them over to husbands, when these girls are completely lacking in morality and good breeding but stuffed with Latinisms?

"Light, more light," said Goethe as he died, but he was referring to that infinite and eternal light, that light of the soul that can never be reached in all its intensity.

—But never,—you can believe it—did he think that the light was in that modernism that today is thrown upon us with its shadow, not with its brilliance.

Feminists?

I know some single ladies (almost always well preserved) who boast about presiding over this or that progressive society. May God forgive me, but when the devil becomes a monk, I wonder why?[1]

Hazard a guess, reader...

I know that if a high-flying woman writer reads my essay, a disdainful smile will curl her lips... Oh! perhaps that mouth has never felt the loving kiss of an idolized husband, or the ineffable kiss of a child that calls her Mother.

The greatness of the woman exists. In self-sacrifice, in duty fulfilled, in the unspeakable tenderness for the one who cries.

Alcestis, timid and sweet, by sacrificing herself for the love of her heart, is a hundred times greater than Atalanta, the daring huntress, wonder of the Greeks who killed her enemies after having vanquished them.[2]

Domination? Power?

And who, being a young and beautiful woman, does not have it?

Which is the greater sovereignty?

That of the pedantic and laughable female lecturer who, from the lectern, preaches ideas of liberty and independence, or that of the pure and angelic woman whose artistic soul, noble and dreamy like a new Beatrice, guides her Dante through the fearsome inferno of life?

So Sappho conquered a poet with her star? I do not doubt it, but... did the poet not want to be conquered in order to achieve being loved?

So there exist women whose talent eclipses that of some men, the sons of the Muses? I do not doubt that either, but the talent of the woman is relative ... very relative ... and I do not want to denigrate my sex by saying that; but tell me: has there been a female Homer or a female Hugo?

Women of vast education and modern ideas, it caused you pity, right?

It doesn't matter: If I have daughters, I prefer them to have the orange-blossom wreath rather than that of victories, and the hymn sung to their ears will sound better if it is the gallant verse of an enamored poet, rather than the strident voice of worldly triumph. I am anxious to see them during the winter soirees lulling the Baby who "came from Europe," while they enjoy ballads by Heine, instead of being extolled by the press, by characterizing them as "modern progressive women."

Triumphs, applause, laurels, all is smoke! All is a lie!

The only truth is love.

The love of husband, of son, of those poor elderly ones who gave us being.

Sovereignty? The Feminine kind!

Because the artist who fashions, the genius who creates, the poet who sings, the warrior who fights, all of them pursue the conquest of glory with the intention of bringing laurels to the feet of the beloved woman.

Let us establish clubs . . . many clubs.

Let us help our leaders by improving their people. Let us do charitable works!

Let us erect rescue houses, by ripping the worker away from the alcoholic claws that imprison him. Let us extend a hand to those innocent maidens who poverty throws into the mud of prostitution and infamy.

Let us quell the hunger of those unredeemed children who like autumn leaves the wind of misfortune blows along the ground of existence without knowing oh! . . . miserable ones, the smile of happiness.

Let us establish clubs, since we want to help our infirm and pained Homeland.

Let us be women without aspiring to be men, let us have a soul before eloquence, let us abound in sentiments more than in rhetoric.

So the path of the woman is sown with thorns?

It is true, but when the hard prose of life hits us, let us raise our eyes to Heaven and lose ourselves in daydreams; because ideality makes us forget suffering. Let us cultivate our spirit with decent books, let us take up the pen at times, not with the pretension of achieving fame and renown, but rather with the hope that our ideas, although small, may reach feminine souls.

And above all, let us not forget the distance that separates us from men, let us always prefer to be admired, exalted, as women, not by exchanging our feminine scepter for the problematic right of "citizenship."

Las mujeres que escriben

La Época
San Antonio, Texas
27 de febrero de 1921

(Contestando la carta abierta de Xóchitl.)

Cuando yo escribiera un artículo, cuyo nombre ahorita no recuerdo, pero que denotaba el fastidio que me causa ver siempre esa tendencia de toda pluma femenina en masculinizarse, nunca creí que se interpretaran tan torcidamente sus conceptos.

Pero he ahí, que una buena amiga a quien aprecio, me ha enviado una carta para que yo le diera cabida en LA ÉPOCA y aunque la citada misiva no deja de zaherirme un poquillo, he cumplido con un deber de cortesía y la carta se dio a la prensa.

¡Dios mío! ¿Es que me expreso tan mal en nuestro divino idioma que no se me entiende? Yo no abomino de la mujer que honradamente lleva al hogar el fruto noble y digno de su trabajo. Mal pudiera yo hablar de la mujer que ha usurpado un puesto en las oficinas masculinas, cuando yo vivo más que nadie del trabajo de un hombre.

Yo he dicho sencillamente, que me duele, que me avergüenza a veces, el que la mujer olvide su sexo y al escribir se ocupe del ministro Fulano, del Presidente Zutano o del Embajador Mengano...

Yo he dicho, que me gusta cuando leo la firma de una mujer, encontrar en aquellas líneas el inefable encanto, la dulzura infinita, la expresión santa, casi divina, que un hombre, por soberano genio que posea, no puede desarrollar jamás. Pero, ¿no es triste, y amargo, q[u]e una mujer cuando escribe, si no lo hace de cintajos y cosméticos, rime poesías ante un amor que nada nos importa, o nos hable de la luna del céfiro suave o de la noche quieta?

Eso es muy bello; [si] un escrito no adereza con su pimienta de romanticismo, claro que sería una flor sin aroma, pero es preciso que ese escrito lleve su moral, su fin, su tendencia.

Todo escritor tiene el deber de moralizar. No basta escribir bien, es preciso saber para qué se escribe.

¿Y el amor? Bien... que nos hable del amor toda escritora,—pero la palabra amor es infinita...

Se ama al niño que huérfano, abandonado, atraviesa solitario la espinada cuesta de la vida.

Se ama a la mujer que caída, en vez de alzarse, se hunde cada vez más, porque no encuentra quien le ayude.

Se ama al hombre, al que vencido, cayó, y silente, va al ocaso, aunque brille aún en su existencia la esperanza, aunque aliente aún en su alma la fé.

¡Hay tantos amores en la vida! . . . Hablemos pues de ellos, que quien nos lea, algo útil pueda encontrar en tal lectura.

Yo no reniego de la mujer, que trabaja cuando a esa mujer, como a mí, no se le enseñe a bordar con primor, ni a tejer con riqueza bellos medios de vida y verdaderos medios para la mujer.

A mí, querida amiga, que dice "[¿]por qué, Loreley, nos fustiga tan fuerte a las mujeres libres-pensadoras?" a mí, lo repito—se me internó en un colegio de monjas como a toda muchacha mimada por la fortuna, se me hartó de francés y de latín olvidando que mi fortuna podía venirse al suelo como se vino y que enmedio de un mar embravecido, huérfana, sola teniendo cerca de mí seres que reclamaban el derecho de vivir no hube más a donde asirme que á la tabla que pasaba y alcancé la orilla redentora del trabajo . . . ¡qué remedio!

Esa tabla era el periodismo. Yo hubiera querido que fuera mejor un taller de modas que un taller de imprenta, yo hubiera querido confeccionar trajes en vez de emborronar cuartillas, yo anhelara mejor usar la máquina SINGER que a la OLIVER . . . El destino no lo quiso, pero no olvidaré nunca que soy mujer primero que ESCRITORA.

En la redacción suspiro por el "home sweet home." Rememoro muchas veces mientras escribo una majadería reporteril; mi piano querido que silencioso me siente solamente una hora apenas por las noches, cuando antes lo acariciaba a todas horas. Muchas veces con lágrimas en los ojos, suspiro doliente por mis flores, por mis pájaros, por los sabrosos pastelillos que solía confeccionar . . . En fin, que seré mujer . . . ¡siempre mujer!

Y yo, mi bella "Xóchitl," he dicho, lo digo hoy y lo repetiré eternamente que ya, que la suerte me puso en este sendero, caminaré por él mientras se llega el día de ascender a la verdadera y única vida: pero a mi paso he de ir deshojando una a una las flores odorantes de mi alma femenina.

Y si fracaso en los próximos libros que daré a luz. . . . Estoy dispuesta, pero jamás he de torcerme. Nunca evolucionaré. Nunca he de convertirme en hombre para abordar ciertos temas que a la mujer nos están vedados . . . De la fantasía que lleva lejos y del ensueño que me avasalla empaparé mi pluma . . .

¿Que abomino de las mujeres hombrunas? ¿que maldigo de los escritos "con bigotes" cuando ahora ni los hombres los llevan? Siempre, amiga mía, . . . ¡siempre!

Un escrito que no es dulce ni emotivo, remeda para mí, una mujer desaliñada y vieja . . . ¿quién puede negarme el derecho de que yo quiera ser joven y bella toda la vida?

De "El Informador"–Guadalajara

Women Who Write

La Época
San Antonio, Texas
27 February 1921

(Answering the open letter from Xóchitl.)

When I might have written a certain article, whose name I can't remember at the moment, but which denoted the annoyance it causes me to always see that tendency of every feminine pen to become masculine, I never thought that the letter's concepts would be interpreted in such a twisted way.

But it happened that a good female friend, whom I value, has sent me a letter for me to give it space in LA EPOCA, and although said missive still derides me a tiny bit, I fulfilled the duty of courtesy and the letter was sent off to be printed.

My God! Can it be that I express myself so poorly in our heavenly language that I am not understood? I do not detest the woman who honorably takes home the noble and worthy fruit of her work. I could not speak badly about the woman who has usurped a place in masculine offices, when I more than anybody make a living at a man's job.

I have simply said that it hurts me, that at times it embarrasses me, the fact that women forget their sex and when writing, she deals with Minister So and So, President Such and Such or Ambassador What's His Name. . . .

I have said that I like it when I read the signature of a woman and find in those lines the ineffable charm, the infinite sweetness, the saintly expression, almost divine, that a man, however great his genius, can never develop. But, is it not sad and bitter that a woman when she writes, if she does not do so about tawdry ornaments and cosmetics, she may rhyme poems about a love that matters nothing to us, or she may speak of the moon, of the soft zephyr, or the tranquil night?

All this is very pretty; if a piece of writing is not well seasoned with its spice of romanticism, of course it would be a flower without aroma, but it is necessary for that writing to have a moral, its objective, its inclinations.

Every writer has a duty to moralize. It is not enough to write well, it is necessary to know to what end one is writing.

And what about love? Good . . . let every woman writer speak of love,—but the word love is infinite.

One loves the orphan child who, abandoned, travels alone the craggy hill of life.

One loves the woman who, once fallen, instead of getting up, she sinks further and further, because she finds no one to help her.

One loves the man, who when vanquished fell, and goes silently into the sunset, although hope still shines in his being, although faith still nourishes his soul.

There are so many loves in life! . . . Then let us speak of them, so that whoever reads us may find something useful in the reading.

I do not reject the woman who works when, as in my case, she is not taught to embroider exquisitely, or to knit together a richly beautiful way of life and true resources for women.

To me, dear friend, who says, "Why, Loreley, do you reprimand us women free-thinkers so harshly?," I, to repeat, was enrolled as a live-in student at a nuns' school like all girls spoiled by fortune, I was stuffed full with French and Latin, forgetting that my fortune could come tumbling down, as it did, and that in the middle of a tumultuous sea, orphaned, alone, having people close to me who claimed the right to live, I had nowhere to hold on except a plank that floated by and I finally reached the redeeming shore of work . . . what a relief!

That plank was journalism. I would have wanted it to be a fashion shop rather than a printing shop, I would have wanted to create suits instead of scribbling on paper, I desired to use a SINGER machine more than an OLIVER. . . . Destiny did not want it to be so, but I will never forget that I am a woman first rather than a WRITER.

In the newspaper office I sigh for "home sweet home." I revive memories many times while I am writing some reporter's nonsense; my beloved piano there that silently I might sit at it for only a brief hour in the evenings, when before I caressed it at all hours. Many times with tears in my eyes, I sigh in pain for my flowers, for my birds, and the delicious little cakes that I used to make. . . . In the end, I will be a woman . . . always a woman!

And I, my lovely "Xóchitl," have said, I say it today and I will repeat it eternally, that since fortune put me on this path, I will follow it while awaiting the day of ascending to the true and only life: but as I go I must strip the petals off one by one of the odiferous flowers of my feminine soul.

And if I fail in the next books that I bring forth . . . I am willing, but I will never turn away. I will never evolve. I will never make myself into a man in order to discuss certain topics that are forbidden to us women. . . . In the fantasy that carries me far and in the daydream that enslaves me will I dip my pen . . .

So do I despise masculine women? Do I curse writings "with mustachios" when now even men do not wear them? Always, my friend, always!

A piece of writing that is neither sweet nor emotive, imitates for me a disheveled old woman . . . who can deny me the right that I want to be young and beautiful my whole life?

From "El Informador"—Guadalajara

Ariana

In 1920 Ariana published her articles "La mujer moderna y el hogar" ("The Modern Woman and the Home") and "Lo que no es el feminismo" ("What Feminism Is Not") in the Spanish-language newspaper *La Prensa* (The Press) (1913–57), which was based in San Antonio, Texas, and owned and operated by Mexican-born Ignacio E. Lozano (Rivas-Rodríguez 77). There is no available biographical information on Ariana, but the rhetorical situation surrounding her writing and the press itself offers some likely details about her life. *La Prensa* was directed to an elite Mexican local, national, and transnational readership, and it circulated from San Antonio into El Paso, Texas; Los Angeles, California; and parts of Mexico (78). The newspaper began during the Mexican Revolution (1910–20), at which time it provided an outlet for Mexican intellectuals to express their dissatisfaction with the Mexican government. Scholar Maggie Rivas-Rodríguez suggests that the newspaper was also assigned in public schools for students who were learning Spanish, because it provided excellent examples of prose (81).

The year Ariana published "La mujer moderna y el hogar" and "Lo que no es el feminismo," the Mexican Revolution was coming to an end, and Mexican people's minds were turning toward reconstruction and envisioning what their new postwar world would be like. These concerns were especially significant for women, since during the war many mexicanas had experienced great change in their societal roles. Numbers served on the battlefield as nurses, caretakers, and even soldiers—known as *soldaderas* and *adelitas*. Women had also, as the writings of many of the mexicanas in this volume make clear, become political leaders, writers, and public intellectuals. Ariana as well as other women such as Sara Estela Ramírez, María Luisa Garza, and Artemisa N. Sáenz Royo were living through a particularly active feminist moment, as U.S. women won the right to vote in 1920, and the years leading up to this victory were marked by persistent and consistent discussions about women's rights.

In "La mujer moderna y el hogar," Ariana engages in this atmosphere of change, and her argument is a unique and important one. While she asserts that the adoption of feminist principles will surely change women's position as a worker and participant in the public sphere, she also argues it should change her position as a wife. She writes that by adopting feminism, the Mexican woman should reject the "humble resignation that adorned [her] grandmothers" and see herself, instead, as her husband's "companion" rather than his "servant." Ariana continues to refine understandings of feminism in her article "Lo que no es el feminismo." In this piece she leverages the rhetorical strategy of negative definition to explain that feminism is *not* marked by the hatred of men, the imitation of men, or the idea that women are better than men. Composing her argument in this way, Ariana likely aimed to dispel assumptions about feminism circulating during the period to clarify the position she and others held.

La mujer moderna y el hogar

La Prensa
San Antonio, Texas
8 de noviembre de 1920

Henos aquí ante el aspecto más espinoso y complicado del problema con que se enfrentan las mujeres de hoy. Sabemos ya que este problema consiste en la modificación que deben sufrir leyes y costumbres para adaptarse al nuevo criterio de la mujer que no se considera ya inferior al hombre sino equivalente a él.

Es indudable que, aceptado tal postulado, la mujer no puede resignarse al papel bastante secundario y a veces hasta depresivo, que le había sido destinado en sociedad.

De aquí surgió en ella el afán de instruirse, de prepararse frente al futuro para gozar de noble independencia o para realizar mejor su deber tradicional rejuvenecido por las nuevas ideas, de buscar garantías para su trabajo y para sus aptitudes. Y de aquí también brotó ese impulso generoso de ampliar su poder para el bien, que exalta a tantas mujeres de hoy. En todas estas fases del problema la mujer va hallando poco a poco, a pesar de obstinadas resistencias, la solución satisfactoria que merece.

Pero queda un punto importantísimo que la mayoría de los teorizantes del feminismo resuelven de una plumada, como si temiesen detenerse a escudriñar sus varios repliegues entre los que se ocultan dificultades hoy casi insuperables.

Trátase de la relación del feminismo con los importantísimos asuntos del amor y del matrimonio, y es tal su trascendencia que mientras no haya sido resuelto, el feminismo alcanzará triunfos más aparentes que reales. No basta, en efecto que a las nuevas ideas de la mujer se conforme lo que podríamos llamar su vida pública, el desarrollo de sus actividades como obrera, empleada, artista o intelectual, electora y elegida. Es preciso prever la influencia y las consecuencias de esas ideas sobre su vida íntima, de esposa y de ama de casa.

Esa influencia, en lo que se refiere al propio desarrollo de la mujer, no puede ser sino altamente benéfica, y las feministas del mundo entero han cantado, con fervoroso entusiasmo, las alabanzas de esa mujer que llaman nueva, cuyo tipo ha aparecido a veces en la historia y que ahora comienza a generalizarse: la mujer fuerte, serena, culta consciente de sus deberes y de sus derechos, de sus aptitudes y responsabilidades, perfecta compañera de su esposo y educadora de sus hijos.

Pero . . . ¿se hallan preparados los que rodean a esa mujer moderna para gozar de las conquistas que ella ha realizado y de los bienes que se adelanta a ofrecerles?

Hablo, naturalmente, de las condiciones de nuestra sociedad, no de otras en que la adaptación a ese nuevo concepto de la feminidad ya se ha efectuado casi por completo, y a veces con muy escasos sacudimientos, tal vez porque a él se hallasen preparados por viejas costumbres y ancestrales tradiciones.

Entre aquellos a quienes Roma desdeñosa apellidó "los bárbaros," las mujeres representaban un papel, no sólo importante sino muy activo y bien visible y tal recuerdo perdura entre sus más o menos civilizados descendientes.

Nosotros, en cambio, hemos recogido la tradición greco-latina, tocada y agravado de islamismo, Gineceo y harén no son exactamente términos semejantes, pero ambos significan reclusión, desde el punto de vista físico, y sumisión, desde el punto de vista moral.

Herederos de estas ideas, muchos hombres de nuestro país, no pueden aceptar con agrado todas las manifestaciones, sí, en gran parte, la necesidad para la mujer de una instrucción verdaderamente sólida y la conveniencia de crearse una posición independiente; pero para ellos—no hablo de honrosas excepciones—la emancipación de la mujer sólo existe en cuanto al mundo exterior: el matrimonio es siempre el último reducto del absolutismo masculino, y la "perfecta casada," muy sinceramente querida en muchos casos, es la "perfecta sumisa" a los gustos, opiniones o caprichos del que la eligió.

Frente a un hombre, por lo demás bueno y amante, pero imbuido de esas ideas, coloquemos al tipo perfecto de la mujer moderna; una mujer a quien el feminismo no ha despojado de su ternura y suavidad, pero que posee una personalidad bien definida y no cuenta entre sus virtudes la humilde resignación que adornaba a nuestras abuelas, una mujer que ama, más consciente y profundamente que muchas esposas de antaño, pero con amor de compañera, no de sierva.

¿Acaso el choque entre esas dos ideologías no destruirá la felicidad? Grave problema. Bien está el desarrollo de ese nuevo espíritu femenino; mas pensemos en que el mundo no se halla por completo preparado para ese cambio, y que en el período de transición y adaptación pueden hundirse en dolor e incomprensión muchas vidas de mujer.

Cuando acerca de esto se reflexiona, compréndanse muchas resistencias tibias, muchas aprobaciones frías, y surge clara la noción de que para lograr el triunfo positivo de los nuevos ideales femeninos, no es preciso catequizar a las mujeres solamente. . . .

The Modern Woman and the Home

La Prensa
San Antonio, Texas
8 November 1920

We have here before us the thorniest and most complicated aspect of the problem that the women of today face. We already know that this problem consists of changes that must be made in laws and customs in order to adapt to the new criteria of the woman who no longer feels inferior to the man, but rather equivalent to him.

There is no doubt, having accepted such a theory, the woman cannot resign herself to the quite secondary and at times even depressing role that had been destined for her in society.

For that reason, there arose in her the desire to educate herself, to prepare herself facing the future in order to enjoy a dignified independence or to better carry out her traditional duty rejuvenated by the new ideas of seeking guarantees for her work and her abilities. And for that reason also that generous impulse blossomed to increase her power for goodness, which uplifts so many women of today. In all these phases of the problem, the woman is finding little by little, in spite of stubborn resistance, the satisfactory solution that she deserves.

But there remains an extremely important point that the majority of theorists of feminism resolve at a pen stroke, as if they were afraid to pause to scrutinize its several recesses among which are hidden today almost insuperable obstacles.

This deals with the relationship of feminism with the very important issues of love and marriage, and its transcendence is such that as long as it has not been resolved, feminism will achieve victories that are more superficial than real. It is not enough, in fact, that the new ideas about women should conform to what we could call her public life, the development of her activities as a worker, employee, artist or intellectual, as voter and as an elected official. It is necessary to foresee the influence and the consequences of these ideas on her intimate life, as a spouse and housewife.

That influence, as far as proper development of the woman is concerned, cannot be anything but highly beneficial, and the feminists of the whole world have sung, with fervent enthusiasm, the praises of that woman whom they call new, whose type has at times appeared throughout history and which is now beginning to become more widespread: the woman who is strong, serene, cultured, conscious of her duties and her rights, of her capabilities and responsibilities, a perfect companion of her husband and educator of her children.

But . . . Are those who surround this modern woman prepared to enjoy the victories that she has achieved and the benefits that she steps forward to offer them?

Of course I am speaking about the conditions of our society, not of others in which the adjustment to that new concept of feminism has already taken effect almost completely, and sometimes with very rare upheavals, perhaps because they have found themselves prepared for it by age-old customs and ancestral traditions.

Among those whom Rome scornfully called "the barbarians," women played a part, not only important, but also very active and highly visible, and this memory endures among its more or less civilized descendants.

We, in contrast, have gathered up the Greco-Roman tradition, touched and worsened by Islamism: Gynecium[1] and harem are not exactly similar terms, but both signify reclusion, from the physical point of view, and submission, from the moral point of view.

Being heirs of these ideas, many men in our country cannot accept with pleasure all of its manifestations, but most of them can accept the woman's need for a truly solid education and the advantage of her creating for herself an independent position; but for them—I am not speaking of the honorable exceptions—the emancipation of the woman only exists with respect to the outside world: Marriage is always the last refuge of masculine absolutism, and the "perfect wife," very sincerely loved in many cases, is the "perfect submissive woman" to the tastes, opinions, or caprices of the one who chose her.

Opposite the man, otherwise good and loving, but imbued with those ideas, we will place the perfect model of the modern woman; a woman whom feminism has not stripped of her tenderness and gentleness, but who does possess a well-defined personality and does not count among her virtues the humble resignation that adorned our grandmothers, a woman who loves, more consciously and deeply than many wives of yore, but with the love of a companion, not of a servant.

Could it be that the clash between those two ideologies will not destroy happiness? A serious problem. The development of this new feminine spirit may be well and good; but let us think about the fact that the world is not completely prepared for that change, and that during the period of transition and adaptation many women's lives may sink into pain and incomprehension.

When one reflects on this, one understands the many lukewarm reactions, the many cold approvals, and what emerges clearly is the notion that in order to achieve the positive victory of the new feminine ideals, it is not necessary to preach to only the women . . .

Lo que no es el feminismo

La Prensa
San Antonio, Texas
12 de octubre de 1920

Como el prejuicio acerca de la desaparición del amor y de la dulzura por virtud del feminismo, otros muchos se levantan en el camino de la mujer; y ya que contra el prejuicio—monstruo prehistórico sin ojos y con mil garras—debemos salir a combatir tú y yo, lectora, todos los días, creo conveniente que declaremos lo que no es el feminismo, o por lo menos "nuestro" feminismo.

No es feminismo usar chaleco, leontina y pelo corto, como la dogmática doctora Madel[e]ine Pelletier, ni vestir por completo el traje masculino, como Jane Dieulafoy, la escritora erudita y viajera infatigable; ni odiar a los hombres como aquella Carolina Legrand, de la comedia de Brieux que a esta frase: "Carolina, una buena noticia," contesta imperturbable:—¿Cuál? . . . ¿Todos los hombres se han muerto?

Ni lo es tampoco, organizar ruidosas protestas contra la tiranía masculina y pelear con los policías en las calles de Londres como la famosa Mrs. Pankhurst, ni creer que las mujeres tienen siempre razón y que los hombres son culpables de cuanto mal existe en el mundo; ni siquiera a juicio, pretender que en todos los países y dentro de brevísimo tiempo, como por arte de encantamiento, se deroguen todas las leyes y se modifiquen las costumbres contrarias a los derechos de la mujer y al desarrollo de la personalidad femenina.

Nada de esto es, en realidad, el feminismo. Para las que representan esencialmente el espíritu nuevo, los hombres no son, por el sólo hecho de serlo, objeto de odio ni de servil imitación: son hermanos a muchos de los cuales es preciso llevar suavemente hacia la comprensión de esa fraternidad. . . . Si los odiáramos, seríamos mucho más injustas de lo que ellos lo han sido, porque su injusticia es el residuo de remotas épocas bárbaras, un legado ancestral, cuya responsabilidad no pertenece a los hombres de hoy; y nosotras, que deseamos preparar el porvenir, nosotras, mujeres de hoy no de hacer [una] cuarentena [de] siglos[,] cometeríamos un delito al admitir en nuestro espíritu algo tan salvajemente primitivo como el odio. Además, las mujeres se han quejado incesantemente, de ser incomprendidas; y el odio es la más intensa forma de la incomprensión.

Las mujeres no deben destruir sino lo indispensable para construir mucho; y el odio destruye siempre demasiado. . . .

Pero que el feminismo derive hacia el odio no es verosímil: las Carolinas Legrand, producto del fortísimo contraste entre la inmensa aspiración que acaba de surgir y la realidad aún sujeta dentro de férreos moldes, son precursoras inquietas y severas que desaparecerán sin que sea necesario atacarlas. Más frecuente es la imitación infantil o desagradable, que no es tampoco feminismo. Imitar a los hombres sería rebajarnos, demostrando que sólo sabemos ser originales en frivolidades; sería convenir en que merecemos nuestro lugar secundario en la sociedad; y sería, por último, hacer que sólo deseamos participación en los asuntos políticos o sociales por capricho fugaz o por estricto egoísmo, y no porque nuestra influencia hubiese de beneficiar en algo al progreso del mundo.

Creer a los hombres culpables sin remisión y a las mujeres inocentes de toda falta, sería establecer un prejuicio y un privilegio contrarios a los que nos han hecho sufrir; y nuestra obra no debe ser sustituir una injusticia por otra, sino lograr igualdad y beneficios para todos. . . . Precisamente no es contra los hombres contra quienes debemos luchar, sino contra todos los privilegios y todos los prejuicios.

La cólera, la impaciencia, tienen mayor excusa; pero no son muy razonables, y . . . ¿no hemos formulado todas nuestras reclamaciones en nombre de la razón? . . . Aunque haya mucha justicia en estas últimas, no debemos desear que por darles una satisfacción rápida, la entrada de la mujer en la vida civil y política asuma los caracteres y las proporciones de una catástrofe geológica. . . .

Odio, imitación, apasionamiento, cólera o impaciencia, son todas manifestaciones externas, superficies inconexas; insignificantes unas y extremadas otras, pero que en ningún caso forman lo esencial del nuevo espíritu femenino. Ellas son como el polvo que se levanta en el camino cuando pasa una gran idea nueva; son la espuma ligera y cambiante oleaje del mar del pensamiento. Confundir con el feminismo todos estos detalles exaltados o pueriles, sería como creer que la política es estruendo de cohetes, música desafinada y gritos de un orador furibundo.

Para los que piensan, la Revolución Francesa no está simbolizada por una guillotina y el feminismo no debe estarlo por las tijeras que destrozan la "Venus del Espejo."

What Feminism Is Not

La Prensa
San Antonio, Texas
12 October 1920

Like the prejudice about the disappearance of love and tenderness by virtue of feminism, many others arise in the woman's path; and since against prejudice—that eyeless prehistoric monster with a thousand claws—we must go forth and fight, you and I, reader, every day, I believe it is appropriate that we declare what feminism is not, or at least "our" feminism.

It is not feminism to wear a vest, watch chain, and short hair, like the dogmatic Doctor Madeleine Pelletier,[2] nor to dress in the complete masculine outfit, like Jane Dieulafoy,[3] the erudite writer and indefatigable traveler; nor to hate men like Carolina Legrand,[4] in the drama by Brieux, that to this phrase, "Carolina, some good news," she answers imperturbably, "What? . . . All the men have died?"

Neither is it to organize noisy protests against masculine tyranny and fight with the police in the streets of London like the famous Mrs. Pankhurst,[5] nor to believe that women are always right and that men are guilty of whatever evil exists in the world; it is also not, in my opinion, claiming that in all countries in a very short time, as if by magic, all laws should be repealed and the customs should be changed that are contrary to women's rights and the development of the feminine personality.

None of this is, in reality, feminism. For those women who fundamentally represent the new spirit, men are not, simply by the fact of being men, objects of hatred or of servile imitation: they are brothers, for many of whom it is necessary to lead gently toward an understanding of that feeling of companionship. If we were to hate them, we would be much more unjust than they have been, because their injustice is the residue of ancient and barbarous eras, an ancestral legacy, whose responsibility does not belong with the men of today; and we women, who desire to prepare the future, we, women of today, not of forty centuries ago, would commit a crime by allowing into our spirit something as savagely primitive as hatred. Furthermore, women have complained incessantly about being misunderstood; and hatred is the most intense form of incomprehension.

Women must not destroy anything except what is absolutely necessary for constructing many things; and hatred always destroys too much. . . .

But to think that feminism may be drifting toward hatred is not credible: the Caroline Legrands of the world, products of the very strong contrast between the immense aspiration that has recently arisen and the reality still confined within iron-clad molds, are restless and stern precursors who will disappear without it being necessary to attack them. More frequent is infantile or disagreeable imitation, which is not feminism either. Imitating men would be to lower ourselves, by showing that we only know how to be original in frivolities; it would be to agree that we deserve our secondary place in society; and it would be, finally, making believe that we only want participation in political or social issues because of a fleeting whim or unbending egotism, and not because our influence might somehow benefit the progress of the world.

To believe that men are guilty without remission and that women are innocent of all faults would be to establish a prejudice and privilege contrary to those who have made us suffer; and our task must not be to substitute one injustice for another, but rather to achieve equality and benefits for all.... As a matter of fact, it is not against men we should fight, but rather against all privileges and all prejudices.

Anger, impatience are more readily excused; but they are not very reasonable, and ... have we not formulated all our demands in the name of reason? ... Although there might be a lot of justice in these demands, we ought not to desire that by giving them swift satisfaction, the entry of women into civil and political life may assume the characteristics and proportions of a geological catastrophe....

Hatred, imitation, fanaticism, anger, or impatience are all eternal manifestations, unconnected surfaces; some of them insignificant and others extreme, but in no case do they constitute the essential element of the new feminine spirit. They are like the dust that arises on the path when a great new idea passes; they are the airy foam and changeable ocean surf of thought. To confuse feminism with all these exalted or childish details would be like believing that politics are the loud noise of fireworks, out-of-tune music, and the shouts of a furious orator.

For those who think the French Revolution is not symbolized by the guillotine, and feminism must not be symbolized by the shears that destroy the "Venus with a Mirror."[6]

Anonymous Feminist Writings from *La Prensa*, San Antonio

The San Antonio–based Spanish-language newspaper, *La Prensa* (The Press), run by Ignacio E. Lozano, took up social issues relating to Mexicans living on both sides of the border. More particularly this press discussed women's place in society and offered space for writers such as Ariana (whose writings are collected here) to speak out on topics related to women's rights. The following anonymous piece, titled "Opiniones de algunas de las feministas que han concurrido al Congreso de La Haya en favor de la paz" (Opinions of some of the feminists who attended the Congress of The Hague in favor of peace), was published on 7 January 1916 in *La Prensa* in a section called "Sección de la Guerra" (War Section). We include this piece because we believe many women published anonymously or, like Ariana, used pseudonyms to shield their identity and avoid ridicule. We thus see anonymous writings as contributing to the very active conversation regarding the role women should play not just in the local San Antonio community but also on the national and international stage.

Offering her *La Prensa* article as a form of international news coverage, the author of "Opiniones" compiles excerpts from speeches given at the 1915 International Congress of Women held at The Hague in the Netherlands. This congress convened in order to assert women's position on the topic of war and to seek a peaceful resolution to World War I. The anonymous *La Prensa* writer articulates her article's purpose and her own research process, explaining, "I scan the columns of the feminist newspapers, including French, North American, English, Dutch, and international ones, because I would like to give you a clear idea of the current state of the feminist cause in the world." Before setting out the excerpts, however, the author identifies the main concerns she believes the speeches convey. She writes that women must take responsibility for the current war for two main reasons: first, mothers are not raising their sons to respect peace and instead are allowing them to grow up glorifying war and conquest, and second, women have not gained the political power to stop the war. Thus, women need to continue their fight for suffrage so they have the opportunity to make their voices heard in consequential civic arenas.

This international perspective would have been particularly meaningful to the mexicana readers of *La Prensa*. At the time, World War I was raging, but Mexico's attention was also regionally transfixed on its own revolution. These feminist arguments regarding the international war would likely have resonated with Mexican women who had similar concerns regarding World War I as well as the conflict on their own soil. Therefore, the translation and reprinting of excerpts from European and American women's speeches could have served as a rhetorical point of identification enabling mexicanas to see similarities between themselves and those speaking at the congress. For example, Austria's Frau Lecher made the claim, "I had never spoken in public ever, I had never participated in a feminist movement; but the horrors of war have brought me to this Congress." Many mexicana readers of *La Prensa* may have likewise seen the war as an exigency for their political activism and civic engagement. Taking the discursive lead from the women at The Hague, the anonymous writer asserts a key feminist principle: "We share equal responsibility with the men who govern, because we have allowed them to govern so absurdly and inhumanely. We are obligated to remedy our neglect. This is the great lesson of the war." Women must claim equal place in society so they are able to remedy the wrongs of those (men) who now govern.

Opiniones de algunas de las feministas que han concurrido al Congreso de La Haya en favor de la paz

La Prensa
San Antonio, Texas
7 de enero de 1916

Recorro las columnas de los periódicos feministas franceses, norteamericanos, ingleses, holandeses, internacionales, porque quisiera dar a ustedes idea clara del estado actual de la causa feminista en el mundo. Por ahora, todos están llenos de esta dolida lamentación: ¡La guerra! Todos, apasionados en la misma anhelante esperanza: ¡La paz!

Reivindicaciones, derechos, sufragio, rebeldías, todo queda reducido a segundo término. La guerra lo llena todo; los mares de la guerra absorben todo el poder de preocupación; el remedio a los males de la guerra acapara toda facultad de ocupación; las mujeres trabajan para endulzar la suerte de los hombres que pelean; trabajan para llenar el hueco de los hombres a quienes la guerra ha obligado a dejar el trabajo. Por ahora, nada piden; dan, dan, dan cuanto tienen con generosidad y tesón; no hay para ellas tarea imposible ni trabajo capaz de amedrentarlas; valerosamente, han hecho suyos todos los deberes, manera elocuentísima de demostrar que están capacitadas para todos los derechos.

Y en esta dura escuela de sudor, sangre y llanto aprenden lecciones inolvidadas, lecciones esenciales para la vida futura de la humanidad. Algunas, las de más autoridad, proclaman las lecciones aprendidas, y en resumen, estas lecciones se reducen a esto: *Los hombres tienen casi toda la culpa de la guerra; pero las mujeres tampoco estamos exentas de responsabilidad; hemos faltado a nuestro deber de dos maneras.*

Primera. Consintiendo que se eduque a nuestros hijos en la falsa idea de heroísmo y de deber patrio. Hasta ahora mismo se ha glorificado en las escuelas el valor militar, las hazañas de sangre, la injusticia de la conquista, el egoísmo colectivo; se ha hecho de la bandera un símbolo, no de patriotismo, sino de imperialismo; en una palabra: se ha inculcado en el corazón de los hombres la idea de que heroísmo significa tanto como desprecio de la vida propia y ajena y arranque para perderla o arrebatarla.

Segunda. Por temor al ridículo, hemos dejado de poner en nuestras reivindicaciones todo el empeño necesario: el día en que las mujeres intervengan en la gobernación de los pueblos en número igual al de los hombres, la guerra habrá concluido de una vez para siempre; esto lo sabemos y lo sentimos. La paz es el primer artículo de nuestro programa y nuestra maternidad lo ha escrito con letras de sangre en nuestro corazón. Pero, madres cobardes, hemos dejado la vida de nuestros hijos en manos de hombres. Hace mucho tiempo que hubiésemos conseguido nuestros derechos políticos si no nos hubiesen asustado, más que las dificultades reales, las burlas de unos cuantos, o demasiado interesados o demasiado indiferentes.

Y esto no puede ser. Somos responsables a medias con los hombres que gobiernan, de haberles dejado gobernar tan absurda e inhumanamente. Estamos obligados a remediar nuestro descuido. Esta es la gran lección de la guerra.

Esta opinión general, que extracto para ustedes, está elocuentemente expresada por varias de las concurrentes al último Congreso de la Haya. A continuación copio fragmentos de algunos de los discursos pronunciados.[1]

De[1] discurso de Jane Addams, la ilustre escritora americana, que ha sido presidenta del Congreso.—Habla en primer lugar de la gran responsabilidad política de las mujeres reconocida como tal ya en algunas naciones (de entre las neutrales, especialmente), y existe, aunque no se conozca, en todas las demás. Y afirma que la reunión de tantas mujeres de diversas nacionalidades en el Congreso de la Haya prueba el progreso del sentimiento internacionalista, esperanza única de un porvenir mejor para la humanidad. Este movimiento internacionalista, que une con tan irresistible fuerza a las mujeres, y que es el fundamento de su asociación no destruye en lo más mínimo el sentimiento nacional. El amor a la Patria puede coincidir o coexistir perfectamente con el amor a la humanidad.

"Espero"—dice—"que las mujeres jóvenes que están aquí verán el cumplimiento de esta organización internacional, que hemos comenzado hace quince años.

"Esta asociación internacional, aunque aún esté poco organizada, ha tenido fuerza bastante para desenvolverse a través de las barreras nacionales. En muchos lugares del frente de la batalla se teme dejar mucho tiempo a los mismos soldados frente a frente, por temor de que acaben por fraternizar. Esta lucha, tan totalmente inútil entre las naciones, hace destrozos hasta en nuestro espíritu: todos, en las naciones neutrales, vivimos en estado de guerra civil, y eso no debe ser. En nuestra época ya no debiera existir conflicto entre el nacionalismo y el internacionalismo. Hace años, las vidas de todos los pueblos del mundo se nos han ido revelando por sus producciones comerciales, por sus periódicos, por las novelas, por su música, por la fotografía y el cinematógrafo y, sobre todo, por los libros de sus poetas y de sus autores dramáticos. De repente, todo esto cesa, y los periódicos no hablan más que de los detalles de la guerra. Nunca había podido aprender el mundo de manera tan espantosa y tan detallada, lo que la palabra *guerra* significa para los soldados, para las mujeres, para los niños, para la civilización, que es la herencia de la humanidad. Penetradas por este sentimiento intolerable, venimos nosotras las mujeres a este Congreso internacional a hacer oír nuestra protesta solemne contra unos [errores] que ahora sí sabemos lo que son.

"Nuestra protesta es importante; pero el mundo progresa de la manera lenta y sin interrupción que ha tenido siempre de progresar: únicamente en proporción de la energía moral desarrollada por hombres y mujeres.

"Nos dicen que muchos soldados heridos, y a quienes no ha sido posible socorrer, llaman constantemente a su madre. En este Congreso se nos ha hablado de heridos que dicen a sus enfermeras: "Nosotros no podemos hacer nada, no podemos más que volver a las trincheras tantas veces como nos sea posible; pero ¿es que las mujeres no pueden hacer algo?" Sólo a sus enfermeras se atreven los soldados a decir estas cosas.

"Vendrá un tiempo en que los que sobrevivan agotados a esta guerra, echen en cara a las mujeres su inacción. Es posible que digan entonces que mientras el patriotismo lanzó a millares de hombres al combate, las mujeres se negaron a afrontar y tomar por suyas responsabilidades, afirmando clara y valerosamente la santidad de la vida y la realidad de las cosas del espíritu."

Del discurso de Kathleen Courtney (danesa).—"La cuestión del voto de las mujeres y la cuestión de la guerra están estrechamente unidas. La causa de las mujeres está perdida si no comprenden que la guerra les concierne directamente. La fuerza brutal no ha triunfado nunca, no ha destruido nunca lo que es verdaderamente digno de vivir. Si las mujeres creen que el derecho es superior al poder, deben defender el ideal de paz y luchar por la supresión de la guerra. Las mujeres que no son pacíficas no tienen derecho a reclamar el derecho del voto."

Del discurso de Frau Lecher (austriaca).—"No había hablado nunca en público, nunca había tomado parte en el movimiento feminista; pero los horrores de la guerra me han traído a este Congreso. He comprendido que el hombre fuerte necesita para regir el mundo la ayuda de la mujer débil. Durante ocho meses he estado palpando los horrores de la guerra en los hospitales de mi país; he visto atroces sufrimientos, soportados sin una queja, y he pensado con desolación: ¿Para qué curar heridos que se han de renovar? Es preciso que todas las mujeres griten al mundo entero: ¡Detened esa efusión de sangre! ¡Devolvednos nuestros maridos, nuestros hijos, nuestros hermanos!"

Del discurso de Lyda Gustava Heymann (alemana).—"He venido al partido feminista convencida de que no hubiésemos llegado a esta civilización contra naturaleza si las mujeres hubieran tenido más influencia en la organización de las relaciones sociales. La influencia de las mujeres traería seguramente, condiciones de vida más normales; pero es indispensable para esto que tengan derechos políticos. En este derrumbamiento de todas las organizaciones sociales preparadas por los hombres, hemos podido darnos cuenta de que quedaba en pie una organización: la de las mujeres que piden el sufragio para trabajar con fuerza y valor en la reconstrucción de la sociedad."

Del discurso de Miss Holbrook (americana).—"Es preciso que las mujeres reaccionen contra la tendencia de los educadores hombres a glorificar la fuerza y la violencia. Es preciso enseñar a los niños a admirar a los héroes y a las heroínas del mundo entero, sin distinción de nacionalidades; es preciso darles conocimientos internacionales y enseñarles a poner todas las artes al servicio del pacifismo. Que las banderas de todas las naciones ondeen en todas las escuelas, que los niños se acostumbren a creer en la fraternidad de los pueblos unidos bajo la paternidad de un solo Dios."

Del discurso de Rosika Schw[i]mmer.—"Las mujeres se habían llegado a figurar que la guerra era negocio exclusivamente masculino. De otra manera hubiesen sucedido las cosas si hubiesen ellas pensado que la guerra les interesa tan directamente como a los hombres. Hasta las victorias de que se alaba su propio país pesan sobre ellas en sufrimiento grave. ¿Qué decir de las mujeres víctimas de las violencias y de la brutalidad de los hombres? ¿Qué decir de los niños y de los males terribles que sufren? Las mujeres que han llegado a ser conscientes de su misión en este mundo, no pueden rechazar la parte de responsabilidad que les corresponda. No deben seguir admitiendo el que la guerra dependa de los hombres solos. Si el crimen debe prolongarse, las mujeres están obligadas a establecer una nueva organización social. De lo contrario, sobrevendrá el agotamiento de la raza humana.... Necesitamos el voto no sólo para ensanchar nuestro campo de acción, sino para defender la raza. ¡Hay que librar al mundo de este militarismo maldito! Los hombres han comprendido lo resueltas que están las mujeres a conseguir sus derechos. Cuando esta primavera el Parlamento danés votó la ley concediendo a las mujeres el derecho al sufragio, no hubo más que un oponente a la adopción de esta ley."

Opinions of Some of the Feminists Who Attended the Congress of The Hague in Favor of Peace

La Prensa
San Antonio, Texas
7 January 1916

I scan the columns of the feminist newspapers, French, North American, English, Dutch, and international ones, because I would like to give you a clear idea of the current state of the feminist cause in the world. For now, all are full of this mournful lamentation: The war! All are passionate about the same eager hope: Peace!

Grievances, rights, suffrage, rebellions, everything has been reduced to second place. The war fills up everything; the seas of the war absorb all the power of preoccupation; the remedy for the evils of the war monopolizes every facet of business; women work to sweeten the fortunes of the men who are fighting; they work to fill the void left by the men whom the war has obligated to leave their jobs. For now, they ask for nothing; they give, give, give whatever they have with generosity and perseverance; no task is impossible for them, no job capable of intimidating them; courageously, they have taken on all duties, an extremely eloquent way of demonstrating that they are qualified for all rights.

And in this hard school of sweat, blood, and tears they are learning unforgettable lessons, lessons essential for the future life of humankind. Some women, those with more authority, proclaim the lessons learned, and in summary, these lessons are reduced to this: *Men have almost all the guilt for war; but women are not exempt from responsibility; we have failed in our duty in two ways.*

First. By consenting that our children be educated in the false idea of heroism and patriotic duty. Right up to the present, military valor has been glorified in the schools, the feats of blood, the injustice of conquest, the collective egotism; the flag has been made a symbol, not of patriotism, but of imperialism; in a word: it has been inculcated in the hearts of men the idea that heroism means just as much as disdain for one's life and that of others and an impulse for losing it or taking it by force.

Second. Out of fear of ridicule, we have neglected to put into our grievances the necessary commitment: the day when women participate in the governing of people in equal numbers to men, war will have ended for once and for all; we know and feel this. Peace is the first article of our program and our motherhood has written it with letters of blood in our hearts. But, cowardly mothers, we have left the lives of our sons in the hands of men. We would have obtained our political rights a long time ago if we hadn't become frightened, more than of the real difficulties, of the taunts of a few people who were either too self-interested or too indifferent.

And this cannot be. We share equal responsibility with the men who govern, because we have allowed them to govern so absurdly and inhumanely. We are obligated to remedy our neglect. This is the great lesson of the war.

This general opinion, which I summarize for you, is eloquently expressed by several of the attendees at the last Congress of The Hague. Below, I copy fragments of some of the speeches given.

From the speech of Jane Addams, the illustrious American writer, who has been the president of the Congress.—She speaks first of women's great political responsibility, already recognized as such in some nations (especially among the neutral ones), and it exists, although it is not known, in all the others. And she affirms that the gathering of so many women of diverse nationalities at the Congress of The Hague proves the progress of the internationalist sentiment, the only hope of a better future for humanity. This internationalist movement, which unites women with such an irresistible force, and which is the foundation of their association, does not at all destroy national sentiment. The love of Country can perfectly coincide, or coexist with, the love of humanity.

"I hope"—she says—"that the young women who are here will see the fulfillment of this international organization, that we started fifteen years ago.

"This international organization, even though it may be only a little organized, has had enough strength to perform well across national barriers. In many places on the battlefront there is a fear of leaving a lot of time to the soldiers themselves face to face, for fear that they will end up fraternizing. This struggle, so totally useless among nations, does damage even to our spirit, every one of us in neutral nations, live in a state of civil war, and that should not be. In our time there should no longer exist a conflict between nationalism and internationalism. For years now, the lives of all peoples of the world we have been revealed to us by their commercial productions, by their newspapers, by novels, by their music, by photography and cinema and, above all, by the books of their poets and their playwrights. Suddenly all this it is ceasing, and newspapers speak only of the details of the war. The world had never been able to learn in such a frightening way and such a detailed one, what the word *war* means for soldiers, for women, for children, for civilization, which is the heritage of humanity. Penetrated by this intolerable feeling, we women come to this international Congress to voice our solemn protest against some horrors that we now do know for what they are.

"Our protest is important; but the world progresses, in the slow way and without interruption which it has always had to progress, only in proportion to the moral energy exerted by the men and women.

"They tell us that many wounded soldiers, whom it has been impossible to aid, call out constantly for their mothers. In this Congress we have been told of soldiers who say to their nurses: 'We can do nothing, we can do nothing more than return to the trenches as many times as we are able to. But cannot the women do something?' Only to their nurses do soldiers dare to say these things.

"The time will come when those that survive this war exhausted may well reproach women for their inaction. It is possible they will then say that when patriotism drove thousands of men into combat, women refused to confront and take on their responsibilities, by stating clearly and courageously the sanctity of life and the reality of the things of the spirit."

From the speech by Kathleen Courtney (Danish).—"The issue of the women's vote and the question of the war are closely tied together. The woman's cause is lost if they do not understand that war concerns them directly. Brute force has never triumphed, it has never destroyed what is truly worthy of living. If women believe that their right is superior to power, they must defend the ideal of peace and fight for the abolition of war. Women who are not peaceful are not entitled to claim the right to vote."

From the speech of Frau Lecher (Austrian).—"I had never spoken in public ever, I had never participated in the feminist movement; but the horrors of war have brought me to this Congress. I have understood that the strong man needs the help of the weak woman to govern the world. For eight months I have been touching the horrors of war in the hospitals of my country; I have seen atrocious suffering, tolerated without complaint, and I have thought with desolation: Why cure wounds that will just be opened again? It is necessary that all women cry out to the whole world: Stop that flow of blood! Return our husbands, our sons, and our brothers to us!"

From the speech by Lyda Gustava Heymann (German).—"I have come to the feminist party convinced that we would not have come to this civilization against nature if women had had more influence in organizing social relationships. The influence of women would surely bring more normal living conditions; but it is indispensable for this to happen for women to have political rights. In this crumbling of all the social organizations prepared by men, we have been able to realize that one organization still stood: that of the women who call for suffrage in order to work with strength and courage in the reconstruction of society."

From the speech by Miss Holbrook (American).—"It is necessary that women react against the tendency of male educators to glorify force and violence. It is necessary to teach children to admire the heroes and heroines of the whole world, regardless of nationality; it is necessary to give them international knowledge and teach them to put all the arts at the service of pacifism. May the flags of all nations wave in all the schools, may children grow accustomed to believing in the brotherhood of peoples united under the paternity of only one God."

From the speech by Rosika Schwimmer.[2]—"Women had reached the point of thinking that war was an exclusively masculine business. Things would have happened differently if they had thought that war concerns them as directly as it does men. Even the victories that their own country praises weigh on them in deep suffering. What can we say about the women victims of the violence and of the brutality of men? What can we say about the children and about the terrible evils they suffer? The women who have become conscious of their mission in this world cannot reject the part of the responsibility which corresponds to them. They should not continue to accept that war depends only on men. If the crime must continue, women are obligated to establish a new social organization. If not, the depletion of the human race will overtake us. We need the vote not only to widen our field of action, but also to defend the human race. We must free the world of this cursed militarism! Men have understood how resolved women are to achieve their rights. When this spring the Danish Parliament voted into law giving women the right of suffrage, there was only one opponent to the adoption of this law."

Anonymous Feminist Writings from *La Prensa*, Los Angeles

La Prensa (The Press) reached several important regions of the United States where there was a large or growing Spanish-speaking populace, such as San Antonio, Los Angeles, and New York. From its various publishing locations, this *La Prensa* published several anonymous feminist writings throughout the early 1900s and into the 1930s. As discussed in the introduction to the anonymous selection from San Antonio-based *La Prensa*, we believe women likely published anonymously as a way for them to write freely with some modicum of protection. In the next article, "Mujeres mexicanas notables" ("Notable Mexican Women"), the writer makes a rhetorical and feminist move similar to many of the contributors to this collection, such as María Rentería and Catalina Dulché Escalante (Catalina D'Erzell), as well as rhetors like Sor Juana Inés de la Cruz: she leverages the strategy of *example* as a means to articulate a progressive vision for women's lives. This anonymous writer's examples range from indigenous military leaders and rulers (Malinalxóchitl and Xiutlatzin) to poets (Sor María de los Dolores) to contemporary heroines (Josefa Ortiz de Domínguez and Leona Vicario). Describing each figure, the writer highlights the characteristics she wants readers to recognize and revere: military strength, effective leadership, beautiful writing, and rhetorical prowess. After moving through these multiple examples, the writer calls readers to consider what the models amount to. She asks, "Will the highly reputed feminist movement finally carry Mexican women into politics?" Given the list of "notable" women the writer has provided, readers would likely answer that mexicanas are indeed ready to take on even greater roles as leaders, thinkers, writers, and rhetors.

One interesting point to consider is where this anonymous writer obtained the facts she includes in this article. While the author references several Mexican male historians such as Carlos de Sigüenza y Góngora, Francisco Sosa, and Carlos María Bustamante, many of the references to indigenous and Mexican historical women, as well as the title of the piece, match closely to the writings of another woman included in this anthology: Laureana Wright de Kleinhans. Throughout her career as literary editor for *Las Hijas [Violetas] del Anáhuac* (The Daughters [Violets] of Anáhuac] (1887–89), Wright de Kleinhans wrote prolifically about the historic actions of mexicanas. Her writings were compiled into a book titled *Mujeres notables mexicanas* (Notable Mexican Women) that was published in 1910, fourteen years after her death. With a similar title to this anonymous piece published in *La Prensa*, Wright de Kleinhans's book highlights relatively unknown women from the four eras of Mexican history: Pre-Columbian/Conquest, Colonial Era, Heroines of Independence, and Contemporaries, and Wright de Kleinhans includes excerpts from their writings when possible. There is a direct correlation between this piece from *La Prensa* and Wright de Kleinhans's historical writings: both writers include a quotation (without reference) about the woman military leader Malinalxóchitl and "the Lady of Tula"—the wife of Texcoco ruler Netzahualpilli. As further evidence of this connection, the anonymous *La Prensa* author discusses indigenous female figures (Malinalxóchitl and Xóchitl) as well as contemporary women (Esther Tapia de Castellanos and Dolores Guerrero) who were also cited in Wright de Kleinhans's book. Whether or not the anonymous writer drew from Wright de Kleinhans's work, it is important to note that both writers relied heavily on the rhetorical power of example to make their claims.

Mujeres mexicanas notables

La Prensa
Los Angeles, California
5 de abril de 1919

La tradición ha conservado ora en los recios caracteres de la historia, ora en los perfiles ideales de la leyenda, nombres célebres de mujeres mexicanas.

De ellas, algunas han alcanzado fama mundial: Sor Juana Inés de la Cruz, doña Josefa Ortiz, Ángela Peralta.... Otras, a pesar de haber realizado grandes actos de heroísmo o de haber ocupado puesto distinguido en las artes o ciencias, su fama quedó circunscrita a algunos relatos de historia patria, como el caso de la madre de los Rayón, y de muchas se perdieron los nombres y sólo uno que otro narrador asienta en un efímero párrafo conservado casualmente a través del tiempo, proezas dignas de inmortalizarse.

En los enmohecidos escritos sacados de la traducción de viejos jeroglíficos indígenas encontramos este fragmento que pone de relieve los adelantos feministas en los remotos tiempos: "Malinalxóchitl, hermana de Huitzitón, gran sacerdote y caudillo de las tribus de Aztlán a que ella acompañó en sus peregrinaciones ayudándolo a dirigir sus tropas. Era Malinalxóchitl heroína de varonil aliento que, al lado de su hermano, en todos los encuentros, se señaló con bizarría en singulares hechos; al valor acompañaba el talento, discreción y conducta en el gobierno, en el que ayudó tanto como en los lances de la guerra."

Notable también fue en su tiempo la principal esposa de Netzahualpilli, cuyo nombre se perdió y es conocida en los relatos históricos como "la señora de Tula." Era tan sabia, dice un historiador, que competía con el rey y con los más sabios de su reino y en poesía "era muy aventajada."

Xiutlatzin, esposa del rey tolteca Mitl, colaboró con su marido en el gobierno con tal acierto que, a la muerte del soberano, se dio por primera vez el caso de que una mujer fuese aclamada por el pueblo como soberana reinante. Durante 59 años esta mujer gobernó al pueblo tolteca con discreción, tino y sabiduría de que muchos reyes carecieron.

En cuanto a casos célebres de amor patrio, podemos asegurar que han abundado en la fémina mexicana. Por desgracia no todos son conocidos, tal como el de Alabahba, india natural de Cholula, a quien la tristemente renombrada Malintzín robó con inteligente astucia, el secreto del plan de batalla de los cholultecas, dando lugar a la cruenta catástrofe en que perecieron más de seis mil indios. La pobre Alabahba, al darse cuenta de que su indiscreción había sido causa de la hecatombe, se ahorcó con su ceñidor.

Valientes y patriotas fueron también las dos mujeres a quienes debió la vida el heredero del trono de Texcoco, usurpado por Tezozomoc. Fugitivo

Netzahualcóyotl, se refugió en la casa de Matlalcihuatín, siendo escondido por ella que supo enfrentarse con los soldados, perseguidores negando con energía tan convincente que los guardias se retiraron seguros de que el príncipe no estaba allí. Interrogada Coxcatcotzín, otra valerosa india, sobre el rumbo que podía haber seguido Netzahualcóyotl, ésta dio una dirección totalmente opuesta, mientras el fugitivo se ponía a salvo.

Entre las narraciones sacadas de la escritura ideográfica de los antiguos pobladores de nuestro país, hay una que podríamos titular "Ilíada India" porque como en la guerra legendaria que cantó Homero fue la hermosura extraordinaria de una mujer causa de sangrientos combates entre varios pueblos cuyos soberanos se prendaban de la bellísima india. Fue [e]sta Atotoxtli, princesa de Culhuacán.

De Xóchitl, la joven tolteca que descubrió el aguamiel, materia prima del pulque, largamente se han ocupado historias y leyendas, así como de la Malint[zí]n, la india enamorada del Conquistador, a quien éste llamara Marina al ser bautizada y a la que se debió en gran parte la caída de la nación mexicana bajo la férula de los españoles.

En la época Colonial, deslumbra el brillo de aquella escritora inteligentísima, cuya obra ha sido celebrada por propios y extraños: Sor Juana Inés de la Cruz y cuyos rasgos biográficos son bien conocidos de todos.

Pero también en ese tiempo vivieron otras mujeres de gran talento, dignas de ser mencionadas en el grupo de mexicanas distinguidas.

En la obra "Relaciones Históricas" de Ixtlilxóchitl, se trata de una india llamada después del bautizo María Bartola y cuyo nombre indio se ha perdido. El escritor alaba con entusiasmo el talento de esta mujer que, apenas terminada la Conquista, escribió en español y en mexicano, el relato de las principales batallas libradas entre españoles y aztecas.

El escritor Sosa en sus "Efemérides históricas y biográficas" dice a este respecto que, "es digno de llamar la atención que en los primeros años posteriores a la caída del Imperio azteca, hubiese habido una mujer afecta a los estudios históricos."

En el siglo XVIII lució María Guerrero, dama de gran instrucción, cosa inusitada en aquellos tiempos en que las mujeres apenas aprendían a leer y escribir. Fue además oradora. En 1731 pronunció en público, con gran éxito, un panegírico latino de Sor Juana Inés de la Cruz y una canción castellana. En 1747 publicó una Elegía latina, con su correspondiente versión castellana, a la muerte de Felipe IV.

En cuanto a la "décima musa," ¿quién no sabe su vida y su obra?

No, ciertamente, geniales como ella, pero sí de talento notable existieron también perdidas en la sombra de los conventos, muchas mujeres ahogadas en el estrecho ambiente claustral.

De aquella incógnita floración hemos podido recoger algunos nombres conservados milagrosamente en anales y memorias dispersos aquí y allá.

La abadesa del convento de Jesús María, llamada Sor Petronila de San José, fue una buena escritora. Dejó un libro titulado "Vidas de Religiosas ejemplares" que mereció los elogios entusiastas del historiador Sigüenza y Góngora.

Con nombre de Sor María de los Dolores, una mujer ciega, atacada además de un raro padecimiento nervioso que la sacudía en horribles convulsiones o la sumía en éxtasis prolongadísimos, vivió en el convento de San Lorenzo, siendo una poeti[s]a inspirada y fecunda que escribió infinidad de composiciones de las que sólo se conservaron algunos bellos romances.

Entre las heroínas de la Independencia, son conocidas y veneradas doña Josefa Ortiz de Domínguez y doña Leona Vicario. La Historia Patria nos narra también la espartana conducta de la madre de los Rayón que prohibió a su hijo Ramón la entrega de la plaza a cambio de la vida de su hermano, proposición hecha por el gobierno español. La heroica dama respondió al ser interpelada en decidir: "Llorar quiero un hijo muerto y no dos traidores."

Hubo otras mexicanas que en aquella época realizaron hechos maravillosos de patriotismo, dignos de ser comentados.

Cuenta el historiador Bustamante el siguiente episodio: En el pueblo de Soto la Marina se hallaba encargado de la defensa, el general don Francisco Xavier Mina. El enemigo guarneció cuidadosamente el río para evitar que los insurgentes se proveyeran de agua. El calor era horrible, los soldados sentían una sed intolerable, pero les era imposible acercarse a la corriente, porque las armas españolas lanzaban sin cesar una lluvia de fuego.

Cuando los soldados comenzaban a desfallecer quemados por el calor del día, seca la garganta, ardorosos los labios, una mujer anónima, desafiando el peligro, acareó agua del río para calmar la sed de aquellos hombres. Innumerables veces atravesó hasta las márgenes del río, las balas caían en torno suyo sin que ninguna hiciera blanco por milagro.

Aquella humilde mujer llamada simplemente María, fue apellidada con el nombre del pueblo salvado, en realidad, por ella.

En las "Memorias para la Historia de las Revoluciones en México," del Lic. Zerecero, se encuentra este interesantísimo relato que pone en relieve una interesante figura de mujer patriota.

Reuníanse en la casa de don Manuel Lazarín y de su esposa, varios jóvenes, decididos partidarios de la causa de Independencia. Cuando se supo en una de aquellas tertulias la captura de Hidalgo y su sentencia de muerte, gran desaliento invadió a todos y fue doña María Rodríguez del Toro de Lazarín, quien tomó la palabra para reavivar las decaídas energías, proponiendo hacer una conspiración que tendría por objeto principal apoderarse del virrey. Desde el día siguiente, doña María de Lazarín se dedicó a conquistarse uno por uno de los jefes de diversos cuerpos del ejército español, haciéndolo con tal maña que, los que no quisieron tomar parte en la conspiración no se atrevieron a delatarla.

El plan estaba muy adelantado, llegando a fijarse el día y la hora en que debía estallar el movimiento. La víspera, uno de los comprometidos, temiendo perecer en la lucha, fue a confesarse con el padre Camargo de la Merced, éste no tuvo empacho en delatar la conspiración y la señora de Lazarín, su esposo y varios de sus compañeros fueron hechos prisioneros.

La heroica mexicana sufrió un encarcelamiento de varios meses, en un calabozo húmedo y frío, sujeta a cruel [maltrato], hasta que contrajo una grave enfermedad.

Las mujeres mexicanas que han descollado en las bellas letras, son numerosas: Gertrudis Tenorio Zavala, yucateca; Esther Tapia de Castellanos, michoacana; Dolores Guerrero, duranguense; Isabel Prieto de Landázuri, tapatía, y otras más.

Y no terminaremos esta revista de mexicanas distinguidas sin recordar a aquella cantante de voz maravillosa que se llamó Ángela Peralta y que fue admirada en el mundo entero.

En la actualidad, las mujeres dedicadas a la ciencia, forman numeroso grupo. Las profesionistas, no son ya, entre nosotros, casos excepcionales.

¿El acentuado movimiento feminista llevará al fin las mujeres mexicanas a la política? . . .

Notable Mexican Women

La Prensa
Los Angeles, California
5 April 1919

Tradition has preserved, sometimes in the vigorous characters of history, sometimes in the ideal profiles of legend, famous names of Mexican women.

Of them, some have achieved worldwide fame: Sor Juana Inés de la Cruz, Doña Josefa Ortiz, Ángela Peralta. . . . Others, in spite of having carried out great acts of heroism or having occupied distinguished posts in the arts or sciences, their fame remained confined to a few stories of national history, like the case of the mother of the Rayón brothers,[1] and of many, the names were lost, and only a few narrators record an ephemeral paragraph fortuitously preserved through time, feats worthy of being immortalized.

In the musty writings taken from translation of old indigenous hieroglyphs, we find this fragment that highlights feminist progress in ancient times: "Malinalxóchitl, sister of Huitzitón, a great priest and military leader of the tribes from Aztlán, whom she accompanied in his pilgrimages by helping him lead his troops. Malinalxóchitl was a heroine of manly spirit who, at her brother's side, in every battle, acquitted herself bravely in singular acts; she combined courage and talent, discretion and management in the government, in which she helped as much as in the wartime expeditions."

Notable also in her time was the principal wife of Netzahualpilli, whose name has been lost and who is known in the historical texts as "the Lady of Tula." She was so wise, says one historian, that she competed with the king and with the wisest men of the kingdom and in poetry "she was most outstanding."

Xiutlatzin, wife of the Toltec King Mitl, collaborated with her husband in the government with such good judgement that, when the sovereign died, there occurred the first instance in which a woman was acclaimed by the people as the reigning sovereign. For fifty-nine years this woman governed the Toltec people with prudence, skill, and wisdom, which many kings lacked.

As for celebrated cases of love of country, we can be assured that such cases have abounded in the female population of Mexico. Unfortunately not all are known, such as that of Alabahba, an Indian, native of Cholula, from whom the sadly remembered Malintzín robbed, by using her clever cunning, the secret of the battle plan of the Cholulans, resulting in the bloody catastrophe in which over six thousand Indians perished. Poor Alabahba, when she realized that her indiscretion was the cause of the disaster, she hanged herself with her sash.

Courageous and patriotic also were two women to whom the heir to the throne of Texcoco, usurped by Tezozomoc, owed his life. The fugitive Netzahualcóyotl took refuge in the house of Matlalcihuatín, being hidden by a woman who knew how to confront the soldier-pursuers, by denying with energy so convincing that the guards left, sure that the prince was not there. When Coxcatcotzín, another courageous Indian woman, was interrogated about the direction that Netzahualcóyotl could have taken, she gave a completely opposite direction, while the fugitive escaped safely.

Among the narrations taken from the ideographic scripts of the ancient inhabitants of our country, there is one we could entitle "the Indian Iliad," because as in the legendary war sung by Homer, the extraordinary beauty of a woman was the cause of bloody combat among several peoples whose sovereigns fell quickly in love with the very beautiful Indian. Her name was Atotoxtli, the Princess of Culhuacán.

To Xóchitl, the Toltec maid who discovered agave juice, the raw material of pulque; a good deal of history and legend is dedicated, as well as to Malintzin, the Indian lover of the Conquistador, whom Cortez called Marina when she was baptized and to whom was owed in large part the fall of the Mexican nation under the rigid authority of the Spaniards.

The colonial epoch was dazzled by the brilliance of that highly intelligent writer: Sor Juana Inés de la Cruz, whose work Mexicans and foreigners have celebrated, and whose biographical details are well known to everyone.

But also during this time there lived other women of great talent, worthy of being mentioned in the group of distinguished Mexican women.

The work "Historical Accounts," by Ixtlilxóchitl, tells of an Indian woman called María Bartola after baptism, and whose Indian name has been lost. The writer enthusiastically praises the talent of this woman who, shortly after the Conquest, wrote, in Spanish and in Nahuatl, the story of the main battles fought between Spaniards and Aztecs.

The writer Sosa in his "Historical and Biographical Dates" says this about Bartola's work: "it is worth mentioning that during the first years after the fall of the Aztec Empire, there was a woman devoted to historical studies."

In the eighteenth century, María Guerrero shone as a highly educated lady, an unusual thing in those times, when women barely learned to read and write. She was also an orator. In 1731 she declaimed in public, with great success, a Latin panegyric by Sor Juana Inés de la Cruz, and a Castilian song. In 1747 she published a Latin Elegy to the death of Felipe IV, with a corresponding Castilian version.

As far as the "Tenth Muse,"[2] who does not know about her life and work?

Many others who were not, certainly, geniuses like her but who had notable talent also existed lost in the shadow of convents, women who were stifled in the restrictive atmosphere of the cloisters.

From that unknown flowering we have been able to collect some names miraculously preserved in annals and memoirs dispersed here and there.

The Abbess of the convent of Jesús María, named Sor Petronila de San José, was a good writer. She left a book titled "Lives of Exemplary Nuns" that earned enthusiastic praise from the historian Sigüenza y Góngora.

A blind woman by the name of Sor María de los Dolores, who was also subject to a rare nervous disorder that would shake her in horrible convulsions or immerse her in extremely prolonged ecstasies, lived in the convent of Saint Lawrence, being an inspired and prolific poet who wrote innumerable compositions of which only some pretty ballads were preserved.

Among the heroines of Independence, Doña Josefa Ortiz de Domínguez and Doña Leona Vicario are well known and venerated. Our national history also tells us about the austere conduct of the mother of the Rayón brothers, who prohibited her son Ramón from surrendering the plaza in exchange for his brother's life, the proposition made by the Spanish government. The heroic lady responded when asked about her decision, "I want to mourn one dead son and not two traitors."

There were other Mexican women of that era who achieved marvelous feats of patriotism, worthy of being commented on.

The historian Bustamante relates the following episode: In the town of Soto la Marina, General Don Francisco Xavier Mina was in charge of the defenses. The enemy garrisoned the river carefully to prevent the insurgents from supplying themselves with water. The heat was horrible, the soldiers felt an intolerable thirst, but it was impossible for them to approach the current, because Spanish arms were launching a continuous rain of fire.

When the soldiers began to pass out, burned by the heat of the day, their throats dry, their lips burning, an unnamed woman, defying danger, carried water from the river to calm the thirst of those men. Innumerable times she crossed to the edge of the river, the bullets were falling around her, miraculously without any of them hitting her. That humble woman, simply named Mary, was surnamed with the name of the town that was saved, really, by her.

In the recollections for the "History of Revolutions in Mexico" by Licentiate Zerecero is found this extremely interesting story that highlights an interesting figure of a patriotic woman.

Several young men, firm partisans of the cause of Independence, met regularly at the home of Don Manuel Lazarín and his wife. When it became known in one of those meetings about Hidalgo's capture and his death sentence, a great discouragement seized everyone, and it was Doña María Rodríguez del Toro de Lazarín who spoke up to revive their failing energy, by proposing to enter into a conspiracy which would have as its principal objective the capture of the viceroy. From the following day, María de Lazarín devoted herself to winning over, one by one, the heads of the various units of the Spanish army, doing so with such cunning that those who refused to take part in the conspiracy did not dare to inform on her.

The plan was quite advanced, to the point that the day and time when the movement would be triggered were assigned. The night before, one of those involved, fearing he would perish in the fight, went to confession with Father Camargo de la Merced, who had no scruples about revealing the conspiracy, and Mrs. Lazarín, her husband, and several of their companions were taken prisoner.

The heroic Mexican woman suffered imprisonment for several months, in a cold and humid jail cell, subject to cruel mistreatment, until she contracted a serious illness.

The Mexican women who have excelled in fine arts are numerous: Gertrudis Tenorio Zavala, from Yucatán; Esther Tapia de Castellanos, from Michoacán; Dolores Guerrero, from Durango; Isabel Prieto de Landázuri, from Jalisco, and many others.

We will not end this review of distinguished Mexican women without remembering that singer with a marvelous voice, who was named Angela Peralta and who was admired throughout the world.

Currently, the women dedicated to science comprise a numerous group. Women professionals among us are no longer exceptional cases.

Will the highly reputed feminist movement finally carry Mexican women into politics? . . .

Aurora Lucero-White Lea

Aurora Lucero-White Lea's (1894–1965) public introduction to New Mexico politics and education began in 1910. As a teenager, Aurora Lucero presented her speech "Shall the Spanish Language Be Taught in the Schools of New Mexico" at a competition held by the Interscholastic Oratorical Association on the campus of New Mexico Normal University (NMNU), now New Mexico Highlands University. Newspaper editors throughout the region republished the speech in Spanish and English (Kanellos et al. 136), and the university published a special bulletin dedicated to it (here). In her speech, Lucero-White Lea responds to the Enabling Act of 1910, a law that required complete fluency in the English language for any person to hold governmental office. Like many Nuevomexicanos, Lucero-White Lea saw this law as another form of discrimination—one that would have severe consequences on the public educational system, for it would prompt teachers toward what twenty-first-century readers would call English-only instruction.

In her speech, Lucero-White Lea argues that New Mexico schools should teach the Spanish language alongside English. She supports her claim by offering a number of reasons to retain Spanish language instruction, and interestingly these reasons point mainly to the loss of the beauty and sophistication of *Spanish* language and literature if this law were enacted. That is, her arguments hinge not so much on the value of Mexican linguistic and literary traditions, but the value of Spanish ones. For example, she writes: "The Spanish language, the language of the Spanish-Americans, the language of the Cortezes, the De Sotos and the Coronados, has been for more than three centuries the home language of the territory." Lucero-White Lea's choice to highlight Spain and Spanish culture rather than the bordering Mexican culture was quite prevalent in New Mexico at this time. As Héctor Calderón writes, contemporary with the moment New Mexico achieved U.S. statehood in 1912, a "set of discursive and cultural practices were set in motion by native writers and scholars" based on "an idyllic 'Old Spain in Our Southwest' to the exclusion of the real historical and social conditions of the majority of New Mexicans" (34). Even as Lucero-White Lea makes this cultural argument that is based on glorifying Spain rather than Mexico, the critical aspect of her overarching project is that she argues for bilingual education in New Mexico's schools. Other contributors to this volume engage in this conversation about the Spanish language and education; see, for example, Jovita Idar's and Leonor Villegas de Magnón's entries.

Lucero-White Lea's commitment to the education of New Mexico's Spanish-speaking population continued throughout her life. She earned her teaching degree in 1915 from NMNU and taught in rural New Mexican communities. After a brief time in California, she enrolled at NMNU to complete the Bachelor of Arts program. From 1925 to 1927, she served as the superintendent of schools for San Miguel County. After earning her master's degree in 1929 at NMNU, she became an assistant professor of Spanish at that institution. In 1934 Lucero-White Lea accepted the role of assistant superintendent of instruction for the New Mexico Public Schools.

Lucero-White Lea's devotion to Nuevomexicano/a culture extended beyond the classroom. She visited New Mexico's villages and published the stories, music, and cultural practices of the villages' isolated populations. Her work on this score is evidenced through such texts as *Folk Dances of the Spanish-colonials of New Mexico* (1937), *The Folklore of New Mexico* (1941), *Los Hispanos: Five Essays on the Folkways of the Hispanos as Seen through the Eyes of One of Them* (1947), *Literary Folklore of the Hispanic Southwest* (1953), and *Juan Bobo: Adapted from the Spanish Folk Tale Bertolodo* (1962). Lucero-White Lea's career as an educator and as a scholar is especially significant when considering the limited opportunities for women to publish and serve in administrative positions during this period.

Shall the Spanish Language Be Taught in the Schools of New Mexico

New Mexico University Bulletin
Albuquerque, New Mexico
1911

The Territory of New Mexico has undergone many changes, politically and socially, it has solved many problems; and now, upon the eve of statehood, a new problem is being discussed in every hamlet, village and city: "Shall the Spanish Language continue to be taught in our public schools?"

It seems beyond all doubt that New Mexico is soon to take her place as one of the states, in the grand sisterhood of commonwealths of this mighty union. That boon which of 60 long years she has sought in vain seems now within her reach, and to all appearances she has but to extend her hand in order to gain it; yet, in her enthusiasm and eagerness to obtain it, she must not forget that she has problems to meet and solve such as no other state ever had.

In order to understand this problem thoroughly, let us state the peculiarities of our achievement. There is to the south of this rich and vast domain a population of more than 60,000,000 people, all descended from the Spanish Conquistadores. To the north, are found the homes of at least 90,000,000 of another people, nearly all of Anglo-Saxon blood, speaking an entirely different language. New Mexico is the meeting ground of these representatives of the Romanic and Germanic races, and no one can fail to see, even now, that their amalgamation is but a question of time. What the final outcome of such a union will be, of course, no one can predict with absolute certainty, but if it be true that history repeats itself under analogous conditions, then we may venture the prediction that a new race will spring from such a union that will far surpass either of its factors in all those traits and characteristics that make man better fitted for high responsibilities. The past history of these two races is a record of glorious deeds and notable achievements. Both have in their natures elements of greatness, and the union of the calm, business like spirit of the Anglo-Saxon with the sanguine, chivalrous enthusiasm of the Castilian will be such a blending of all that is best in human nature that we fail to see how anything better for the weal of humanity could possibly happen.

A difficulty presents itself at the very beginning, no matter how eager one may be that a new race should people these plains and hills, his hopes will be blasted if the essential means are ignored, means efficacious to the desired end. One of these is the cultivation of a thorough acquaintance, one with the other—the Anglo-Saxon with the Castilian—the Anglo-American with the Spanish-American. How can this be done unless each understands the other's language?

Spanish in the Schools of New Mexico

In New Mexico, English and Spanish are the leading languages of the territory. The English language is the language of the government, the national language, the language in which the great bulk of the business of the territory is transacted. The Spanish language, the language of the Spanish-Americans, the language of the Cortezes, the De Sotos and the Coronados, has been for more than three centuries the home language of the territory. Now, however, it has been proposed by the President and the Congress of the United States to deprive the territory of this language; that is, they seem to wish to break into fragments at a single blow this strong and marvelous link in the chain of events, which has connected and held together the history of the Old and the New World; for this is exactly what the Spanish language has done, is doing, and will continue to do as long as it is not eliminated from the public schools and driven out of the territory.

In the act of enabling New Mexico to become a state, passed by Congress, it was provided that none except those who speak, read and write the English language with sufficient correctness shall be eligible to the legislature of the new state, or to any of the state public offices. It is claimed by some of those who passed this act that the Spanish-American will become a better citizen by depriving him of the use of his vernacular. In resorting to such a course, it would seem that the contrary effect might be produced in him by the unwarranted interference of Congress with his natural rights, and instead of becoming a better, he might be made a worse citizen. Yet the Spanish-Americans of New Mexico have never been bad citizens. They have more than once proved their loyalty to the government and their love for the "Stars and Stripes" as their conduct in the Civil and the Spanish-American wars, and in many of the Indian wars, abundantly testifies.

It is impossible to understand why, in view of such a record, the people of New Mexico should be so unceremoniously deprived of a right which flows from the very essence of their manhood, for the right of language in man is a God-given right, and as such it is guaranteed and secured to him by the federal constitution when it declares that the natural rights of all men are inalienable. To single out New Mexico, then, for such unprecedented treatment, at the very moment that she is welcomed into sisterhood, is not only a gratuitous insult to the intelligence of her people, but it is also a proceeding as untenable in principle as it seems to be outrageous in its intent.

Man is by nature fond of distinction in anything that is praiseworthy. Everyone loves the praise of others, and to obtain it tries to become as accomplished as he can. We are accustomed to recognize the superiority of the person who has a command of one or more foreign languages. Consequently, as an accomplishment in the individual, the study of languages should be encouraged in the schools of any country that values intellectual attainments in its citizens. Why, then, should this most enlightened nation prevent the study of the Spanish language in the schools of New Mexico, where that language is even now the language of the majority of the people, and especially since it is as cultured and refined as any of the modern languages and far surpasses them in dignity, beauty, and majesty?

A few Spanish words are sufficient to set in motion all the finer and nobler sentiments of our nature. Take for instance, the entrancing patriotic image pictured by Espronceda[1] when, in appealing to the Spanish people to rescue their country from the regime of the pusi[l]lanimous Charles IV, who was absolutely dominated by France:

> "Del cetro de sus Reyes los pedazos
> Del suelo ensangrentados recogía,
> Y nuevo trono en sus robustos brazos
> Levantado, a su Príncipe ofrecía."[2]

This passage from Espronceda is but a single, isolated instance of the richness of Spanish poetry. Pathos, tragedy, indomitable courage, patriotism, and the passionate appeal to action—all are eloquently and sublimely compressed into four short lines.

There is a host of Spanish writers who have beautified and ennobled Spanish literature to at least as high a degree as have the Chaucers, Drydens, Miltons, Byrons, and Websters uplifted the English language. We have our De Vegas, Calderons, Escriches, Castellars, Bellos and Arbledas, whose talents make them fully the compeers of the best Saxon bards and prose writers and whose pens have made Spanish literature the delight of scholars in every age and clime: while towering above them all stands that colossal genius, the author of "Don Quixote," whose superb merit is universally acknowledged and whose fame is rivaled but not surpassed by that of the great bard of Avon.

Yet this grand array of illustrious scholars, not to mention a vast number of others no less brilliant, will be lost to the youth of New Mexico when the Spanish language ceases to be taught in her schools.

Then consider the great commercial importance of this language. Besides being spoken in Spain and the Philippines, it is spoken in all countries south of the United States. These countries offer an unlimited field for the investment of American energy and enterprise. The advice of Horace Greeley to the young of our country: "Go West," was heeded and the West became a blooming garden and a mighty empire; but the West is now filling up rapidly and those young men must soon turn south to these Spanish-American countries. If then we would cultivate their friendship and good will, get them to do business with us, admit us into their society, we should be able to greet them with a "[¿]Cómo está usted?" as well as that they should be able to greet us with a "How do you do?"

Our public schools must have the Spanish language for the same reason that other modern languages are taught in them: they must have it as the inseparable companion of her sister, the English; they must have it if we wish that our youth shall be fully prepared to meet the duties which are awaiting them in all the Spanish-American countries—duties which they will in vain try to perform, without a thorough knowledge of the Spanish language.

The Spanish language is the language of our fathers, it is our own language, and must be now and hereafter the language of our children and our children's children. It is the language handed down to us by the discoverers of this New World. We are American citizens, it is true, and our conduct places our loyalty and patriotism above reproach. We want to learn the language of our country, and we are doing so; but we do not need, on that account, to deny either our origin or our race or our language or our traditions or our history or our ancestry, because we are not ashamed of them; and we will not do it, because we are proud of them.

The Spanish, next to the English, is the language most widely spread throughout the world; and though now the sun sets on the dominions of the actual successor of Charles V, it does not set, nor will it ever, on the dominion of the Spanish language. It is spoken in the far-off Philippines, and far along, from frozen mountain peaks to blooming valleys, it leaps with ever-increasing echo from Mexico and Central America down to the Straits of Magellan. All the islands cradled in the bosom of the Atlantic rejoice in its grandeur and its majesty. Lastly, it is spoken, written, and sung in Spain—romantic Spain—the land of knighthood and the mother of heroes, the power that saved Europe from the fate of the Roman Empire, the hand that first unraveled the mystery of the sea, to give a New World to civilization, and to hoist the ensigns of Christianity on the Teocalis of the Incas and the Montezumas.

Such is the language against which it is proposed to close the doors of the public schools of this territory. A language with such a record, such a history, such traditions and backed, as is the Spanish[,] by the moral influence of so many civilized countries, deserves a place not only in the public schools of New Mexico, where it belongs by inheritance and the right which three centuries of permanency therein give it, but in the best colleges of the United States in the proudest seats of learning in the world.

Therefore, in the name of all that is noble, grand and beautiful in the literature of the world; in the name of the broadening of the field of our business interests, and in the expansion of trade relations with our immediate neighbors;

in the name of the Anglo-Saxon youth of this territory who are everywhere endeavoring, with an earnestness fully worthy of the excellent cause, to learn the Spanish; in the name of the rights which the people of New Mexico have as citizens of this great republic; in the name of its duty to them, as contracted most solemnly before the world at Guadalupe Hidalgo; in the name of honesty and justice, let us by all means see to it that the Spanish language is not driven from the public schools of New Mexico.

Elena Arizmendi Mejía

Elena Arizmendi (1884–1949), born in Mexico City, was a political activist and feminist writer. Living in Mexico and the United States throughout her life, she developed a cross-border perspective. As a mexicana, she trained to be a nurse in San Antonio, Texas, from 1909 to 1911 at the Santa Rosa Training School for Nurses, headed by the Sisters of the Incarnate Word (Cano, *Se* 31–32, 57). At Santa Rosa, she received the latest in medical training, learned English, and gained a deep understanding of U.S. culture and the opportunities it offered women. Her time in the states was not without struggle, though, as she experienced severe discrimination during her nursing apprenticeship (61). These experiences, along with a call to serve her country during a time of war, prompted Arizmendi to leave Santa Rosa months before graduation and spearhead the creation of the Cruz Blanca Neutral (the Neutral White Cross) in Mexico, an organization that would serve the medical needs of unattended soldiers in the Mexican Revolution (75–94).[1] Arizmendi named her organization Cruz Blanca Neutral because, like the Red Cross, it treated anyone who was injured or in need. (This was not the case with Mexican governmental medical attention on the battlefield, which aided only the soldiers from its particular "side.") For her care of wounded soldiers, Arizmendi was awarded the distinctive medal of honor from La Gran Liga Obrera (The Great Workers League) in Mexico in 1911 ("Medalla" 3). But even though she was celebrated for her work, Arizmendi also received a good deal of scrutiny due to the fact that as a woman, she was taking on a public and political role. These criticisms would later galvanize her feminist ideas and rhetorical activity.

Biographical details on Arizmendi would not be complete without mentioning her connection to José Vasconcelos, a prominent leader and writer in Mexico during the Revolution. Vasconcelos immortalized Arizmendi and their love affair in his autobiographical writings, *Memorias* (Memories), edited in four volumes: *Ulises criollo* (Creole Ulysses), *La tormenta* (The Storm), *El desastre* (The Disaster), *El proconsulado* (The Proconsulship),

(1935–39), in which he used the name "Adriana" to represent her (Cano, *Se* 13). Due to the public attention Arizmendi received by virtue of Vasconcelos's writings, she moved to New York City, and it was during her time there that she became active in the U.S. feminist movement. As she learned about the movement and its ideals, she realized that there was a distinction between Anglo-centric feminism and Latin American feminism.

At an international level, she saw the need for greater representation and respect for the version of feminism Latin American women embraced and promoted. In order to accomplish this goal, in 1922 Arizmendi formed the International League of Iberian and Latin American Women. Also known as Liga de Mujeres de la Raza, this international women's group was made up of Spanish-speaking women professionals as well as local and world leaders from Uruguay, Colombia, Peru, and Mexico. Arizmendi translated this international understanding of feminism into a journal published out of New York City titled *Feminismo Internacional* (International Feminism) in 1922. As the journal's founder and director, Arizmendi sought and published the writings of Latin American women writers such as Carmen de Burgos of Colombia, María Felicidad González of Paraguay, and Miguelina Acosta Cárdenas of Peru, while also including many other women's (and men's) writings from Europe and Mexico (Arizmendi, *Femenismo* 1). Arizmendi published extensively in her journal about the Liga Internacional de Mujeres Ibéricas e Hispanoamericanas, focusing on its social merits and achievements. Arizmendi's work garnered international attention. For example, Virgilina de Souza Salles, editor of São Paulo, Brazil's *Revista Femenina* (Female Magazine), published five articles in her press about Arizmendi throughout the 1920s.

In the next entry, which was originally published in Los Angeles, California's Spanish-language newspaper *El Heraldo de México* (The Mexican Herald) in 1922, Arizmendi articulates both the need for the league to serve as a guiding force for Latin American women and her plans to start *Feminismo Internacional*. Here, she weighs the positive and negative consequences of feminism for her Mexican readers, citing that it has benefitted women in terms of education, professional opportunity, and domestic and marital life. Arizmendi argues, however, that feminism fails women when they receive no guidance on how to actualize its philosophies, leaving women to reason (wrongly, Arizmendi makes clear) that feminist principles justify such practices as divorce and the abandonment of the home. Arizmendi introduces *Feminismo Internacional* as the women's journal that will take on this much needed guiding role and direct women to interpret and put into action feminist principles in ways that make sense within their cultural communities.

El feminismo y la Liga Internacional de Mujeres Ibéricas e Hispano-Americanas

El Heraldo de México
Los Angeles, California
1 de octubre de 1922

El feminismo, o sea el movimiento mundial en favor de la libertad intelectual y económica de la mujer, ofrece una gran confusión en la copiosa variedad de sus aspectos. Este movimiento que ha determinado el desarrollo físico, intelectual y económico de la mujer de los grandes centros, cada vez más activo y más complejo ha llegado a lo excesivo y sus crecientes imposiciones son ya imposibles de evitar. No habiendo un elemento que lo nivele éste podría encontrarse apoyando las acciones en las leyes, en las buenas tradiciones y en la religión.

Si se ha de intentar una clasificación del feminismo, se debe dividir en dos órdenes fundamentales: sus benéficos y sus funestos resultados. Penetremos primero en el carácter de la expresión de este movimiento que define bien su ideal, en sus manifestaciones de utilidad positiva que presenta a hijas; esposas y madres transformadas en ciudadanas perfectas.

Como consecuencia del movimiento en favor de la mujer, a la hija ya no se le sujeta a una dependencia financiera forzada, fundada en el falso sentido de seguridad, en el fracaso de no poder reconocer que la prosperidad de hoy, puede convertirse en penuria de mañana. Se ha logrado que a la joven se le eduque asegurándole un porvenir al igual que sus hermanos varones; y así, se encuentra ella, actualmente, en mejores condiciones económicas, con un oficio, una profesión o una educación formal. Si llega a perder el sostén que generalmente facilita la familia, o el marido, no necesita lamentarse exclamando: "Si me hubieran enseñado algo con lo que ahora pudiera ganarme el sustento..." Está armada para luchar en contra de la indigencia; además, se la orienta, ilustrándola en el sentido real de lo que es la vida, para ponerla a salvo de las malas pasiones de muchos hombres, a quienes la ignorancia les ofrece una senda fácil para sus conquistas, que siembran la sociedad de víctimas de la injusticia humana.

Cuando por razones ajenas a su voluntad, la mujer se conserva soltera, une a sus atractivos femeniles la belleza de su espíritu, enriquecido por una educación superior; no limita su interés a su persona, o a un círculo reducido, su instinto maternal, propio del sexo, le sugiere mil maneras de ser útil a toda la sociedad. Y debido a esto, ¡cuántos niños huérfanos, jóvenes desvalidos y ancianos menesterosos han encontrado protección, cuidados y tranquilidad y dicha!

Como esposa, los sentimientos de la mujer se han depurado de emociones extrañas al amor: ella sabe atender a su subsistencia, y no contrae nupcias meramente impulsada por la necesidad de encontrar en el marido un seguro de vida. Su entusiasmo y su amor por el hogar son más firmes porque ella tiene también mayor conciencia de lo que son deberes de esposa y de madre. Su instrucción le permite apreciar mejor los esfuerzos del hombre y darle un justo valor a su trabajo. Y con frecuencia se puede admirar a una mujer satisfecha de poder colaborar con éxito en las empresas del marido.

Debido a una concienzuda y previa preparación para el objeto el hogar está organizado y administrado con habilidad. Y al saber regular la mujer sus faenas, encuentra siempre tiempo para seguir cultivándose y cultivar inteligentemente, en el marido la ilusión. De esta manera conserva frescas las relaciones conyugales y cimienta la base de la felicidad de la familia toda.

Como madre ha adquirido una visión clara de la realidad; tiene la certeza de que sus funciones no deben limitarse a su ternura, su paciencia y a rodear a la familia de comodidades; por eso estimula constantemente su imaginación y su inteligencia con métodos escogidos y científicos. Su instinto de madre armoniza con su cultura que tiene reflejo siempre en la sociedad.

Por esta honda razón, hoy la mujer como esposa y como madre, tiene más oportunidades de engrandecer y hacer más interesante su vida; y al poner en juego todas sus facultades, se presenta más fuerte y más completa.

Fortalecidas las dotes de la mujer pueden ofrecer el cuadro más asombroso, el tipo de mujer capaz de distribuir sus ocupaciones de tal manera, que le es posible conciliar la atención que demanda una profesión. Pero esto sólo es posible cuando la educación recibida ha sido edificada en las bases del hogar y no fuera de él.

Estas mujeres, madres perfeccionadas, porque han logrado conquistarse a sí mismas; que despliegan el esplendor de sus méritos porque han desarrollado su carácter dentro de la mejor universidad, que es el hogar, tienen la posibilidad de comprender bien la naturaleza de sus hijos, a quienes sabiamente dirigen, para entregarlos al mundo con el sello invisible y perdurable de su personalidad.

Así es como las mujeres han comprendido que los valores intelectuales no son meros pasatiempos, o elegancias de la civilización para quedar bien en sociedad. Los resultados adquiridos son un medio seguro para enseñar que las mujeres pueden cultivar sus energías sin neutralizar las características de su sexo.

El hombre que ha estudiado este punto de vista del feminismo ha podido darse cuenta de que, al permitir que la mujer se eleve, se eleva él a sí mismo; y que, al dejarla caer, él se hunde con ella; porque no puede existir el uno sin el otro; porque uno y otro se complementan: Los hombres que se han identificado con el ideal que aboga por las necesidades intelectuales y económicas de la mujer, han obtenido un conocimiento amplio de los valores humanos, y por eso, sin vacilar ya más, substituyen los orgullos sin fundamento, el egoísmo y la vanidad ancestral masculinos, por la razón y la justicia.

Probado está que el movimiento en favor de la mujer ha logrado que la gran mayoría de los hombres cultos sean en el presente, una fibra del corazón de la mujer, que participa de sus palpitaciones y vibra sin disonancias, en sus congojas y en sus regocijos. De esto proviene que el hombre comparte con la mujer todos los puestos, en todas las formas nobles y superiores de las actividades humanas. Al unir su influencia ambos sexos han hecho más fuertes las sociedades, de las que hoy son las primeras del mundo.

De estos seres que cumplen con su alta misión de padres, y que al mismo tiempo se estimulan para conservar latentes sus cualidades humanas, brota exuberante el altruismo y con él dan inspiración y combaten los legítimos intereses humanos. Descendientes de esas mujeres de hombres privilegiados, son ese enjambre de mujeres samaritanas, que ya sea solas o al lado del hombre, practican el bien en favor de los demás, desempeñando un papel muy importante en el escenario social.

Su fuerza tiene por impulso el movimiento ascendente del feminismo; y el benéfico imperio de éste, alcanza a los que aún lo combaten y lo desconocen. La demostración de su grandeza titánica se manifiesta actualmente en Ginebra, Suiza, en una serie de sesiones que está celebrando la "Convención Internacional del Sufragio"; y en el magno congreso femenino que celebra el "Consejo Internacional de la Mujer" en este mes de septiembre en Cristianía, Noruega. Para el efecto, 22 consejos internacionales de mujeres, han enviado comisiones de representantes. Sus amplísimos programas, que abarcan todas las cuestiones de interés universal, serán discutidos en el palacio parlamentario donde tendrán efecto las sesiones.

Estos hechos de significación trascendental, simbolizan el triunfo adquirido por el movimiento en favor de la mujer, por el sincero reconocimiento de cuanto hay en él luminoso y de grande.

El otro aspecto del feminismo se nos presenta como los barcos veleros que son arrastrados por el viento al desplegar sus velas; barcos que siguen un curso sin destino a falta de un capitán experto, de un piloto conocedor que maneje el timón. Aunque se tiendan sus velas, a esas naves les falta la dirección que puede salvarles de los peligros que las rodean y van a estrellarse contra ellos.

Así va la aptitud de muchas mujeres, desviada sin rumbo fijo, ni freno que las domine y guíe. Su vida extraviada constituye un fracaso. Vemos c[ó]mo la libertad, sin sujeción a preceptos o leyes, ha convertido en esclavas de la frivolidad, del placer, de la ambición y del egoísmo sin límites, a centenares de jóvenes doncellas, casadas, y aun ancianas que podrían ser muy respetables.

La libertad mal entendida destruye la idea del deber como una realidad seria, extravía los sentimientos de moralidad y por consiguiente produce efectos desastrosos en los seres que sacrifican todos los valores de la vida al goce material que los consume.

Por otra parte, muchas de estas mujeres, a quienes les es posible formar un hogar y una familia, rechazan esta idea por temor de perder lo que ellas llaman su "personalidad." ¿No har[í]an mejor estas mujeres en cultivar su corazón ya que no tienen cabeza?

Otro aspecto interesante lo presentan algunas mujeres ilustradas que se empeñan en que las gentes inválidas, decrépitas o analfabetas no tengan descendientes; pero ellas, sanas, vigorosas y cultas, ¿no debieran tenerlos? La sociedad se los reclama. Si trabajan por la humanidad, ¿por qué se niegan?

Hay otra manifestación de desorientación que se revela en algunas de las que han entrado de lleno en política y las que desean relacionar todas las ideas y todos los esfuerzos de otras mujeres como los rayos que parten de un mismo centro.

Es muy encomiosa la labor del movimiento de las ideas que se desenvuelven alrededor de la vida administrativa y legislativa de un país; pero ¿cuántas mujeres habrán tenido que perder su optimismo al verse lanzadas a la lucha de las pasiones de los politicastros y de los partidos que las sujetan a intrigas y a demandas comprometedoras? [É]sta es la causa por la cual aún los mismos hombres se retiran de la política, además, ¿a dónde iría a parar el mundo si todas las mujeres lucharan por ser jueces, senadoras, gobernadoras o ministras?

Esta parte del feminismo nos presenta otro problema de vital importancia: en estos grandes centros, la vida no sólo de hombres sino de miles de mujeres describe un círculo vicioso que señala la ansiedad constante por tener un puesto en el lugar de la competencia que se encuentra en todas las esferas del engrandecimiento material.

Todas las energías las despliegan fuera del hogar, de este santuario que ofrece al que lo cuida, amenidad, poesía y alegría. Los afectos de familia que son los que alimentan los sentimientos generosos, también los subordinan a los estremecimientos del triunfo material. Y como generalmente los seres que no saben hacer felices a otros, son los más exigentes, no es extraño ver cómo se precipita la desintegración de multitud de familias. Si se observan las estadísticas oficiales más recientes sobre divorcios en la Unión Americana, se verá que éstos van en aumento creciente. Así, en 1896 hubo 42,397; en 1906 hubo 72,062 y en el 1916 llegaron a 112,036.

Esto pide una urgente restauración en el orden social. Pero se presenta la gran dificultad de dos puntos de vista irreconciliables: en primer lugar, el hombre que se aleja del hogar subyugado al egoísmo personal o colectivo, y en segundo lugar, la mujer que lo sigue por no quedarse atrás. Mientras tanto los seres que constituyen la familia se dispersan porque falta en el hogar la chispa eficaz que haga levantar la llama de un ideal vivificante.

Asistimos al naufragio de muchas vidas y no podemos menos que preocuparnos por nuestro provenir.

Ahora bien, la formación del feminismo en algunos países hispanoamericanos (vuelta) a donde este movimiento ha transformado y trastornado a muchas mujeres. Sin hacer a un lado su influencia benéfica y la inspiración soñadora que es la amiga del combate, debemos encararnos con la trascendencia que envuelve cuando viene el desconocimiento de la importancia que tiene el hogar, para poder preservar las naciones y la raza.

Si bien es cierto que en algunos de nuestros países tenemos instituciones feministas de mucho prestigio, también es verdad que éstas son débiles de fuerza, por lo precario de su situación y por el alejamiento en que viven de otras, las representantes de los ideales más elevados del feminismo. No cabe duda alguna que a estas propagandistas del bien corresponde facilitar los elementos convenientes para integrar un organismo propio y cabal, que sea el orgullo colectivo de la mujer de habla española. Estas nobles damas pueden hacer que un feminismo bien depurado exista en nuestros países, y que sirva también para guardar el equilibrio al hacer resistencia y contener los destentados impulsos que pretenden obrar sin un régimen fundado.

No olvidemos que para actualizar esta importante empresa se ha establecido la Liga Internacional de Mujeres Ibéricas e Hispanoamericanas. En ella figuran ya muchas damas distinguidas que solas, y como representantes de sus respectivas sociedades están uniendo sus esfuerzos para combatir los prejuicios y obstáculos que siempre salen al paso y llegar a la conquista de nuestro justo y desinteresado ideal.

Como el asunto que nos ocupa interesa vivamente a nuestra mitad o sea al hombre, le hemos dirigido una invitación con objeto de crear opiniones afines a las ideas de la Liga. La aquiescencia por parte de ellos ha quedado demostrada con el valioso apoyo que ya nos presta la prensa de habla española, y el que igualmente nos brindan altos personajes de nuestra raza.

Los puntos de nuestro programa se basan en el valor moral, social e intelectual, así es que pueden conformarse al de otras sociedades establecidas, las cuales, aunque figuren en la Liga, quedan independientes y con toda libertad de acción. Sin embargo, integrando una fuerza colectiva organizada serán más potentes.

Tenemos una cláusula en nuestras bases que indica la conveniencia de que sean presidentas honorarias de la Liga, la reina de España y las esposas de todos los presidentes de las repúblicas americanas, porque hemos comprendido la parte importante que a ellas corresponde. Estas dignas señoras no pueden ser indiferentes a la parte que concierne a las relaciones internacionales que las mujeres tratamos de hacer más estrechas: y tampoco pueden ser indiferentes de la mujer en favor del bien público.

Debe advertirse que la cooperación de estas damas en la manera que se estipula no compromete la autonomía de la Liga: esta sociedad no se hace partícipe de la actitud política que observen los gobiernos. La bandera de la Liga significa la solidaridad de los hombres y de las mujeres cultas de la raza. Su legislación está fundada en nuestras buenas tradiciones y costumbres y uso oficial de nuestro idioma.

Nuestro programa es, lograr un acercamiento entre todas las mujeres altruistas que luchan por la reivindicación de la mujer, como hija, esposa, madre y ciudadana.

Con objeto de encontrar el complemento de la unión espiritual que buscamos, en nuestras bases figura una cláusula que dice así: "Serán socias honorarias de la Liga, las señoras de reconocidos méritos morales e intelectuales." Estas señoras integrarán la personalidad social de la mujer de habla española, ante nosotras mismas y ante el extranjero, que hasta hoy, nos desconoce.

Pero como nosotras no somos suficientemente competentes para intentar siquiera calificar prendas que son tan comunes en las mujeres de la raza, con objeto de poder solucionar este problema difícil, las representantes de la Liga en esta ciudad, hemos decidido acudir al auxilio del público para poder con su ayuda llegar a una solución.

Como el periodismo es un complemento de todas las funciones que interesan al organismo social; hemos buscado el valioso concurso de la prensa de habla española. Ella con su complacencia habitual, para todo lo que es en beneficio nuestro, explorará la opinión del público y nos descubrirá quiénes son las mujeres más notables, de la época actual, en España y demás países de Hispano América.

Por conducto de la misma prensa se dará a conocer el final de esta investigación, según el fallo que dé un jurado calificador. Este jurado estará integrado por altas y conocidas personalidades residentes en New York que generosamente nos han brindado su cooperación. Los nombres de estas personas prominentes, que formarán el jurado, se darán a conocer próximamente.

Centro Femenino de Información
P.O. Box 12 G.P.O
New York City, [s]eptiembre 23 de 1922.

Feminism and the International League of Iberian and Hispanic-American Women

El Heraldo de México
Los Angeles, California
1 October 1922

Feminism, that is to say, the worldwide movement in favor of women's intellectual and economic freedom, presents great confusion in the profuse variety of its forms. This movement, which has determined the physical, intellectual, and economic development of women in large urban centers, ever more dynamic and complex, has arrived at an excessive point and its increasing impositions are now impossible to avoid. Without any mechanism to level off its growth, it could be found supporting its objectives through laws, solid traditions, and religion.

If a classification of feminism is to be attempted, it should be divided into two distinct and fundamental classes: its beneficial attributes and its disastrous results. Let us delve into the mode of expression of this movement that well defines its ideals, in the manifestations of positive usefulness that it offers to daughters; wives and mothers transformed into perfect citizens.

As a consequence of the movement in favor of women, a daughter is no longer subjected to forced financial dependence, based on the false sense of security, on the failure of not being able to recognize that today's prosperity can become tomorrow's penury. One achievement has been that the young woman is educated by assuring her a future equal to that of her brothers; and that way, she currently finds herself in a better economic status, with an occupation, a profession, or a formal education. If she happens to lose the support that the family or her husband usually provides, she has no need to complain by exclaiming: "If only they had taught me something that I could now earn a living from . . ." She is armed to fight against indigence; furthermore, she has been oriented, by instructing her in the true meaning of what life really is, in order to save her from the evil passions of many men, to whom ignorance offers an easy path to their conquests, who sow society with victims of human injustice.

When for reasons beyond her control, the woman remains single, she combines her feminine attractions with the beauty of her spirit, enriched by a higher education; she does not limit her interests to herself, or to a small social circle; her maternal instinct, inherent in her sex, suggests to her a thousand ways to be useful to all of society. And by virtue of this, how many orphaned children, disabled youngsters, and needy older persons have found protection, care, tranquility, and happiness!

As a wife, the feelings of the woman have been purified of emotions foreign to love: she knows how to attend to her sustenance, and she does not take the marital vows merely driven by the necessity of finding in a husband a life insurance policy. Her enthusiasm and her love for the home are stronger because she also has greater awareness of what the duties of a wife and mother are. Her education allows her to better appreciate the efforts of the man and give fair value to his work. And often one can admire a woman who is satisfied to be able to collaborate successfully in the husband's enterprises.

Due to her conscientious and prior preparation for the objective, the home is ably organized and administrated. And because the woman knows how to manage her tasks, she always finds time to continue cultivating herself and to intelligently cultivate in her husband the illusion. In this way she keeps marital relations fresh and lays the foundation of the basis of happiness of the entire family.

As a mother she has acquired a clear vision of reality; she is certain that her functions should not be limited to her tenderness, patience, and to surrounding her family with comforts; for that reason, she constantly stimulates her imagination and her intelligence through selected scientific methods. Her maternal instincts are in harmony with her level of culture, which is always reflected in society.

For this profound reason, today the woman as a wife and mother has more opportunities to enlarge her life and make it more interesting; and by putting into play all her capacities, she appears stronger and more complete.

The woman's talents, being strengthened, can offer a most amazing picture, the type of woman capable of distributing her activities in such a way that it is possible for her to reconcile the attention which a profession demands. But this is possible only when the education received has been built on the foundation of the home and not outside it.

These women, perfected mothers, because they have been able to conquer themselves; who display the splendor of their merits because they have developed their character within the best university, which is the home. They have the possibility of understanding well the nature of their children, whom they wisely lead, to release them into the world with the invisible and lasting stamp of their personality.

That is how women have understood that intellectual values are not mere pastimes, or elegant touches of civilization for fitting in with society. The results achieved are a sure means to show that women can develop their energies without neutralizing the characteristics of their sex.

The man who has studied this point of view of feminism has been able to realize that, by permitting the woman to rise, he himself rises; and that by letting her fall, he sinks with her; because the one cannot exist without the other, because the two complement each other: Men who have identified with the ideal that advocates the intellectual and economic needs of the woman have obtained a broad knowledge of human values, and for that reason, without further vacillation, they substitute the ancestral masculine traits of unfounded pride, egotism, and vanity for reason and justice.

It is a proven fact that the pro-woman movement has caused the great majority of cultured men to be, nowadays, a fiber of the woman's heart that shares in its palpitations and vibrates without dissonance, during her anguish and her rejoicing. From this comes the fact that man shares with the woman all positions, in all noble and advanced forms of human activities. Upon combining their influence, both sexes have made societies stronger, of those that are today the very finest in the world.

From these people who fulfill their high mission as parents and at the same time encourage each other to keep their latent human qualities, altruism bursts forth exuberantly, and with it, they give inspiration and fight for legitimate human interests. The descendants of these women by privileged men, are the throng of good Samaritan women, who either alone or beside their men, carry out good deeds for others, fulfilling a very important role in the social scene.

Their strength is driven by the ascendant feminist movement; and the beneficial dominion of it reaches to those who still fight it and ignore it. The demonstration of its titanic greatness is currently seen in Geneva, Switzerland, in a series of sessions that the "International Suffrage Convention" is holding; and in the great women's congress that the "International Council of Women" is celebrating this month of September in Christiania, Norway. To this end, twenty-two international councils of women have sent commissions of representatives. Its wide-ranging programs, which cover all the issues of universal interest, will be discussed in the parliamentary palace where the sessions will be held.

These events of transcendental significance symbolize the triumph obtained by the movement on behalf of women, because of the sincere recognition of how much there is in it that is luminous and great.

The other aspect of feminism is presented to us like sailboats that are carried along by the wind, once the sails are unfurled; boats that follow a course without destination because they lack an expert captain, or a knowledgeable pilot who steers the rudder. Although they extend their sails, these boats lack the direction that could save them from the dangers that surround them and against which they are going to crash.

So goes the talent of many women, drifting without a fixed course, and without any restraint to direct and guide them. Their disoriented lives constitute a failure. We see how freedom, without subjection to precepts or laws, has transformed into slaves of frivolity, pleasure, ambition, and egotism without limit hundreds of young maidens, married women, and even elderly women who could be respectable.

Badly understood liberty destroys the idea of duty as a serious reality, leads feelings of morality astray, and therefore produces disastrous effects in the beings who sacrifice all life's values to the material enjoyment that consumes them.

On the other hand, many of these women, for whom it is possible to form a home and family, reject this idea for fear of losing what they call their "personality." Wouldn't these women do better to cultivate their hearts, since they have lost their heads?

Another interesting aspect is revealed by some educated women who insist on the fact that invalid, decrepit, or illiterate people should not have descendants; but they, healthy, vigorous, and cultured, should they not have them? Society demands that of them. If they work for humanity, why do they refuse?

There is another manifestation of disorientation that is revealed in some of those who have fully entered politics, and those who desire to connect all the ideas and all the efforts of other women like spokes that originate from the same center.

Praiseworthy, indeed, is the work of the movement of ideas that develop around the administrative and legislative life of a country; but how many women may have had to lose their optimism upon seeing themselves thrown into the struggle of the passions of petty politicians and the factions that subject them to intrigues and compromising demands? This is the cause for which even men themselves retire from politics, furthermore, what would become of the world if all the women were to fight to be judges, senators, governors, or ministers?

This part of feminism presents us with another problem of vital importance: in these great centers, the lives not only of men but also of thousands of women portray a vicious circle that points out the constant anxiety to secure a position in the place of competition which is found in all the spheres of material expansion.

All the energies are displayed outside of the home, of that sanctuary that offers to the one who tends to it, amenity, poetry, and joy. The familial affections that are those that nourish generous feelings also subordinate them to the trembling of material triumph. And since generally the beings who do not know how to make others happy are the most demanding ones, it is not strange to see how the disintegration of a multitude of families is precipitated. If the most recent official statistics on divorce in the United States are examined, it will be seen that these are increasing. Thus, in 1896 there were 42,397; in 1906 there were 72,062; and in 1916 the number reached 112,036.

This requires an urgent restoration in the social order. But the great difficulty of two irreconcilable points of view presents itself: in the first place, the man who distances himself from the home, subjugated to personal or collective egotism, and in second place, the woman who follows him so as not to remain behind. Meanwhile, the beings that constitute the family become dispersed because the home lacks the effective spark to raise the flame of a life-giving ideal.

We are present at the shipwreck of many lives and we can do nothing less than worry about our future.

Now then, the formation of feminism in some Hispano-American countries (returns) to where this movement has transformed and disturbed many women. Without ignoring the beneficial influence and the visionary inspiration which is the friend of the struggle, we must come face to face with the transcendence that envelops everything when ignorance arrives about the importance the home has, in order to be able to preserve the nations and the people.

While it is true that in some of our countries we have very prestigious feminist institutions, it is also true that they are a weak force, because of their precarious situation and because of the estrangement in which the others exist, the representatives of the highest ideals of feminism. There is no doubt whatsoever that these propagandists of the good have the duty to facilitate the appropriate elements in order to constitute a proper and complete organism, which will be the collective pride of the Spanish-speaking woman. These noble ladies can make a highly refined feminism exist in our countries, and one that will also serve to keep the equilibrium while resisting and containing any unlawfully held impulses that seek to operate without an established system of government.

Let us not forget that in order to modernize this important undertaking the International League of Iberian and Hispanic-American Women has been established. This institution already includes many distinguished ladies who alone, and as representatives of their respective societies, are joining their efforts to combat the prejudices and obstacles that always intercept and come to conquer our just and unselfish ideals.

Since the issue that occupies us is of lively interest to our other half, that is the men, we have sent them an invitation with the objective of establishing opinions similar to the ideas of the League. Their assent has been demonstrated with the valuable support that the Spanish-speaking press has already lent to us, and that offered to us, similarly, by exalted persons of our race.

The points of our program are based on moral, social, and intellectual merit, so that they can conform to that of other established societies, which, although they participate in the League, remain independent and with total freedom of action. Nevertheless, by constituting an organized collective force they will be stronger.

We have a clause in our program statement that points out the advisability of there being honorary female presidents of the League: the Queen of Spain and the wives of all the presidents of the American republics, because we have understood the important role that corresponds to them. These worthy ladies cannot be indifferent to the role that is concerned with international relations that we women are trying to make tighter; and neither can they be indifferent to the women who are in favor of the public's well-being.

It should be noted that the cooperation of these first ladies in the way that is stipulated does not compromise the autonomy of the League: this society will not be a participant in the political mind-set that governments adhere to. The flag of the League signifies the solidarity of men with the cultured women of the people. Its legislation is founded on our good traditions and customs and the official use of our language. Our program is to achieve a meeting of the minds among all altruistic women who fight for the revindication of the woman as daughter, wife, mother, and citizen.

With the objective of finding the complement of the spiritual union that we seek, in our program statement there is a clause that states, "Women of recognized moral and intellectual merits will be honorary members of the League." These ladies will constitute the social personality of the Spanish-speaking woman, before us and before the foreigner who, up to now, has refused to accept us.

But since we are not sufficiently competent to attempt to even identify the good qualities that are so common in the women of the people, with the objective of being able to solve this difficult problem, we, the representatives of the League in this city, have decided to call for the help of the public to be able to reach a solution.

Since journalism is a complement in all the functions that concern the social organism; we have sought out the valuable assistance of the Spanish-speaking press. The press, with its usual forbearance with respect to all things of benefit to us, will explore public opinion and discover for us those who are the most notable women of the present era, in Spain and the rest of the countries of Hispanic-America.

By way of the same press, the results of this investigation will be made known, according to the decision that a qualifying jury will render. This jury will be composed of elevated and well-known personalities, residents of New York who have generously offered us their cooperation. The names of these prominent persons who will make up the jury will soon be made known.

Feminine Center of Information
P.O. Box 12 G.P.O.
New York City, September 23, 1922

Catalina Dulché Escalante (Catalina D'Erzell)

Born in Silao, Guanajuato, Mexico, Catalina Dulché Escalante (1897–1950) was a successful journalist, author, artist, and playwright for almost four decades who wrote under the pseudonym Catalina D'Erzell. During a time when Mexican women's rights were under debate, Escalante entered this conversation by articulating her arguments through a wide variety of genres: newspaper editorials, stories, interviews, plays, and more. Her active and prolific participation in the Spanish-language press suggests the wide reach of her writings as well as recognition and popularity. Her plays were well received, with some being performed over one hundred times, and, like her journalism, they often addressed concerns relevant to women (Jones 489). As Willis Knapp Jones explains, Escalante "not only wrote about women but also helped to bring more mexicana writers into literary and dramatic society"; she thus "opened theatre doors to a great number of women writers at this period of Mexico's drama history" (489).

Escalante's practice of opening doors for other mexicana writers is evidenced in the next piece. This article, "La mujer y el arte: Teresa Farías de Isassi" ("The Woman and Art: Teresa Farías de Isassi") was published in 1920 through the Los Angeles–based Spanish-language newspaper, *El Heraldo de México*. Here, Escalante reviews the plays and writings of renowned mexicana playwright and novelist Teresa Farías de Isassi and praises her work. Under the heading "Lecturas Para El Sexo Femenino" (Readings for the feminine sex), Escalante's review recommends Farías de Isassi's writings to the women readers of *El Heraldo*. Significant to this review is the way Escalante frames her celebration of Farías de Isassi: the artist is exceptional because of her modesty, her maternal instincts, her feminine disposition, and her feminine voice. Escalante writes, "To my way of thinking, in order that the woman writer not make herself disagreeable by resolutely taking on the freedom of expression, characteristic of men, she should never stop being feminine. And Mrs.

Farías de Isassi never stops being feminine." A significant turn at the end of this review piece, however, occurs when she notes the way Farías de Isassi's four-year-old daughter, Graziella, followed her mother's example by writing a play. Escalante thus focuses readers' attention on a feminine model of literacy and the role educated women played for their children.

Escalante's journalistic and dramatistic career was long and prolific. The rhetorical force behind her writing is evident, as her work was well recognized and widely read, winning awards such as the Palmas Academicas de Francia (Baeza Ventura 127). While her early writing focused more on traditional understandings of femininity and womanhood, her later work theorized women's everyday condition much differently. Her 1937 article in San Antonio, Texas's *La Prensa* (The Press) titled "Se acabaron las mujeres musas" (The women muses have disappeared) reflects this shift. Here, she focuses on women's rights, expounds on the changing conceptions of women, and argues how they were no longer the giddy, romantic muses of men as in times past. In "Lo de matrimonios a plazo" (The matter of fixed-term marriages), published in El Paso's *El Continental* (The Continent) in 1937, Escalante engages the controversy of fixed-term marriages emerging in San Luis Potosí, Mexico. Lastly, in her article "Mujer revolucionaria" (Revolutionary woman), also published in *El Continental* in 1937, she asserts that Mexican women should be given the right to vote—a right they would not win until 1953. These are only a small sampling of her many writings that stretched over several decades.[1]

La mujer y el arte. Teresa Farías de Isassi

El Heraldo de México
Los Angeles, California
8 de enero de 1920

Quien haya hablado una vez tan sólo con la señora Farías de Isassi, quien siquiera la haya mirado silenciosamente mientras sus labios se mueven vertiendo frases de admirable y sutil lírica, podrá comprender el entusiasmo mío por su talento. Cada uno de sus pensamientos es una delicadeza, cada uno de sus conceptos una enseñanza. Tuve la fortuna de escucharle la lectura de uno de los capítulos de su obra filosófica "Ante el enigma," inspirada en su última visita a la florecida tumba del gran escritor Víctor Hugo. "Ante el enigma," es decir: ante la muerte, donde surge la interrogación tremenda: "¿morir es morir o es nacer?" Y Teresa Farías de Isassi contesta con brava inspiración, sin basarse en opiniones de sabios autores, sino dejando llevar su mano sobre el papel, únicamente al dictado de su cerebro creador. Y pregunta a su vez, atrevida y lógicamente: "¿No es acaso mayor milagro convertirse de embrión en hombre, que volver de hombre a embrión?" Esta obra que pronto publicará es sencillamente admirable y junto con sus dramas en preparación "Religión de Amor" y "Páginas de la Vida," elevará a su autora a las cumbres del triunfo.

Y a pesar de esto, Teresa Farías de Isassi es modesta. Habla con naturalidad, sin alardes vanidosos, sin fatuidad y al escucharle expresar una idea profunda, llega a parecernos sencillísima, porque al pasar por sus labios, adquiere un colorido de naturalidad pasmosa.

Es además... ¡madre! Y quizá ¿por qué no? tiene su estilo tal galanura, tal feminidad de la que nunca se desprende, porque su mesa de trabajo está colocada cerca de una cuna blanca en la que una cabecita orlada de rizos negros descansa y unas largas pestañas derraman su sombra obscura en derredor de dos ojos dormidos.... Y cuando una mujer escribe y la potencia de su cerebro hace aparecer involuntariamente sus frases demasiado varoniles, bástale oír de pronto la vocecita cadenciosa de un niño o mirar la sonrisa inocente de su boca, para que bajo sus frases se adivine a la madre, a la amante, y de todos modos a la mujer.

En mi concepto, para que la escritora no se haga antipática al tomar decididamente la libertad de expresión, atributo de los hombres, debe de no dejar de ser femenina nunca. Y la señora Farías de Isassi jamás deja de serlo. Tengo a la vista su bello drama "Como las Aves," premiado recientemente en el concurso literario abierto por la Dirección de Bellas Artes. Por boca de uno de sus personajes dice la señora Isassi: "Las almas son como las aves. No están hechas para arrastrarse entre el fango de la tierra, sino para volar entre las diafanías del firmamento. No están hechas para los abismos, sino para las más altas cumbres, para las más altas cimas. No están hechas para alimentarse de lodo, están hechas para saturarse de azul, para embriagarse de la luz, para inundarse de sol. Su alma podrá haber sido detenida en su ascensión. El polvo de la tierra podrá haber entorpecido sus alas; pero sabrá sacudirlas, sabrá hacer el esfuerzo supremo, sabrá subir de nuevo." He admirado este pasaje, sinceramente, pero más, mucho más, la frase con que termina el drama, porque es todo un poema y porque es netamente femenina: "Sí, aquí estoy, en mi puesto," dice ante una cuna la mujer que al mirarla no se ha atrevido a huir con el hombre amado. ¡En mi puesto! Es decir, en el de la mujer honrada, de la madre buena, de la sacrificada amante, de la esposa fiel. Y la señora Farías de Isassi hace una hermosa síntesis de estas virtudes en las tres palabras de su poema.

Yo no puedo menos de poner a los pies de la señora Isassi, mi humilde admiración y comprender y decir, que mujeres como ella honran a México, ya que Teresa Farías de Isassi es una eminente escritora.

En el saloncito gracioso decorado de bellas pinturas debidas al pincel de la señora Farías de Isassi (también posee el arte del color) llegó a mis oídos la argentina nota de su voz melodiosa de niña, que resulta extraña expresando ideas hondas y explicando complicados problemas . . . Y, de pronto, tras la entornada puerta, otra voz de cristal, muy parecida a la de la escritora, trinó alegremente . . . y entonces ví serenarse aquella frente blanca, que penetra con la sutileza de su pensamiento los "enigmas," y las almas.

Y su boca acalló el verbo conceptuoso y ardiente en que estallaba a cada instante un pasionalismo delicadísimo, para murmurar orgullosamente, es mi hija. . . .

Vino Graziella, la niña morena de los ojos sombreados, que habla cantando, y quedóse extática ante la multitud de planillas escritas que se esparcían a nuestro alrededor y encarándose conmigo dijo con toda la ingenuidad de sus cuatro años:

—Yo no quería entrar. . . .
—¿Por qué?
—Estaba ocupada . . .
—[¿]Qué hacías . . . ?
—. . . ¡escribir un drama . . . !

The Woman and Art: Teresa Farías de Isassi

El Heraldo de México
Los Angeles, California
8 January 1920

Anyone who has spoken just one time with Mrs. Farías de Isassi, anyone who has even silently watched her while her lips move articulating phrases of admirable and subtle lyricism, will be able to understand my enthusiasm for her talent. Each one of her thoughts is a delicacy, each one of her concepts is instructive. I had the good fortune of hearing her reading one of the chapters of her philosophical work "Facing the Enigma," inspired by her last visit to the flower-bedecked tomb of the great writer Victor Hugo. "Facing the Enigma," that is to say: facing death, where the tremendous question arises: "Does dying mean death or birth?" And Teresa Farías de Isassi replies with brave inspiration, without basing her opinions on sage authors, but rather letting her hand glide over the paper, at the sole dictate of her creative mind. And she in turn asks, daringly and logically: "Is it not a greater miracle to be converted from an embryo into a man, than to return from man to embryo?" This work that she will publish soon is simply admirable, and along with the dramas she has in preparation, "The Religion of Love" and "Pages of Life," will elevate their author to the heights of victory.

And in spite of this, Teresa Farías de Isassi is modest. She speaks naturally, without any vain boasting, without fatuity, and upon hearing her express a profound idea, it seems to us to be very simple, because when it passes her lips, it takes on a coloring of amazing naturalness.

Besides, she is . . . a mother! And perhaps (why not?) her style has such elegance, such femininity from which she never detaches herself, because her work table is situated close to a white cradle in which rests a little head trimmed by black curls and long lashes cast their dark shadow around two sleepy eyes. . . . And when a woman writes and the power of her mind involuntarily makes some of her phrases appear too masculine, it is sufficient for her to suddenly hear the rhythmic little voice of a child or to look at the innocent smile on her lips, so that beneath her phrases one can envision the mother, the lover, and in all aspects the woman.

To my way of thinking, in order that the woman writer not make herself disagreeable by resolutely taking on the freedom of expression characteristic of men, she should never stop being feminine. And Mrs. Farías de Isassi never stops being feminine. I am looking at her lovely drama *Like the Birds*, which recently won a prize in the literary competition held by the Editorial Board of Fine Arts. Mrs. Isassi states, through a speech of one of her characters:

"Souls are like birds. They are not made to crawl through the slime of the earth, but rather to fly among the diaphanous lights of the firmament. They are not made for abysses, but rather for the highest mountaintops, for the high peaks. They are not made to feed upon mud, they are made to be saturated with blue, to become inebriated with light, to be inundated by sunshine. Her soul might have been detained in its ascension. The dust of the earth might have numbed her wings; but she will know how to shake them out, she will know how to make the supreme effort, she will know how to rise again." I have admired this passage, sincerely, but more, much more, have I admired the sentence that ends the drama, because it is a poem in itself and because it is purely feminine: "Yes, here I am, in my place," says the woman in front of a cradle, which when she looks at it she has not dared to run away with the man she loves. In my place! That is, in that of the honorable woman, of the good mother, of the self-sacrificing lover, of the loyal wife. And Mrs. Farías de Isassi makes a beautiful synthesis of these virtues in those three words of her poem.

I can only place at the feet of Mrs. Isassi my humble admiration, and to understand and say that women like her honor Mexico, since Teresa Farías de Isassi is an eminent writer.

In the charming little room decorated with pretty pictures from the brush of Mrs. Farías de Isassi (who also possesses the art of color), the silvery note of her melodious voice, like a girl's voice, reached my ears, which seemed strange expressing profound ideas and explaining complicated problems. . . . And suddenly, from behind the slightly open door, another crystalline voice, very like the voice of the writer, trilled happily . . . and then I saw her pale forehead become calm, the one that penetrates with the subtlety of her thought the "enigmas," and souls.

And her mouth hushed the conceptual and ardent speech from which burst forth at every moment, an extremely delicate "passionalism" in order to murmur proudly, "This is my daughter . . ."

Graziella came in, the bronze-skinned child with the shadowy eyes, who speaks as if singing, and she stopped enraptured in the presence of the many written pages that were scattered around us, and facing me she said with all the naiveté of her four years:

—I didn't want to come in. . . .
—Why?
—I was busy . . .
—What were you doing . . . ?
—. . . writing a play . . . !

Notes

Works Cited

Index

Notes

INTRODUCTION: *UNA INVITACIÓN*

1. We label many of the mexicana rhetors' arguments collected here as feminist. While this label may seem anachronistic, because the term *feminist* was not in wide circulation during the time we focus on, we use it to describe these women's efforts to reflect on and revise their sociopolitical roles and to argue for expanded personal and political rights.

2. Following the practice of scholars such as A. Gabriel Meléndez, Clara Lomas and Gabriela Baeza Ventura, Frankie Hutton and Barbara Straus Reed, and many others, we use the word *press* interchangeably with *newspaper*.

3. *Las Hijas del Anáhuac* changed its name to *Violetas del Anáhuac* in 1888. When we refer to the publication in general we use the form *Las Hijas [Violetas] del Anáhuac*. When referring to a particular moment within the history of the publication, we reference the title used at that time, either *Las Hijas del Anáhuac* or *Violetas del Anáhuac*.

4. One of the readings collected here, Aurora Lucero-White Lea's "Shall the Spanish Language Be Taught in the Schools of New Mexico" was published in both the English- and Spanish-language press (Kanellos et al. 136). We publish the English version here, because that was the only version available to us.

5. There are two caveats to this description of the rhetors in this volume. First, *Mestiza Rhetorics* contains a published letter from Paz, who identifies herself as Cuban. We chose to include this letter because it was published in *Violetas del Anáhuac* and because Paz is writing to and praising the Mexican newspaperwomen publishing in that press. Paz's letter reveals the reach and significance of a newspaper that was directed by mexicanas, dedicated to mexicana concerns, and composed mainly of mexicana contributions. Second, we include Aurora Lucero-White Lea's published speech, "Shall the Spanish Language Be Taught in the Schools of New Mexico," in which she argues that Mexican students in New Mexico schools should receive Spanish-language instruction. In this piece, she bases her claims on the connections Spanish-language instruction has to the Spanish literary tradition rather than the Mexican one. We include her piece because it reflects the complex negotiations educators made as they thought through bilingual education in the borderlands.

6. For more information on the Mexican nationalist movement in the United States called El México de Afuera, see Juanita Luna Lawhn, "María Luisa Garza: The Novelist of *El México de Afuera*."

7. For detailed explanation of the caste system of Colonial Mexico, see Frederick.

8. As Frederick makes clear, *mulato* referred to the racial mix of European with African or black heritage; *pardo* referred to anyone born in the Americas with

an unidentified mixture of European, Amerindian, or black African, and *español* referred to anyone of pure Spanish blood. *Mestizo*, then, specifically referred to the mixture of Spanish and indigenous race.

9. The time period of this anthology (1887–1922) represents a moment right before the critical writings of Mexican philosopher José Vasconcelos, who documented the apex of *mestizaje* in *La raza cósmica* (1925). Previous to Vasconcelos, the concept of *mestizaje* was popularized in Latin America in such texts as Cuban philosopher, writer, and journalist José Martí's 1892 "Our America." In this essay, Martí wrote about the mixing of cultures and peoples and labeled this reality "our *mestizo* America." What solidified the Mexican identity with *mestizaje* was the 1876 presidential election of Porfirio Díaz, who was himself a *mestizo* descending from both Mixtec Indians and Spaniards. A cross section of Mexicans at this time would have identified themselves as *mestizo*. For extended reading on this topic, see Bonfil Batalla, Farr, Hedrick, Lund, Paredes, and Vento.

10. See chapter 2 of Ramírez's *Occupying Our Space* for a thorough discussion of *mestiza* rhetoric.

11. In *Borderlands/La Frontera*, Anzaldúa defines the U.S.-Mexican border as a borderland, *una herida abierta* (an open wound). She writes, "borders are set up to define the places that are safe and unsafe, to distinguish an us from a them. A border is a dividing line, a narrow strip along a steep edge. A borderland is a vague and undetermined place created by the emotional residue of an unnatural boundary" (25). Thus, as many scholars have noticed and explored, Anzaldúa's border is often understood as the physical site of division between the United States and Mexico. However, it can also be read as more of an ideological, experiential site of division and distinction that inflects, defines, and disrupts daily life.

12. See also Bessette, Christoph, Eves, Gold and Hobbs, Hogg, Logan, Moulder, Pough and Richardson, and Wang, among many others.

13. See also Elyazghi, Gilyard and Nunley, Jackson and Richardson, Kells, Lipson and Binkley, and Mao, among many others.

14. As noted by Olson and De los Santos, the reference to *América* indicates an imperative of rhetorical scholars to study rhetorical history, practice, and theory that emerged from the entire hemisphere, not just the United States (194).

15. For historical information on Mexican women workers and their activism, see Sonia Hernández.

16. See Dingo, Hesford, Queen, and Richards, for example.

17. We should also note that in the original Spanish-language articles, there were at times minor errors or typos—indiscretions found in many newspapers of this period, English and Spanish alike. In the Spanish versions, we chose to correct errors using brackets, so readers can see our insertions and corrections. For the English version, we translated the correction without the brackets.

18. See chapter 4 in Enoch's *Refiguring Rhetorical Education* for a discussion of how Laredo teachers such as Idar troubled this conservative depiction of the mexicana teacher.

19. Subsequent corrections and edits to the translations were done by Dr. Neil J. Devereaux.

LAUREANA WRIGHT DE KLEINHANS

1. The color purple has long been identified with the feminist movement outside of Mexico as well. From the suffrage movement in England and the United States to the contemporary moment, activists have displayed purple, along with gold and white, in protest artifacts and clothing to indicate their allegiances with the cause. Purple in the form of lavender has also been identified with lesbian activism.

2. The helots in Ancient Greece were a population of slaves and subjugated peoples of Laconia and Messenia, areas ruled by Sparta. These people were poorly treated and could be killed during an autumn ritual without repercussion. This Greek reference suggests that Mexican women were similarly subjugated by men.

3. Available resources could not clarify this reference.

CATALINA ZAPATA DE PUIG

1. As noted in the introduction, the title *Las Hijas del Anáhuac* changed to *Violetas del Anáhuac* in 1888. Zapata de Puig published her article under the title *Violetas*.

2. Hemeroteca Digital Nacional de México holds issues 6 and 8 from 5 and 19 June 1882; the complete number of editions published is not known.

3. Zapata de Puig would also publish her poem "Mi Lira" (My lira) in *Diario del Hogar* in 1882.

4. El Semanario de las Señoritas Mejicanas can be located online through the Hemeroteca Digital Nacional de México database.

CONCEPCIÓN MANRESA DE PÉREZ

1. As noted in the introduction, the title of *Las Hijas del Anáhuac* changed to *Violetas del Anáhuac* in 1888. Concepción Manresa de Pérez published under the title *Las Hijas*.

2. In addition to "Mujeres de nuestra época," Manresa de Pérez published two other essays in *Las Hijas* [*Violetas*] *del Anáhuac*, "La memoria" (Memory) and "El trabajo" (Work).

3. The Temple of Minerva is an ancient Roman temple dedicated to the goddess Minerva, who was the goddess of wisdom and sponsor of arts and trade.

4. The author may have used the currency of the French franc for consistency purposes in order to give the reader an idea of the value of each budget listed. The elite readers would have had knowledge of the franc due to the French occupation from 1862 to 1867. The franc was also circulating widely at the time.

PAZ

1. As noted in the introduction, the title of *Las Hijas del Anáhuac* changed to *Violetas del Anáhuac* in 1888. Paz published under the title *Violetas*.

2. Guatimozín is another name for Cuauhtémoc, the last Aztec Emperor of Tenochtitlán (1520–21). Cuauhtémoc means "one that has descended like an eagle." He is regarded as an important figure in Mexican history and lore.

JUANA BELÉN GUTIÉRREZ DE MENDOZA AND ELISA ACUÑA Y ROSSETTI

1. There is no direct translation for Chinaco.

2. Ponciano Arriaga was the name of a political and intellectual dissident during the prerevolutionary uprisings.

3. For more information regarding Juana Belén Gutiérrez de Mendoza, see Ramírez, *Occupying Our Space*, chapter 4.

4. Belem was the prison in Mexico City where many of the journalists were housed after being arrested.

5. The Convention referenced here points to the Anti-reelection Convention held in April 1910, where the attendees nominated Francisco Madero for president.

6. Mr. Madero here refers to Francisco I. Madero, the 1910 presidential nominee to take the place of the dictator of Porfirio Díaz. After Díaz was ousted on 25 May 1911, Madero became the highest political leader of the country. He was later voted in as president with 90 percent of the vote in October 1911. His time in office would be short-lived. In 1913, amidst the chaotic grab for power during the Revolution, he was assassinated in a coup carried out by Victoriano Huerta.

HERMILA GALINDO

1. The Congreso Feminista de Yucatán did not necessarily indicate the formation of a formal feminist movement in Mexico. While the Mexican Revolution opened many doors of opportunity for women, the term *feminist* was beginning to surface in conferences and articles both pro- and anti-feminist. For details on the 1916 congress, see Foppa.

2. Galindo wrote two speeches for the Feminist Congresses: "La mujer en el porvenir" (The woman of the future) and "Estudio de la Srita. Hermila con motivo de los temas que han de absolverse en el segundo congreso feminista de Yucatán" (A study by Miss Hermila Galindo on the occasion of the topics to be resolved in the Second Feminist Congress of Yucatán). However, she did not deliver these speeches. The reason for her absence is unclear, but it may have been due to commitments to other speaking engagements. The entire transcript of the 1916 Primer Congreso Feminista de México can be found in the Latin American Women Writers database at the University of Arizona.

3. *Indolatino* refers to the European and Indigenous cultural blending. It is also another word for *mestizo*. The Indo-Latin approach was the policy of Mexico that took into consideration the population of people from this mixed background. This approach was also a response to Woodrow Wilson's renewed Manifest Destiny

in Latin America. The book can be found in the University of Texas at El Paso Special Collections.

4. The title of her journal, *La Mujer Moderna*, was the same title as that of Andrea and Teresa Villarreal's women's journal started in San Antonio, Texas, in 1909. While they shared a name, these two journals were distinct.

5. For scholarship regarding republican motherhood in the United States, see the works by Cott, Kraditor, and Welter.

6. For more on Hermila Galindo see Macías, Ramírez, and Valles Ruiz.

7. 16 September marks Mexican Independence Day; it commemorates the day in 1810 when Mexicans initiated the Mexican War of Independence.

8. This is a reference to Venustiano Carranza Garza, who was at the time president of Mexico, until his assassination on 21 May 1920.

9. The text Galindo is quoting from here is unclear.

10. Marie-Jeanne Phlipon Roland (1754–1793) was known simply as Madame Roland. Along with her husband, Jean-Marie Roland de la Platière, she was a public supporter of the French Revolution and jailed. There, she wrote *Mémoires de Madame Roland* (1795).

11. Ernest Renan was a French archeologist who traveled extensively throughout the Middle East. Galindo is referencing his sister, Henriette, who supported him in his travels, research, and writings. She died during their travels. Renan would later write a memoir on the significance of his sister, *Ma Soeur, Henriette*.

12. Victoriano Huerta became president of Mexico in 1913 after he led a coup d'etat against President Francisco Madero.

13. The "H." in front of Veracruz stands for *Heroica*. Heroica is a designation given to Mexican cities that have had been sites of major events that contributed to the defense of national sovereignty. At the time *El Pueblo* was published, Veracruz had been given the distinction four times.

JOVITA IDAR (A. V. NEGRA AND ASTREA)

1. There are at least three scholars who in their writings briefly discuss Jovita Idar's involvement in *La Crónica*: José Limón, "El Primer Congreso Mexicanista de 1911: A Precursor to Contemporary Chicanismo"; Laura Gutiérrez Witt, "Cultural Continuity in the Face of Change: Hispanic Printers in Texas"; and Clara Lomas, "Revolutionary Women and the Alternative Press in the Borderlands."

2. In her introduction to Leonor Villegas de Magnón's *The Rebel*, Clara Lomas writes that from 1898 through 1914, Jovita Idar wrote "under the pseudonym A. V. Negra (which translates phonetically to 'Black Bird')" ("Revolutionary" xv). And according to Texas and borderlands scholar Sonia Hernández, Idar also wrote under the pseudonym Astrea. Hernández notes, "Indeed, [Idar's] writings, often under the pseudonym of 'Astrea,' cut across national and gender boundaries, addressing gender equity and other issues affecting the Mexican community on both sides of the border" (94). Idar signed her own name to *La Crónica* articles

titled "El eterno problema" (The eternal problem) vol. 2, no. 89 (15 Sep. 1910), p. 6; "En memoria de mi padre" (In memory of my father) Memorial Issue (18 Apr. 1914), p. 2; "En memoria de mi inolvidable amiga" (In memory of my unforgettable friend) vol. 2, no. 86 (27 Aug. 1910), p. 3. Idar's subject for the final piece listed is Sara Estela Ramírez. See Enoch's *Refiguring Rhetorical Education* for a study of Idar's educational essays written under the pseudonym A. V. Negra. Without the knowledge that Idar also used the pen name Astrea, Enoch wrote about Astrea's feminist writings in "'*Para la Mujer*': Defining a Chicana Feminist Rhetoric at the Turn of the Century."

3. The reference here is to Benito Juárez (1806–72), the president of Mexico who served five terms from 1858 to 1872. He is one of the most revered heroes of Mexico because he was the first president with indigenous origins (Zapotec). As a soldier, he fought against the French occupation of Mexico, and, above all else, was a progressive leader dedicated to democratic principles.

4. On 10 October 1910 women gained the right to vote in California; it was the sixth U.S. state to ratify women's suffrage.

LEONOR VILLEGAS DE MAGNÓN

1. In chapter 4 of *Refiguring Rhetorical Education*, Enoch explores Villegas de Magnón's work as a teacher, educating through the pages of *La Crónica*.

2. For a detailed description and analysis of El Primer Congreso, see Limón.

3. Francisco I. Madero was the political leader who challenged Porfirio Díaz on his sixth presidential move in 1910. Díaz had served five terms, and after his resignation of power, Madero took office. Victoriano Huerta forced Madero to resign, and Madero was later assassinated (with José María Pino Suárez) on what is known as *La decena tragica*.

4. We assume here that Villegas de Magnón is referring to an article previously published in *La Crónica*.

SARA ESTELA RAMÍREZ

1. The root word of *corregidora* is *corregir*, which means "to correct." In turn, the term could have a rough translation of "the one who corrects," but there is no direct translation for *corregidora*. Historically, according to the Oxford Spanish dictionary, the masculine word *corregidor* could mean mayor.

2. Enoch examines this poem in "'*Para la Mujer.*'"

MARÍA RENTERÍA

1. For more on the early development of Chicana feminist activities, see *Chicana Feminist Thought: The Basic Historical Writings*, edited by Alma M. García (Routledge, 1997).

2. Rentería is likely referring to José María Morelos (1765–1815), Mexican revolutionary and Roman Catholic priest.

ANDREA VILLARREAL GONZÁLEZ

1. The title *La Mujer Moderna* was the same as that of Hermila Galindo's women's journal, but the two periodicals were distinct. Galindo initiated hers in September 1915 in Mexico City.

ISIDRA T. DE CÁRDENAS

1. Lomas notes that Cárdenas could have been writing under the direction of male supporters behind the scenes. Leon Cárdenas (the relation to Isidra is not known) held the post of Secretary of Education in Mexico, and Lomas suggests that he and other men may have prompted Isidra and her collaborators to steer the newspaper in certain directions ("Transborder" 60).

2. The phrase of Nation of Hidalgo refers to the country of Mexico. Miguel Hidalgo, a Mexican national hero to this day, was the priest who instigated the 1810 War of Independence against Spain.

3. While the reference to Ludovico is unclear, Manuel Estrada Cabrera (1857–1924) was president of Guatemala at the time of this article. He was known for his despotic and cruel tactics against the workers of Guatemala.

4. A Tartar here refers to a savage or ill-tempered person.

5. Juan Sarabia was a public intellectual and journalist who openly criticized Porfirio Díaz for his government and international policies.

6. Díaz wrote and signed the Plan of Tuxtepec in 1876 to remove Sebastian Lerdo de Tejada from the Mexican presidency. Revolutionaries of 1910 referred to this document because in it Díaz espoused liberal principles that he later disavowed as dictator.

7. This reference to "el llorón de Icamole" (the cry-baby of Icamole) reminds readers that Díaz broke into tears after he saw the disastrous performance of his troops in the Battle of Icamole. This reference frames him as a coward.

8. The phrase "Mexican Estrada Cabrera" refers to the brutal, anti-labor president of Guatemala. The author is putting Porfirio Díaz in the same disrespected camp as Estrada Cabrera when it comes to lack of support and even brutality against the common worker.

ARTEMISA N. SÁENZ ROYO (XÓCHITL)

1. A traditional drink in Central Mexico, pulque is the fermented sap of the maguey plant. It has been produced for millennia, beginning with the indigenous cultures of Mexico.

2. The newspaper does not make note of the title of the book.

3. Sáenz Royo is likely referring to John Stuart Mill's 1869 essay "The Subjection of Women."

4. Princess Marie of Edinburgh (1875–1938) became the Queen of Romania through marriage to Prince Ferdinand of Romania. She is best known for working

alongside her three daughters as nurses in aid of the soldiers in Moldavia during World War I.

5. Sáenz Royo is referring to Queen Mary of Teck, wife of King George V, who ascended to the throne in England in 1910. During the war, Mary visited wounded soldiers.

6. The reference here is likely to U.S. President Woodrow Wilson's daughter, Margaret Wilson. After Margaret's mother died in 1914 and while her father was still in office, Margaret took on the role of first lady.

7. This is likely a reference to Elizabeth of Bavaria, Queen of Belguim at the turn of the twentieth century. She was well known and beloved for establishing a nursing unit and visiting soldiers during World War I.

8. José Venustiano Carranza Garza was a leader in the Mexican Revolution who eventually became president of Mexico from 1917 to 1920.

9. Salvador Alvarado was a general in the Constitutionalist Army under Carranza and later became governor of Yucatán. Alvarado was the progressive governor who initiated the First Feminist Congress in Mexico in January 1916. Called by Governor Alvarado, a second Congress was held in December of that same year in order to clarify a statement for women's voting rights. Less than half the women returned for the second congress, which failed to produce sufficient votes to support suffrage.

MARÍA LUISA GARZA (LORELEY)

1. Garza refers to a Spanish proverb, "When the devil has had his fill of flesh, he [takes holy orders as] a monk." Garza is stating that she knows unmarried women who are feminists because they have nothing to lose, since they have no hope of marrying and assuming traditional women's roles.

2. In Greek mythology, Alcestis is a princess known for her love for her husband; Atalanta was a virgin huntress who refused to marry.

ARIANA

1. In ancient Greek culture, the Gynecium was the inner sanctum of the home, the space designated specifically for women.

2. Madeleine Pelletier (1874–1939) was the first French woman to complete a medical degree in psychiatry. With this medical knowledge, she challenged the idea that women were inferior to men. She was known for her radical stance as a feminist. Pelletier's last days were spent in an insane asylum, where she was committed after suspicion of conducting abortions.

3. Jane Dieulafoy is known for the work she conducted with her husband, Marcel Dieulafoy, traveling and studying anthropological sites in Persia, which they visited twice. During her travels, she performed a kind of masculinity by wearing her hair short and dressing in pants and suits. For women at this time, dressing in this way was illegal in France, but an exception was made for Dieulafoy by the government, citing travel permissions.

4. Caroline Legrand was a French actress.

5. Emmeline Pankhurst (1858–1928) led British women in their fight for equal rights. In 1889, she founded the Women's Franchise League, which proposed that married women have the right to vote. Her radical work as a suffragette led to several arrests.

6. Ariana is referring to feminist Mary Richardson's vandalism of Titian's painting *Venus with a Mirror*. In 1914, Richardson smuggled shears into London's National Gallery and badly damaged the painting, possibly in retaliation for suffragette Emmeline Pankhurst's arrest the previous day. Richardson objected to the painting's portrayal of a woman as goddess of love. She also stated that it was appalling the way men stood and stared at it all day long. After this incident, Mary Richardson was nicknamed "Slasher Mary" by the press.

ANONYMOUS FEMINIST WRITINGS FROM *LA PRENSA*, SAN ANTONIO

1. The writer uses quotation marks to indicate the speeches of the presenters and the congress. The exact accuracy of these quotations translated into Spanish is unclear. However, the inclusion of these speeches—paraphrased or even misquoted as they may be—indicates this writer's investment in the congress and her interest in other women's rhetorical and political interventions. We retain the quotation marks to reflect how the article was originally published in *La Prensa*.

2. Rosika Schwimmer (1877–1948) was a pacifist and feminist. A Jewish woman born in Hungary, she found the Hungarian Feminist Association in 1904, served as secretary for the International Woman Suffrage Association in 1913 before speaking at the International Congress of Women in 1915.

ANONYMOUS FEMINIST WRITINGS FROM *LA PRENSA*, LOS ANGELES

1. In her selection in this volume, María Rentería recovers this "forgotten" mother: Mrs. Rafaela López Aguado de Rayón.

2. The writer is referring to Sor Juana Inés de la Cruz here.

AURORA LUCERO-WHITE LEA

1. José de Espronceda (1808–1842), born and educated in Spain, was one of the most important, as well as politically rebellious, Spanish Romantic poets. His works include the novel *Sancho Saldaña* and other long lyrical poems, "El estudiante de Salamanca" (The student from Salamanca) and "El diablo mundo" (The devil world). The poem Lucero references is one of Espronceda's historical poems titled "El dos de mayo" (The second of May).

> 2. From the scepter of his Kings, the pieces
> from the soil, bloodied, he collected,
> And a new throne in his strong arms
> Lifted up, to his Prince he offered up.

ELENA ARIZMENDI MEJÍA

1. Cruz Blanca Neutral, formed in 1911 in Juárez, Mexico, was not associated with La Cruz Blanca, which was organized in 1913 by Leonor Villegas de Magnón and Jovita Idar.

CATALINA DULCHÉ ESCALANTE (CATALINA D'ERZELL)

1. Catalina D'Erzell's writings are readily available in Hispanic American Newspapers, 1808–1980, a database provided by Readex at the University of Arizona, among other libraries.

Works Cited

COLLECTED WORKS

Unless otherwise noted, all translations are by Joel Bollinger Pouwels, with subsequent edits by Neil J. Devereaux.

Ariana. "La mujer moderna y el hogar." *La Prensa*, 8 Nov. 1920, pp. 7–8. Arte Público Hispanic Historical Collection. Latino/Hispanic Historical Collection Series 1.

———. "Lo que no es el feminismo." *La Prensa*, 12 Oct. 1920, pp. 9+. Arte Público Hispanic Historical Collection. Latino/Hispanic Historical Collection Series 1.

Arizmendi Mejía, Elena. "El feminismo y la Liga Internacional de Mujeres Ibéricas e Hispano-Americanas." *El Heraldo de México*, vol. 8, no. 1427, 1 Oct. 1922, pp. 4+. America's Historical Newspapers.

Cárdenas, Isidra T. de. "¡Unifiquémonos!" *La Voz de la Mujer*, vol. 50, no. 9, 6 Sept. 1907, pp. 2–3. Arte Público Hispanic Historical Collection: Series 2.

Dulché Escalante, Catalina (Catalina D'Erzell). "La mujer y el arte. Teresa Farías de Isassi." *El Heraldo de México*, no. 575, 8 Jan. 1920, pp. 5+. America's Historical Newspapers.

Galindo, Hermila. "La mujer como colaboradora en la vida pública." *El Pueblo*, vol. 2, no. 188, 11 Apr. 1915, pp. 2+. Hemeroteca Nacional Digital de México.

———. "¡Laboremos!" *Sol de libertad Hermila Galindo: feminista, constitucionalista y primera censora legislativa en México*, edited by Rosa María Valles Ruiz, Instituto de Cultura del Estado de Durango, 2010, pp. 226–27.

Garza, María Luisa (Loreley). "[¿]Feministas . . . ? [¡]No! Femeninas!" *La Época*, vol. 4, no. 283, 12 Sept. 1920, pp. 3+. America's Historical Newspapers, 1808–1980.

———. "Las mujeres que escriben." *La Época*, vol. 7, no. 307, 27 Feb. 1921, pp. 9+. Hispanic American Newspapers, 1808–1980.

Gutiérrez de Mendoza, Juana Belén. "¡Ecce Homo!" *Mujeres y Revolución, 1900–1917*, edited by Ana Lau Jaiven and Carmen Ramos-Escandón, Instituto Nacional de Estudios Históricos de la Revolución Mexicana, 1993, pp. 182–83.

———. "Vésper siempre ocupará su puesto." *Vésper: Justicia y Libertad*, vol. 5, no. 1, 8 May 1910, p. 1. Benson Latin American Collection Digital Delivery System.

Gutiérrez de Mendoza, Juana Belén, and Elena Acuña y Rossetti. "A los mexicanos." *Vésper: Justicia y Libertad*, 15 May 1903, pp. 3+. Benson Latin American Collection Digital Delivery System.

Idar, Jovita (Astrea). "Debemos trabajar." *La Crónica*, 23 Nov. 1911, p. 2. Arte Público Hispanic Historical Collection: Series 1.

——— (Astrea). "Para la mujer que lee." *La Crónica*, 26 Oct. 1911, pp. 3–4. Arte Público Hispanic Historical Collection Series 1.

——— (A. V. Negra). "Por la raza: la conversación del nacionalismo." *La Crónica*, 17 Aug. 1911, p. 1. Arte Público Hispanic Historical Collection: Series 1.

——— (A. V. Negra). "Por la raza: la niñez mexicana en Texas." *La Crónica*, 10 Aug. 1911, p. 1. Arte Público Hispanic Historical Collection: Series 1.

"La Liga Femenil Mexicanista." *La Crónica*, vol. 3, no. 48, 30 Nov. 1911, p. 4. Arte Público Hispanic Historical Collection: Series 1.

"Liga Femenil Mexicanista." *La Crónica*, vol. 3, no. 41, 19 Oct. 1911, p. 1. Arte Público Hispanic Historical Collection: Series 1.

Lucero-White Lea, Aurora. "Shall the Spanish Language Be Taught in the Schools of New Mexico." *New Mexico Normal University Bulletin*, no. 23, Jan. 1911, n.p., New Mexico Highlands University.

Manresa de Pérez, Concepción. "Mujeres de nuestra época." *Las Hijas del Anáhuac*, vol. 1, no. 2, 4 Dec. 1887, pp. 7, 19. C. L. Sonnichsen Special Collections.

"Mujeres mexicanas notables." *La Prensa*, vol. 7, no. 44, 5 Apr. 1919, pp. 7+. America's Historical Newspapers, 1808–1980.

"Opiniones de algunas de las feministas que han concurrido al Congreso de La Haya en favor de la paz." *La Prensa*, vol. 3, no. 424, 7 Jan. 1916, pp. 7+. America's Historical Newspapers: 1808–1980.

Paz. "Á las Violetas del Anáhuac." *Las Hijas del Anáhuac*, vol. 1, no. 15, 11 Mar. 1888, pp. 173–74. C. L. Sonnichsen Special Collections.

Ramírez, Sara Estela. "¡Surge! A la mujer." *La Crónica*, 9 Apr. 1910, p. 3. Arte Público Hispanic Historical Collection: Series 1.

Rentería, María. "Leona Vicario y Rafaela López." *La Crónica*, 19 Oct. 1911, p. 2. Arte Público Hispanic Historical Collection: Series 1.

Sáenz Royo, Artemisa (Xóchitl). "La mujer en el pasado, en el presente y en el porvenir." *La Época*, 31 Oct. 1920, pp. 15–17. Arte Público Hispanic Historical Collection: Series 1.

Villarreal González, Andrea. "A qué venimos." *Mujeres y Revolución, 1900–1907*, edited by Ana Lau Javien and Carmen Ramos-Escondón, Insituto Nacional de Estudios Históricos de la Revolución Mexicana, 1993, pp. 192–93.

Villegas de Magnón, Leonor. "Adelanto de los mexicanos de Texas." *La Crónica*, 21 Sept. 1911, pp. 4+. Arte Público Hispanic Historical Collection: Series 1.

———. "Evolución Mexicana." *La Crónica*, 7 Sept. 1911, p. 1. Arte Público Hispanic Historical Collection: Series 1.

Wright de Kleinhans, Laureana. "Capítulo xxi. La lectura." *Educación y superación femenina en el siglo XIX: dos ensayos de Laureana Wright*, edited by Lourdes Alvarado, U Nacional Autónoma de México, 2005.

———. "La mujer artista y artesana." *El Tiempo*, 17 Dec. 1891, pp. 2–4. Arte Público Hispanic Historical Collection: Series 1.

———. "Saludo y prospecto." *Las Hijas del Anáhuac*, vol. 1, no. 1, 4 Dec. 1887, pp. 1+. C. L. Sonnichsen Special Collections.

Zapata de Puig, Catalina. "La mujer de este siglo." *Las Hijas del Anáhuac*, vol. 1, no. 13, 26 Feb. 1888, pp. 151–53. C. L. Sonnichsen Special Collections.

SOURCES CITED

Album Recreativo, vol. 1, no. 8, 5 June 1882, pp. 1–4. Hemeroteca Nacional Digital de México.

Alvarado, Lourdes. *Educación y superación femenina en el siglo XIX: dos ensayos de Laureana Wright*. U Nacional Autónoma de México, 2005.

Anzaldúa, Gloria. *Borderlands/La Frontera: The New Mestiza*. Aunt Lute, 1987.

Arizmendi, Elena. *Feminismo Internacional: Revista Mensual Ilustrada*, vol. 1, nos. 1, 2, 5–7, 10, 1923. Arte Público Hispanic Historical Collection: Series 2.

Arrieta Corral, Eduardo. "Juana Belén Gutiérrez de Mendoza, olvidada heroína del periodismo político mexicano." *Tres revolucionarios de México: Tomas Urbina, Orestes Pereyra, Juana Belén Gutiérrez*, edited by Eduardo Arrieta Corral, Antonio Arreola, and Javier Guerrero Romero, Comisión de Reinhumación y Homenaje, 1991, pp. 11–20.

Baca, Damián. *Mestiz@ Scripts, Digital Migrations, and the Territories of Writing*. Palgrave MacMillan, 2008.

Baca, Damián, and Victor Villanueva, editors. *Rhetorics of the Americas: 3114 BCE to 2012 CE*. Palgrave MacMillan, 2009.

Baeza Ventura, Gabriela. *La imagen de la mujer en la crónica del "México de afuera."* U Autónoma de Ciudad Juárez, 2006.

Beals, Carleton. "The Mexican as He Is." *The North American Review*, vol. 214, no. 791, Oct. 1921, pp. 538–46.

Bellos, David. "Fictions of the Foreign: The Paradox of "Foreign-Soundingness."" *In Translation: Translators on Their Work and What it Means*, edited by Esther Allen and Susan Bernofsky, Columbia UP, 2013, pp. 31–43.

Benavides, Adán and Agnes L. McAlester. *Independent Newspapers in Mexico in the Nineteenth Century: Guide to the Microfilm Set*. Nettie Lee Benson Latin American Collection, U of Texas Libraries.

Bessette, Jean. *Retroactivism in American Lesbian Collectives: Composing Pasts and Futures*. Southern Illinois UP, 2017.

Biesecker, Barbara. "Coming to Terms with Recent Attempts to Write Women in to the History of Rhetoric." *Philosophy & Rhetoric*, vol. 25, no. 2, 1992, pp. 140–61.

Bizzell, Patricia, and Herzberg, Bruce, editors. *The Rhetorical Tradition: Readings from Classical Times to the Present*. 2nd ed., Bedford/St. Martin's, 2001.

Bokser, Julie. "Reading and Writing Sor Juana's Arch: Rhetorics of Belonging, *Criollo* Identity and Feminist Histories." *Rhetoric Society Quarterly*, vol. 42, no. 2, 2012, pp. 143–66.

———. "Sor Juana's *Divine Narcissus:* A New World Rhetoric of Listening." *Rhetoric Society Quarterly*, vol. 40, no. 3, 2010, pp. 224–46.

Bonfil Batalla, Guillermo. *México Profundo: Reclaiming a Civilization*. Translated by Philip A. Dennis, U of Texas P, 1996.

Browdy de Hernandez, Jennifer, editor. *Women Writing Resistance: Essays on Latin America and the Caribbean*. South End P, 2005.

Calderón, Héctor. *Narratives of Greater Mexico: Essays on Chicano Literary History, Genre, and Borders.* U of Texas P, 2004.
Campbell, Karlyn Kohrs. *Man Cannot Speak for Her: Key Texts of the Early Feminists.* Praeger, 1989.
Cano, Gabriela. "Las feministas en campaña: la primera mitad del siglo XX." *Debate Feminista*, no. 4, 1990, pp. 269–92.
———. *Se llamaba Elena Arizmendi.* Tusquets Editores, 2010.
Cano, Gabriela, and Georgette José Valenzuela, editors. *Cuatro estudios de género en el México urbano del siglo XIX.* Programa Universitario de Estudios de Género, U Nacional Autónoma de México, 2001.
Castillo, Debra A., and María-Scorro Tabuenca Córdoba. *Border Women: Writing from La Frontera.* U of Minnesota P, 2002.
Christoph, Julie Nelson. "Reconceiving Ethos in Relation to the Personal: Strategies of Placement in Pioneer Women's Writing." *College English*, vol. 64, no. 6, 2002, pp. 660–79.
Cisneros, Josue David. *The Border Crossed Us: Rhetorics of Borders, Citizenship, and Latina/o Identity.* U of Alabama P, 2014.
Cockcroft, James D. *Intellectual Precursors of the Mexican Revolution, 1900–1913.* U of Texas P, 1968.
———. *Latinos in the Struggle for Equal Education: The Hispanic Experience in the Americas.* Franklin Watts, 1995.
Cortés, Carlos. "The Mexican American Press." *The Ethnic Press in the United States*, edited by Sally M. Miller, Greenwood P, 1987, pp. 247–60.
Cotera, Martha. "Feminism: The Chicana and Anglo Versions–A Historical Analysis." *Chicana Feminist Thought: The Basic Historical Writings*, edited by Alma M. García, Routledge, 1997, pp. 223–31.
Cott, Nancy. *The Bonds of Womanhood: 'Woman's Sphere' in New England, 1780–1835.* Yale UP, 1977.
Crane, Stephen. "The Main Streets of This City." *Stephen Crane in the West and Mexico*, edited by Stephen Katz, Kent State UP, 1970, pp. 66–69.
De León, Arnoldo, editor. *War Along the Border: The Mexican Revolution and Tejano Communities*, Texas A&M UP, 2012.
Dingo, Rebecca. *Networking Arguments: Rhetoric, Transnational Feminism, and Public Policy Writing.* U of Pittsburgh P, 2012.
Donawerth, Jane, editor. *Rhetorical Theory by Women before 1900.* Rowman & Littlefield, 2002.
Dulché Escalante, Catalina. "Lo de matrimonios a plazo." *El Continental*, vol. 12, no. 124, 5 Nov. 1937, pp. 4+. American Historical Newspapers.
———. "Mujer revolucionaria." *El Continental*, vol. 12, no. 130, Nov. 11, 1937, pp. 4+. American Historical Newspapers.
———. "Se acabaron las mujeres musas." *La Prensa*, vol. 25, no. 279, Nov. 18, 1937, pp. 3+, American Historical Newspapers.

E. A. "Loreley y el Congreso de Mujeres en México." *Feminismo Internacional*, 1 July 1923, p. 11. Arte Público Hispanic Historical Collection: Series 2.

"El Estudiante." *La Crónica*. Translated by Jessica Enoch and Raquel Morán Tellez, vol. 3, no. 41, 19 Oct. 1911, p. 1. Arte Público Hispanic Historical Collection Series 1.

"El segundo año de vida de La Crónica en su segunda época." Translated by Lisa Lawson and Raquel Morán Tellez, *La Crónica*, vol. 2, no. 104, 31 Dec. 1911, p. 6+. Arte Público Hispanic Historical Collection Series 1.

Enoch, Jessica. "'Para la Mujer': Defining a Chicana Feminist Rhetoric at the Turn of the Century." *College English*, vol. 67, no. 1, 2004, pp. 20–37.

———. *Refiguring Rhetorical Education: Women Teaching African American, Native American, and Chicano/a Students, 1865–1911*. Southern Illinois UP, 2008.

Eves, Rosalyn Collings. "A Recipe for Remembrance: Memory and Identity in African American Women's Cookbooks." *Rhetoric Society Quarterly*, vol. 24, no. 3, 2005, pp. 280–97.

Ezzaher, Lahcen Elyazghi. *Three Arabic Treatises on Aristotle's Rhetoric: Commentaries of al-Farabi, Avicenna, and Averroes*. Southern Illinois UP, 2015.

Farr, Marcia. "Playing with Race in Transnational Space: Rethinking Mestizaje." *English and Ethnicity*, edited by Janina Brutt-Griffler and Catherine Evans Davies, Palgrave, 2006, pp. 229–258.

Fernheimer, Janice. "Talimidae Rhetoricae: Drashing Up Models and Methods for Jewish Rhetorical Studies." *College English*, vol. 72, no. 6, 2010, pp. 577–89.

Foppa, Alaída. "The First Feminist Congress in Mexico, 1916." Translated by Helene F. de Aguilar. *Signs*, vol. 5, no. 1, 1979, pp. 192–99.

Frederick, Jake. "Without Impediment: Crossing Borders in Colonial Mexico" *The Americas*, vol. 67, no. 4, 2011, pp. 495–515.

García, Mario T. *Desert Immigrants: The Mexicans of El Paso, 1880–1920*. Yale UP, 1981.

Garner, Paul. *Porfirio Díaz: Profile in Power*. Longman, 2001.

Gibson, Karen Bush. *Jovita Idar*. Mitchell Lane P, 2003.

Gilyard, Keith and Vorris Nunley, editors. *Rhetoric and Ethnicity*. Heinemann, 2004.

Glenn, Cheryl. *Rhetoric Retold: Regendering the Rhetorical Tradition from Antiquity to the Renaissance*. Southern Illinois UP, 1997.

Gold, David, and Catherine Hobbs. *Educating the Southern Woman: Speech, Writing, and Race at the Public Women's Colleges, 1884–1945*. Southern Illinois UP, 2013.

Grider, Sylvia Ann, and Lou Halsell Rodenberger. *Texas Women Writers: A Tradition of Their Own*. Texas A&M UP, 1997.

Grossman, Edith. *Why Translation Matters*. Yale UP, 2011.

Gutiérrez, Félix. "Spanish-Language Media in America: Background, Resources, History." *Journalism History*, vol. 4, no. 2, Summer 1977, pp. 34–41, 65–67.

Gutiérrez-Witt, Laura. "Cultural Continuity in the Face of Change: Hispanic Printers in Texas." *Recovering the U.S. Hispanic Literary Heritage*, edited by Erlinda Gonzales-Berry and Chuck Tatum, vol. 2, Arte Público P, 1996, pp. 260–78.

Hart, John Mason. *Revolutionary Mexico: The Coming and Process of the Mexican Revolution*. U of California P, 1997.

Hedrick, Tace. *Mestizo Modernism: Race, Nation, and Identity in Latin American Culture, 1900–1940*. Rutgers UP, 2003.

Hernández, Sonia. *Working Women into the Borderlands*. Texas A&M UP, 2014.

Hernández Carballido, Elvira. *Dos Violetas del Anáhuac*. DEMAC, 2010.

Hesford, Wendy. *Spectacular Rhetorics: Human Rights Visions, Recognitions, Feminisms*. Duke UP, 2011.

Hogg, Charlotte. *From the Garden Club: Rural Women Writing Community*. U of Nebraska P, 2006.

———. "Including Conservative Women's Rhetoric in an 'Ethics of Hope and Care.'" *Rhetoric Review*, vol. 34, no. 4, 2015, pp. 391–408.

Horner, Bruce, and John Trimbur. "English Only and U.S. College Composition." *College Composition and Communication*, vol. 53, no. 4, 2002, pp. 594–630.

Houck, David, and David Dixon. *Women and the Civil Rights Movement, 1954–1965*. U of Mississippi P, 2011.

Hutton, Frankie and Barbara Straus Reed, editors. *Outsiders in 19th-Century Press History: Multicultural Perspectives*. Bowling Green Popular P, 1995.

Iberia: El Periódico de Literatura, Ciencias, Artes, Agricultura, Comercio, Industria y Mejoras Materiales, vol. 5, no. 786, 23 Oct. 1869. Hemeroteca Nacional Digital de México.

Jackson II, Ronald L., and Elaine B. Richardson, editors. *Understanding African American Rhetoric: Classical Origins to Contemporary Innovations*. Routledge, 2003.

Johnson, Nan. *Gender and Rhetorical Space in American Life, 1866–1910*. Southern Illinois UP, 2002.

Jones, Willis Knapp. *Beyond the Spanish American Footlights*. U of Texas P, 1966.

Kanellos, Nicolás. "A Socio-Historic Study of Hispanic Newspapers in the United States." *Recovering the U.S. Hispanic Literary Heritage*, edited by Ramón Gutierrez and Genaro Padilla, vol. 1, Arte Público P, 1993, pp. 107–28.

Kanellos, Nicolás, Kenya Dworkin y Méndez, José B. Fernández, Erlinda Gonzaléz-Berry, Agnes Lugo-Ortiz, and Charles Tatum, editors. *Herencia: The Anthology of Hispanic Literature of the United States*, Oxford UP, 2002.

Kells, Michelle Hall. *Héctor P. García: Everyday Rhetoric and Mexican American Civil Rights*. Southern Illinois UP, 2006.

Knight, Alan. *The Mexican Revolution*. Vols. 1 & 2, U of Nebraska P, 1990.

Kraditor, Aileen. *Up from the Pedestal: Selected Writings in the History of American Feminism*. Quadrangle, 1968.

Lau, Ana. "Expresiones políticas femeninas en el México del siglo XX: el Ateneo Mexicano de Mujeres y la Alianza de Mujeres de México (1934–1953)." *Orden social e identidad de género México, siglos XIX y XX*, edited by María Teresa

Fernández Aceves, Carmen Ramos-Escandón, and Susie Porter, U de Guadalajara, 2006, pp. 93–124.

Lau Javien, Ana, and Carmen Ramos-Escandón, editors. *Mujeres y Revolución, 1900–1917*. Instituto Nacional de Estudios Históricos de la Revolución Mexicana, 1993.

León, Arnoldo de. *They Called Them Greasers: Anglo Attitudes toward Mexicans in Texas, 1821–1900*. U of Texas P, 1983.

Lima Costa, Claudia de, and Sonia E. Álvarez. "Dislocating the Sign: Toward a Translocal Feminist Politics of Translation." *Signs*, vol. 39, no. 3, 2014, pp. 557–63.

Limón, José. "El Primer Congreso Mexicanista de 1911: A Precursor to Contemporary Chicanismo." *Aztlán*, vol. 5, no. 1, 1974, pp. 85–117.

Lipson, Carol, and Roberta A. Binkley, editors. *Rhetoric Before and Beyond the Greeks*. State University of New York P, 2004.

Logan, Shirley Wilson. Introduction. *With Pen and Voice: A Critical Anthology of Nineteenth-Century African American Women*. Southern Illinois UP, 1995, pp. xi-xvi.

———. *"We are Coming": The Persuasive Discourse of Nineteenth-Century Black Women*. Southern Illinois UP, 1995.

———, editor. *With Pen and Voice: A Critical Anthology of Nineteenth-Century African American Women*. Southern Illinois UP, 1995.

Lomas, Clara. Introduction. "Revolutionary Women and the Alternative Press in the Borderlands." *The Rebel: Leonor Villegas de Magnón*, edited by Clara Lomas, Arte Público P, 1994, pp. xi-lvi.

———. "Transborder Discourse: The Articulation of Gender on the Borderlands in the Early Twentieth Century." *Gender on the Borderlands: The Frontiers Reader*, edited by Antonia Castañeda, U of Nebraska P, 2007, pp. 51–74.

Lomas, Clara, and Gabriela Baeza Ventura, editors. *Recovering the U.S. Hispanic Literary Heritage*. Vol. 8, Arte Público P, 2012.

Luna Lawhn, Juanita. "María Luisa Garza: Novelist of *El México de Afuera*." *Double Crossings / Entre Cruzamientos: Anthology of Research Articles Delivered at: 9th International Conference of Latino Cultures in North America*, edited by Mario Martín Flores and Carlos von Son, Ediciones Nuevo Espacio, 2001, pp. 83–96.

Lund, Joshua. *The Impure Imagination: Toward a Critical Hybridity in Latin American Writing*. U of Minnesota P, 2006.

———. *The Mestizo State: Reading Race in Modern Mexico*. U of Minnesota P, 2012.

Lunsford, Andrea. "Toward a Mestiza Rhetoric: Gloria Anzaldúa on Composition and Postcoloniality." *JAC*, vol. 18, no. 1, 1998, pp. 1–27.

Macías, Anna. *Against All Odds: The Feminist Movement in Mexico to 1940*. Greenwood P, 1982.

Mao, Lu Ming. *Reading Chinese Fortune Cookie: The Making of Chinese American Rhetoric*. Utah UP, 2006.

Martinez-Echazábal, Lourdes. "Mestizaje and the Discourse of National/Cultural Identity in Latin America, 1845–1959." *Latin American Perspectives*, vol. 25, no. 3, 1998, pp. 21–42.

"Medalla á la Srita. Arizmendi." *El Regidor*, vol. 23, no. 118, 20 July 1911, p. 3. America's Historical Newspapers.

Meléndez, A. Gabriel. *Spanish-Language Newspapers in New Mexico, 1834–1858*. U of Arizona P, 2005.

Melero, Pilar. "Sara Estela Ramírez and Andrea Villarreal González: Revolutionary Voices?" *Recovering the U.S. Hispanic Literary Heritage*, edited by Antonia I. Castañeda and A. Gabriel Meléndez, vol. 6, Arte Público P, 2006, pp. 182–98.

———. *Mythological Constructs of Mexican Feminity*. Palgrave MacMillan, 2015.

Menchaca, Martha. *Recovering History, Recovering Race: The Indian, Black, and White Roots of Mexican Americans*. U of Texas P, 2002.

Mendieta Alatorre, Ángeles. *Juana Belén Gutiérrez de Mendoza: Extraordinaria Precursora de la Revolución Mexicana*. U México, D.F., Copilco, 1983.

Meyer, Doris. "Reading Early Neomexicano Newspapers: Yesterday and Today." *Recovering U.S. Hispanic Literary Heritage*, edited by María Herrera-Sobek and Virginia Sánchez-Korrol, vol. 3, Arte Público P, 2000, pp. 402–11.

Montejano, David. *Anglos and Mexicans in the Making of Texas, 1836–1986*. U of Texas P, 1987.

Moulder, M. Amanda. "'By Women, You Were Brought Forth into This World': Cherokee Women's Oratorical Education in the Late Eighteenth Century." *Educating the Southern Woman: Speech, Writing, and Race at the Public Women's Colleges, 1884–1945*, edited by David Gold and Catherine Hobbs, Routledge, 2014, pp. 19–37.

Moya, Paula M. L. "Chicana Feminism and Postmodernist Theory." *Signs*, vol. 26, no. 2, 2001, pp. 441–83.

Murguía de Aveleyra, Mateana. "Laureana Wright de Kleinhans." *Violetas del Anáhuac*, 10 June 1888, pp. 314–17. Hemeroteca Nacional Digital de México.

Napiorski, Maria Patricia. "The Politics of Border Crossing: A Transnational Encounter in the Work of María Luisa Garza." *Hispanic Journal*, vol. 29, no. 2, 2008, pp. 39–53.

"Nueva sociedad." *La Libertad*, vol. 1, no. 258, 8 December 1878, pp. 3. Hemeroteca Nacional Digital de México.

Orellana Trinidad, Laura. *Hermila Galindo: una mujer moderna*. Instituto Nacional de Bellas Artes, 2001.

Olson, Christa, and René Agustín De los Santos. "Expanding the Idea of América." *Rhetoric Society Quarterly*, vol. 45, no. 3, 2015, pp. 193–98.

Palomo Acosta, Teresa. "LA CRÓNICA." *Handbook of Texas Online*, Texas State Historical Association, 10 June 2010, www.tshaonline.org/handbook/online/articles/ee106. Accessed 4 June 2015.

Paredes, Américo. *Between Two Worlds*. Arte Público P, 1991.

Pérez, Emma. *The Decolonial Imaginary: Writing Chicanas into History*. Indiana UP: 1999.

Pough, Gwendolyn, and Elaine Richardson. *Home Girls Make Some Noise: Hip Hop Feminism Anthology*. Parker, 2007.

Pouwels, Joel Bollinger. *Political Journalism by Mexican Women during the Age of Revolution 1876–1940.* Edwin Mellen P, 2006.

Powell, Malea. "Rhetorics of Survivance: How American Indians Use Writing." *College Composition and Communication*, vol. 53, no. 3, 2002, pp. 396–434.

Queen, Mary. "Transnational Feminist Rhetorics in a Digital World." *College English*, vol. 70, no. 5, 2008, pp. 471–89.

Ramírez, Cristina D. *Occupying Our Space: The Mestiza Rhetorics of Mexican Women Journalists and Activists, 1875–1942.* U of Arizona P, 2015.

Ramos Escandón, Carmen. "Quinientos años de olvido: historiografía e historia de la mujer en México." *Secuencia: nueva época*, no. 36, 1996, pp. 121–50.

Ratcliffe, Krista. *Rhetorical Listening: Identification, Gender, Whiteness.* Southern Illinois UP, 2005.

Richards, Rebecca. *Transnational Feminist Rhetorics and Gendered Leadership in Global Politics: From Daughters of Destiny to Iron Ladies.* Lexington Books, 2014.

Ritchie, Joy, and Kate Ronald, editors. *Available Means: An Anthology of Women's Rhetoric(s).* U of Pittsburgh P, 2001.

Rivas-Rodríguez, Maggie. "Ignacio E. Lozano: The Mexican Exile Publisher Who Conquered San Antonio and Los Angeles." *American Journalism*, vol. 21, no. 1, 2004, pp. 75–89.

Rodríguez, America. *Making Latino News: Race, Language, Class.* Sage, 1999.

Romano, Susan. "The Historical Catalina Hernández: Inhabiting the Topoi of Feminist Historiography." *Rhetoric Society Quarterly*, vol. 37, no. 4, 2007, pp. 453–80.

Romero, Manuel M. "Impresiones de la prensa." *Las Hijas del Anáhuac*, vol. 1, no. 3, 18 Dec. 1887, p. 36. Hemeroteca Nacional Digital de México.

Royster, Jacqueline Jones. *Traces of a Stream: Literacy and Social Change among African American Women.* U of Pittsburgh P, 2000.

Royster, Jacqueline Jones, and Gesa Kirsch. *Feminist Rhetorical Practices: New Horizons for Rhetoric, Composition, and Literacy Studies.* Southern Illinois UP, 2012.

Ruiz, Vicki L. *From out of the Shadows: Mexican Women in Twentieth-Century America.* Oxford UP, 1998.

Ruiz, Vicki, and Virginia Sánchez Korrol. *Latinas in the United States: A Historical Encyclopedia.* Indiana UP, 2006.

Salvídar-Hull, Sonia. *Feminism on the Border: Chicana Gender Politics and Literature.* U of California P, 2000.

Sáenz Royo, Artemisa. "México para los mexicanos." *El Pueblo*, vol. 2, no. 344, 17 Sept. 1915, pp. 4+. Hemeroteca Nacional Digital de México.

Serviss, Tricia. "Femicide and Rhetorics of *Coadyuvante* in Ciudad Juárez: Valuing Rhetorical Traditions in the Americas." *College English*, vol. 75, no. 6, 2013, pp. 608–28.

Shaver, Lisa. *Beyond the Pulpit: Women's Roles in the Antebellum Religious Press.* U of Pittsburgh P, 2012.

Sohn, Katherine Kelleher. *Whistlin' and Crowin' Women of Appalachia: Literacy Practices since College.* Southern Illinois UP, 2006.

Souza Salles, Virgilina de. "Congreso Femenismo." *Revista Femenina*, vol. 13, no. 151, 1926, p. 105.

"Sra. Leonor Villegas de Mag[n]ón." *La Crónica*, 12 Sept. 1911, p. 1, Arte Público Hispanic Historical Collection Series 1.

Tovar, Inés Hernández. "Sara Estela Ramírez: The Early Twentieth-Century Texas-Mexican Poet." 1984. U of Houston, PhD dissertation.

Tuñón Pablos, Julia. *Women in Mexico: A Past Unveiled.* Translated by Alan Hynds. U of Texas P, 2005.

———, editor. *Voces a la mujeres: antología del pensamiento feminista mexicano, 1873–1953.* U Autónoma de la Ciudad de México, 2011.

Two Republics, vol. 33, no. 39, 14 Aug. 1891, p. 2. Hemeroteca Nacional Digital de México.

Valles Ruiz, Rosa María. *Hermila Galindo: Sol de libertad: Feminista, constitucionalista y primera censora legislativa en México.* Instituto de Cultura del Estado de Durango, 2010.

Vaughan, Mary Kay. "Women, Class and Education in Mexico, 1880–1928." *Latin American Perspectives*, vol. 4, nos. 1/2, 1977, pp. 135–52.

Vento, Arnoldo Carlos. *Mestizo: The History, Culture and Politics of the Mexican and the Chicano—The Emerging Mestizo-Americans.* University of America, 1998.

Venuti, Lawrence, editor. *Rethinking Translation: Discourse, Subjectivity, Ideology.* Routledge, 1992.

Villaneda, Alicia. *Justicia y Libertad: Juana Belén Gutiérrez de Mendoza.* Documentación y Estudios de Mujeres, 1994.

Wang, Bo. "'Breaking the Age of Flower Vases': Lu Yin's Feminist Rhetoric." *Rhetoric Review*, vol. 28, no. 3, 2009, pp. 246–64.

Welter, Barbara. "The Cult of True Womanhood: 1820–1860." *American Quarterly*, vol. 18, no. 1, Summer 1966, pp. 151–74.

You, Xiaoye. *Writing in the Devil's Tongue: A History of English Composition in China.* Southern Illinois UP, 2010.

Zapata de Puig, Catalina. "Mi Lira." *Diario del Hogar*, vol. 8, no. 118, 31 Jan. 1889, pp. 3+. Hemeroteca Nacional Digital de México.

Zavella, Patricia. "Reflections on Diversity among Chicanas." *Frontiers*, vol. 12, no. 2, 1991, pp. 73–85.

Index

Page numbers followed by n *indicate notes.*
The page number 9 in italics denotes a map.

Acosta Cárdenas, Miguelina, 204
activism, 227n1, 230n1
Acuña y Rossetti, Elisa, 3, 19, 67; biography, 68–69; editorial collaborations, 69–70, 119
—writings: "A los mexicanos" ("To the Mexicans") (Gutiérrez de Mendoza and Acuña y Rossetti), 16, 69–70, 71–74 (español), 75–78 (English text)
Addams, Jane, 180–81, 183–84
"Adelanto de los mexicanos de Texas" ("Progress of Mexicans in Texas") (Villegas de Magnón), 111, 115–16 (español), 116–18 (English text)
adelitas, 167
Adriana. *See* Arizmendi Mejía, Elena
Alabahba, 188, 192
"A la mujer" (To woman) (Magón), 19
El Álbum de la Mujer: Ilustración Hispano-Americana (Women's Album: Hispanic-American Illustration), 23
Album Recreativo (Recreational Album), 43
Alcestis, 232n2
Allen, Ruth, 18
Alma Femenina (Feminine Spirit), 154
"A los mexicanos" ("To the Mexicans") (Gutiérrez de Mendoza and Acuña y Rossetti), 16, 69–70, 71–74 (español), 75–78 (English text)
Altamirano, Ignacio Manuel, 25
Alvarado, Lourdes, 6
Alvarado, Salvador, 232n9
Álvarez, Sonia E., 12, 14
América, 226n14

Americanization, 12
America's Historical Newspapers, 6, 20
Los amores de Gaona: Apuntes realistas de Loreley (The Many Loves of Gaona: Realistic Reflections from Loreley) (Garza), 156
Anáhuac (term), 25
Ancient Greece, 227n2
Anna Macías, Anna, 19
anonymous writings, 21; feminist writings from *La Prensa*, Los Angeles, 186–87; feminist writings from *La Prensa*, San Antonio, 177–78; on La Liga Femenil Mexicanista (The Mexican Feminine League), 122–27
—specific works: "Liga Femenil Mexicanista" ("Mexicanist Feminine League") (Anonymous), 123 (español), 124–25 (English text); "La Liga Femenil Mexicanista" ("The Mexicanist Feminine League") (Anonymous), 126 (español), 127 (English text); "Mujeres mexicanas notables" ("Notable Mexican Women"), 3, 10, 186–87, 188–91 (español), 191–95 (English text); "Opiniones de algunas de las feministas que han concurrido al Congreso de La Haya en favor de la paz" (Opinions of Some of the Feminists Who Attended the Congress of The Hague in Favor of Peace) (Anonymous), 177–78, 179–82 (español), 182–85 (English text)
Anti-reelection Convention (April 1910, Mexico), 228n5
El Anunciador (The Announcer), 154

Anzaldúa, Gloria, 3, 5, 11
"A qué venimos" ("What We Have Come For") (Villarreal), 135–36, 137–38 (español), 138–39 (English text)
archives, 20–21
Ariana, 5, 8, 135, 177; biography, 167–68
—writings: "Lo que no es el feminismo" ("What Feminism Is Not"), 167–68, 173–74 (español), 175–76 (English text); "La mujer moderna y el hogar" ("The Modern Woman and the Home") (Ariana), 167–68, 169–70 (español), 171–72 (English text)
Aristotle, 5
Arizmendi Mejía, Elena, 5, 7, 17, 19; biography, 203–4
—writings: "El feminismo y la Liga Internacional de Mujeres Ibéricas e Hispano-Americanas" ("Feminism and the International League of Iberian and Hispanic-American Women"), 205–10 (español), 211–16 (English text)
Arizona, 17
Arnold, Lisa, 13
Arriaga, Camilo, 69
Arriaga, Ponciano, 228n2
Arrieta Corral, Eduardo, 68
Arte Público Hispanic Historical Collection, 6, 20
artistas y artesanas (artists and artisans): "La mujer artista y artesana" ("The Woman Artist and Artisan") (Wright de Kleinhans), 26, 37–39 (español), 40–42 (English text)
Astrea, 97, 229–30n2. *See also* Idar, Jovita
—writings: "Debemos trabajar" ("We Must Work"), 26, 97, 107–8 (español), 108–9 (English text); "Para la mujer que lee" ("To the Woman Who Reads"), 97, 104 (español), 105–6 (English text)

Atalanta, 232n2
Atotoxtli, 189, 192
Aurora, 119

Baca, Damián, 3–5, 13
Baeza Ventura, Gabriela, 6, 156
Bartola, María, 189, 193
Battle of Icamole, 231n7
Beals, Carleton, 18
Belem prison (Mexico City), 228n4
bellas letras (fine arts), 191, 194; *Venus with a Mirror* (Titian), 233n6
Benson Latin American Collection, 20
Biesecker, Barbara, 8
Bizzell, Patricia, 5
Bokser, Julie, 4–5
border, U.S.-Mexico, 11–12, 226n11
Browdy de Hernandez, Jennifer, 5
Burgos, Carmen de, 204
Bustamante, Carlos María, 186, 189, 194

C. L. Sonnichsen Special Collections, 20
Calderón, Héctor, 196–97
California, 17, 230n4
Camargo de la Merced, Father, 190, 194
Canagaraja, Suresh, 13
Cano, Gabriela, 6
Cárdenas, Isidra T. de, 8, 19, 231n1; biography, 140–41
—writings: "¡Unifiquémonos!" ("Let Us Unite!"), 140–41, 142–43 (español), 144–45 (English text)
Cárdenas, León, 231n1
Carranza Garza, José Venustiano, 85, 229n8, 232n8
—writings about: *La doctrina Carranza y el acercamiento indolatino* (The Carranza Doctrine: An Indo-Latin Approach) (Galindo), 85–86; *El Venustiano Carranza que yo conocí* (The Venustiano Carranza That I Knew) (Sáenz Royo), 146

"Carta abierta" ("An Open Letter") (Paz), 10, 61–62, 63–64 (español), 65–66 (English text)
caste system, 2–3, 225n7
Castillo, Debra A., 5
Castillo, Guadalupe, 17
Chicana feminist activities, 230n1
children—writings about: "La infancia" (Childhood) (Zapata de Puig), 44; "Por la raza: la niñez mexicana en Texas" ("For the Mexican People: Mexican Children in Texas") (Negra), 3, 97, 98–99 (español), 99–100 (English text)
Chinaco, 68
Cisneros, Josue David, 15
citizenship, 20
clothing, 232n3
Cockcroft, James, 15
coercive nationalism, 155
Colegio Zaragoza, 85
Colorado, 17
colors of protest, 227n1
Congreso de la Haya (Congress of The Hague)—writings about: "Opiniones de algunas de las feministas que han concurrido al Congreso de La Haya en favor de la paz" (Opinions of Some of the Feminists Who Attended the Congress of The Hague in Favor of Peace) (Anonymous), 177–78, 179–82 (español), 182–85 (English text)
Congreso Feminista de México (Feminist Congress of Mexico), 228n2, 232n9
Congreso Feminista de Yucatán (Feminist Congress of Yucutan), 85, 228nn1–2
El Congreso Mexicanista (Mexican Congress), 111
Constitutionalist Congress (Mexico), 86
El Continental (The Continent)— articles: "Lo de matrimonios a plazo" (The matter of fixed-term marriages) (D'Erzell), 218; "Mujer revolucionaria" (Revolutionary woman) (D'Erzell), 218
Correa Zapata, Dolores, 24
corregidora (word), 230n1
La Corregidora, 119
Cotera, Martha, 128
Cortés, Carlos, 17
Courtney, Kathleen, 181 (español), 184 (English text)
Coxcatcotzín, 189 (español), 192 (English text)
Crane, Stephen, 18
La Crónica (The Chronicle), 17, 229–30n2, 230n1; contributors, 96–97, 110–11, 119, 122, 128; location, 9, 9; microfilm collection, 20
—articles, essays, poetry: "Adelanto de los mexicanos de Texas" ("Progress of Mexicans in Texas") (Villegas de Magnón), 111, 115–16 (español), 116–18 (English text); "Debemos trabajar" ("We Must Work") (Astrea), 26, 97, 107–8 (español), 108–9 (English text); "Evolución mexicana" ("Mexican Evolution") (Villegas de Magnón), 26, 111, 112–13 (español), 113–14 (English text); "Leona Vicario y Rafaela Lopez" (Rentería), 7, 128–29, 130–32 (español), 132–34 (English text); "Liga Femenil Mexicanista" ("Mexicanist Feminine League") (Anonymous), 123 (español), 124–25 (English text); "La Liga Femenil Mexicanista" ("The Mexicanist Feminine League") (Anonymous), 126 (español), 127 (English text); "Para la mujer que lee" ("To the Woman Who Reads") (Astrea), 97, 104 (español), 105–6 (English text); "Por la raza: la conservación del nacionalismo" ("For the Mexican People: The Preservation of

La Crónica (continued)
Nationalism") (Negra), 97, 101–2 (español), 102–3 (English text); "Por la raza: la niñez mexicana en Texas" ("For the Mexican People: Mexican Children in Texas") (Negra), 3, 97, 98–99 (español), 99–100 (English text); "¡Surge! A la mujer" ("Rise Up! To Womankind") (Ramírez), 119, 120–21 (English text), 120 (español)
"Crónicas Femeninas" (Women's Chronicles) (Garza), 154
La Cruz Azul Mexicana (Mexican Blue Cross), 156
La Cruz Blanca (Mexican White Cross), 96, 110, 234n1
Cruz Blanca Neutral (Neutral White Cross), 203, 234n1
Cuauhtémoc (Guatimozín), 61, 228n2

"Debemos trabajar" ("We Must Work") (Astrea), 26, 97, 107–8 (español), 108–9 (English text)
La decena trágica, 230n3
de Jesús de León, María, 122
del Alba, María, 24
de la Merced, Father Camargo, 190
de Lima Costa, Claudia, 12, 14
De los Santos, René Agustín, 4
El Democrata Fronterizo (The Democratic Frontier), 119
D'Erzell, Catalina (Catalina Dulché Escalante), 2. *See also* Escalante, Catalina Dulché
—writings: "Lo de matrimonios a plazo" (The matter of fixed-term marriages), 218; "Mujer revolucionaria" (Revolutionary woman), 218; "La Mujer y el Arte: Teresa Farías de Isassi" ("The Woman and Art: Teresa Farías de Isassi"), 217–18, 219–20 (español), 221–22 (English text); "Se acabaron las mujeres musas" (The women muses have disappeared), 218

Devereaux, Neil J., 13–14, 227n19
Diario del Hogar (Daily Home Journal), 16, 68, 227n3
Díaz, Porfirio, 3, 15–16, 19, 67, 226n9, 228n6, 230n3, 231nn6–8
Dieulafoy, Jane, 232n3
Dieulafoy, Marcel, 232n3
Diotima, 5
La doctrina Carranza y el acercamiento indolatino (The Carranza Doctrine: An Indo-Latin Approach) (Galindo), 85–86
"El dos de mayo" (The second of May) (Espronceda), 233n1

"¡Ecce homo!" (Behold the Man!) (Gutiérrez de Mendoza), 70, 79–80 (español), 80–81 (English text)
El Eco del Golfo (The Gulf's Echo), 96
education, women's, 19, 25–26, 54
—writings about: "Adelanto de los mexicanos de Texas" ("Progress of Mexicans in Texas") (Villegas de Magnón), 111, 115–16 (español), 116–18 (English text); *Educación errónea de la mujer y medios practicos para correjirla* (The erroneous education of women and practical means of correction), 25–26, 31–33 (Spanish–language transcription), 34–36 (English text); "La lectura" ("Reading") (Wright de Kleinhans), 25–26, 31–33 (Spanish–language transcription), 34–36 (English text); "Para la mujer que lee" ("To the Woman Who Reads") (Astrea), 97, 104 (español), 105–6 (English text); "Shall the Spanish Language Be Taught in the Schools of New Mexico" (Lucero), 7, 196, 198–202 (English text)
elitism, 111
Elizabeth of Bavaria, 232n7
El Paso, Texas, 17
Enabling Act, 196

English language, 12, 196
Enoch, Jessica, 4–5
La Época (The Epoch), 10, 154
—articles: "[¿]Feministas . . . ? [¡]No! Femeninas" ("Feminists . . . ? No! Feminine Women") (Garza), 155, 157–59 (español), 159–62 (English text); "La mujer en el pasado, el presente y en el porvenir" ("Women in the Past, Present, and Future") (Sáenz Royo), 146–47, 148–50 (español), 151–53 (English text), 155; "Las mujeres que escriben" ("Women Who Write") (Garza), 10, 146–47, 155, 163–64 (español), 165–66 (English text)
Escalante, Catalina Dulché (Catalina D'Erzell), 2, 186; biography, 217–18
—writings: "Lo de matrimonios a plazo" (The matter of fixed-term marriages) (D'Erzell), 218; "Mujer revolucionaria" (Revolutionary woman) (D'Erzell), 218; "La Mujer y el Arte: Teresa Farías de Isassi" ("The Woman and Art: Teresa Farías de Isassi") (D'Erzell), 217–18, 219–20 (español), 221–22 (English text); "Se acabaron las mujeres musas" (The women muses have disappeared) (D'Erzell), 218
Escucha (Listen) (Garza), 156
Escuela Nacional Secundaria para Niñas (National Secondary School for Girls), 19
Escuela Normal para Señoritas (Young Women's Normal School), 19
"La Esmeralda" mine, 67
español (term), 2–3, 226n8
Espronceda, José de, 233n1
Estrada Cabrera, Manuel, 231n3, 231n8
"El Estudiante" (The Student) (Idar), 96
El Estudiante (The Student), 96
"Estudio de la Srita. Hermila con motivo de los temas que han de absolverse en el segundo congreso feminista de Yucatán" (A study by Miss Hermila Galindo on the occasion of the topics to be resolved in the Second Feminist Congress of Yucatán) (Galindo), 228n2
ethnic identity, 11
Evolución (Evolution), 96
"Evolución mexicana" ("Mexican Evolution") (Villegas de Magnón), 26, 111, 112–13 (español), 113–14 (English text)
example (strategy), 186–87
Excélsior (Excelsior), 16

Farías de Isassi, Graziella, 218
Farías de Isassi, Teresa—writings about: "La Mujer y el Arte: Teresa Farías de Isassi" ("The Woman and Art: Teresa Farías de Isassi") (D'Erzell), 217–18, 219–20 (español), 221–22 (English text)
feminism—writings about: *Feminismo Internacional* (International Feminism), 154, 204; "El feminismo y la Liga Internacional de Mujeres Ibéricas e Hispano-Americanas" ("Feminism and the International League of Iberian and Hispanic-American Women"), 205–10 (español), 211–16 (English text); *Historia politico-social-cultural del movimiento femenino en México, 1914–1950* (Political, Social, and Cultural History of the Feminine Movement in Mexico, 1914–1950) (Sáenz Royo), 147; "Lo que no es el feminismo" ("What Feminism Is Not") (Ariana), 167–68, 173–74 (español), 175–76 (English text); "Mujeres mexicanas notables" ("Notable Mexican Women"), 3, 10, 186–87, 188–91 (español), 191–95 (English text)
feminist (label), 225n1, 228n1

"[¿]Feministas...? [¡]No! Femeninas" ("Feminists...? No! Feminine Women") (Garza), 155, 157–59 (español), 159–62 (English text)
Feminist Congress of Mexico (Congreso Feminista de México), 228n2, 232n9
Feminist Congress of Yucatán (Congreso Feminista de Yucatán), 85, 228nn1–2
Fernheimer, Janice, 4
fine arts (*bellas letras*), 191, 194; *Venus with a Mirror* (Titian), 233n6
Flores de Peña, Soledad, 111
Flores y Espinas (Flowers and Thorns), 43
Folk Dances of the Spanish-colonials of New Mexico (Lucero), 197
The Folklore of New Mexico (Lucero), 197
Foucault, Michel, 5
Frederick, Jake, 2–3
French franc, 227n4
future directions, 228n2

Gaceta Popular, La (The Popular Gazette), 25
Galindo, Hermila, 6–8, 19, 229n4, 231n1; biography, 85–87
—writings: *La doctrina Carranza y el acercamiento indolatino* (The Carranza Doctrine: An Indo-Latin Approach), 85–86; "Estudio de la Srita. Hermila con motivo de los temas que han de absolverse en el segundo congreso feminista de Yucatán" (A study by Miss Hermila Galindo on the occasion of the topics to be resolved in the Second Feminist Congress of Yucatán), 228n2; "¡Laboremos!" ("Let Us Labor!"), 86, 88–89 (Spanish–language transcription), 89–90 (English text); "La mujer como colaboradora en la vida pública" ("Woman as Collaborator in Public Life"), 86–87, 91–92 (español), 93–95 (English text); "La mujer en el porvenir" (The woman of the future), 228n2
García, Alma M., 230n1
García, María P., 140
García, Mario T., 15
Garza, María Luisa (Loreley), 2, 5–7, 17–21, 146, 167, 232n1; biography, 154–56; location, 10–11
—writings: *Los amores de Gaona: Apuntes realistas de Loreley* (The Many Loves of Gaona: Realistic Reflections from Loreley), 156; "Crónicas Femeninas" (Women's Chronicles) column, 154; *Escucha* (Listen), 156; "[¿]Feministas...? [¡]No! Femeninas" ("Feminists...? No! Feminine Women") (Garza), 155, 157–59 (español), 159–62 (English text); "Las mujeres que escriben" ("Women Who Write"), 10, 146–47, 155, 163–64 (español), 165–66 (English text); *La novia de Nervo* (Nervo's Girlfriend), 156; *Tentáculos de fuego* (Tentacles of Fire), 156; *La verdadera misión de la mujer* (The True Mission of Women), 146, 155
gender roles, 18, 54, 86; debate regarding, 146–47
Gimeno de Flaquer, Concepción, 23
Glenn, Cheryl, 4
Gondra, Isidro Rafael, 43
González, María Felicidad, 204
La Gran Liga Obrera (The Great Workers League), 203
Grossman, Edith, 12
Guadalajara, México, 10
Guatemala, 231n3
Guatimozín (Cuauhtémoc), 61, 228n2
Guerrero, Dolores, 187, 190, 194
Guerrero, María, 189, 193
Gutiérrez, Félix, 17

Gutiérrez de Mendoza, Juana Belén, 3, 7–8, 19, 67; biography, 67–68; editorial collaborations, 69–70, 119; location, 11
—writings: "A los mexicanos" ("To the Mexicans") (Gutiérrez de Mendoza and Acuña y Rossetti), 16, 69–70, 71–74 (español), 75–78 (English text); "¡Ecce homo!" (Behold the Man!), 70, 79–80 (español), 80–81 (English text); "*Vésper* siempre ocupará su puesto" ("Vesper Will Always Occupy Its Post"), 70, 82–83 (español), 83–84 (English text)
Gutiérrez-Witt, Laura, 229n1
Gynecium, 232n1

The Hague Congress (Congreso de la Haya)—writings about: "Opiniones de algunas de las feministas que han concurrido al Congreso de La Haya en favor de la paz" (Opinions of Some of the Feminists Who Attended the Congress of The Hague in Favor of Peace) (Anonymous), 177–78, 179–82 (español), 182–85 (English text)
helots, 227n2
hembrismo (extreme female submission), 18
Hemeroteca Digital Nacional de Chihuahua, 6
Hemeroteca Digital Nacional de México, 6, 227n2
El Heraldo de México (The Mexican Herald), 204; location, 9, 9
—articles: "El feminismo y la Liga Internacional de Mujeres Ibéricas e Hispano-Americanas" ("Feminism and the International League of Iberian and Hispanic-American Women"), 205–10 (español), 211–16 (English text); "La Mujer y el Arte: Teresa Farías de Isassi" ("The Woman and Art: Teresa Farías de Isassi") (D'Erzell), 217–18, 219–20 (español), 221–22 (English text)
Hernández, Sonia, 226n15, 229n2
Hernández Carballido, Elvira, 25
Heroica (designation), 229n13
Herrera, Lucía G., 44
Herzberg, Bruce, 5
Heymann, Lyda Gustava, 181 (español), 185 (English text)
Hidalgo, Miguel, 231n2
Las Hijas [Violetas] del Anáhuac (Daughters [Violets] of Anáhuac), 7, 24–25, 227nn1–2, 227n4; contributers, 53, 61; male audience, 44–45; microfilm collection, 20; name change, 25, 225n3, 227n1
—articles: "Carta abierta" ("An Open Letter") (Paz), 61–62, 63–64 (español), 65–66 (English text); "La infancia" (Childhood) (Zapata de Puig), 44; "La mujer de este siglo" (The Woman of This Century) (Zapata de Puig), 43–45, 46–48 (español), 49–52 (English text); "Mujeres de nuestra época" ("Women of Our Era") (Manresa de Pérez), 53–54, 55–57 (español), 58–60 (English text); "Saludo y Prospecto" ("Greeting and Prospectus") (Wright de Kleinhans), 24, 27–28 (español), 29–30 (English text), 44
El Hijo de Ahuizote (The Son of the Gadfly), 16, 68
Hispanic American Newspapers, 1808–1980 (database), 6, 20, 234n2
Hispanic press, 6–7
Los Hispanos: Five Essays on the Folkways of the Hispanos as Seen through the Eyes of One of Them (Lucero), 197
Historia de una vida: del caos a la luz (History of a Life: From Chaos to the Light) (Sáenz Royo), 147

Historia politico-social-cultural del movimiento femenino en México, 1914–1950 (Political, Social, and Cultural History of the Feminine Movement in Mexico, 1914–1950) (Sáenz Royo), 147
historical context, 15–20
El Hogar, 20
Holbrook, Miss, 181–82 (español), 185 (English text)
Horner, Bruce, 13
Huerta, Victoriano, 228n6, 229n12, 230n3

Idar, Clemente, 96
Idar, Eduardo, 96
Idar, Jovita (A. V. Negra and Astrea), 7, 21, 197, 229–30n2; biography, 96–97, 110, 122; location, 12
—writings: "Debemos trabajar" ("We Must Work"), 26, 97, 107–8 (español), 108–9 (English text); "El Estudiante" (The Student), 96; "Para la mujer que lee" ("To the Woman Who Reads"), 97, 104 (español), 105–6 (English text); "Por la raza: la conservación del nacionalismo" ("For the Mexican People: The Preservation of Nationalism"), 97, 101–2 (español), 102–3 (English text); "Por la raza: la niñez mexicana en Texas" ("For the Mexican People: Mexican Children in Texas"), 3, 97, 98–99 (español), 99–100 (English text)
Idar, Nicasio, 96
identity, ethnic, 11
ideology, gendered, 18
Ilíada India (Indian Iliad), 189, 192
La Ilustración: Semanario de las Señoritas (The Enlightenment: The Weekly for Young Ladies), 43
El Imparcial de Texas (The Impartial of Texas), 154

Independence Day (Mexico), 229n7
indigenous women, 187
Indo-Latin approach, 228n3
indolatino (term), 228n3
"La infancia" (Childhood) (Zapata de Puig), 44
El Informador (The Reporter), 10, 147
International League of Iberian and Hispanic-American Women (Liga Internacional de Mujeres Ibéricas e Hispanoamericanas o Liga de Mujeres de la Raza), 204
—writings about: "El feminismo y la Liga Internacional de Mujeres Ibéricas e Hispano-Americanas" ("Feminism and the International League of Iberian and Hispanic-American Women"), 205–10 (español), 211–16 (English text)
Interscholastic Oratorical Association, 7
Ixtlilxóchitl, 189, 193

Jones, Willis Knapp, 217
José Ignacio Gallegos Caballero Public Library, 20
José Valenzuela, Georgette, 6
journalistic resistance, 96–97
Juan Bobo: Adapted from the Spanish Folk Tale Bertolodo (Lucero), 197
Juárez, Benito, 15, 230n3

Kanellos, Nicolás, 6–7
Kirsch, Gesa E., 11
Kleinhans, Sebastián, 23
Knight, Alan, 15

"¡Laboremos!" ("Let Us Labor!") (Galindo), 86, 88–89 (Spanish-language transcription), 89–90 (English text)
Lady of Tula (señora de Tula), 187, 188 (español), 192 (English text)

language: multilingualism, 13–14; translation, 12–14. *See also specific languages*
language instruction, 196–97, 225n5
—writings about: "Adelanto de los mexicanos de Texas" ("Progress of Mexicans in Texas") (Villegas de Magnón), 111, 115–16 (español), 116–18 (English text); "Shall the Spanish Language Be Taught in the Schools of New Mexico" (Lucero), 7, 196, 198–202 (English text)
Laredo, Texas, 9, 9, 17, 226n18
Latin American Women Writers database, 20
Lau Jaiven, Ana, 6
lavender (color), 227n1
Lawhn, Juanita Luna, 225n6
Lazarín, Manuel, 189, 194
Lazarín, María Rodríguez del Toro de, 189, 194
Lecher, Frau, 178, 181 (español), 185 (English text)
"La lectura" ("Reading") (Wright de Kleinhans), 25–26, 31–33 (Spanish-language transcription), 34–36 (English text)
Legrand, Caroline, 232n4
León, Kendall, 4–5
"Leona Vicario y Rafaela López" (Rentería), 7, 128–29, 130–32 (español), 132–34 (English text)
Lerdo de Tejada, Miguel, 85
Lerdo de Tejada, Sebastian, 231n6
lesbian activism, 227n1
La Libertad (Liberty), 43
Liceo Hidalgo, 23
Liceo Mexicano, 23
Liga de Mujeres de la Raza (Liga Internacional de Mujeres Ibéricas e Hispanoamericanas, International League of Iberian and Latin American Women), 204
—writings about: "El feminismo y la Liga Internacional de Mujeres Ibéricas e Hispano-Americanas" ("Feminism and the International League of Iberian and Hispanic-American Women"), 205–10 (español), 211–16 (English text)
La Liga Femenil Mexicanista (The Mexican Feminine League), 7, 20, 96–97, 122; goals, 128–29
—anonymous writings on, 122–27; "Liga Femenil Mexicanista" ("Mexicanist Feminine League") (Anonymous), 123 (español), 124–25 (English text); "La Liga Femenil Mexicanista" ("The Mexicanist Feminine League") (Anonymous), 126 (español), 127 (English text)
Liga Internacional de Mujeres Ibéricas e Hispanoamericanas (International League of Iberian and Hispanic-American Women), 204
—writings about: "El feminismo y la Liga Internacional de Mujeres Ibéricas e Hispano-Americanas" ("Feminism and the International League of Iberian and Hispanic-American Women"), 205–10 (español), 211–16 (English text)
Limón, José, 15, 96, 111, 229n1
listening, rhetorical, 12–13
Literary Folklore of the Hispanic Southwest (Lucero), 197
locations, 9, 9–14
"Lo de matrimonios a plazo" (The matter of fixed-term marriages) (D'Erzell), 218
Logan, Shirley Wilson, 22
Lomas, Clara, 5, 13, 96, 141, 229nn1–2
López Aguado de Rayón, Rafaela, 233n1
—writings about: "Leona Vicario y Rafaela López" (Rentería), 7, 128–29,

writings about (*continued*)
130–32 (español), 132–34 (English text)
"Lo que no es el feminismo" ("What Feminism Is Not") (Ariana), 167–68, 173–74 (español), 175–76 (English text)
Loreley. *See* Garza, María Luisa
Los Angeles, California, 9, 9
Lozano, Ignacio E., 167, 177
Lozano Vargas, Elvira, 44
Lucero-White Lea, Aurora, 7, 97; biography, 196–97; location, 12
—writings: *Folk Dances of the Spanish-colonials of New Mexico*, 197; *The Folklore of New Mexico*, 197; *Los Hispanos: Five Essays on the Folkways of the Hispanos as Seen through the Eyes of One of Them*, 197; *Juan Bobo: Adapted from the Spanish Folk Tale Bertolodo*, 197; *Literary Folklore of the Hispanic Southwest*, 197; "Shall the Spanish Language Be Taught in the Schools of New Mexico," 7, 196, 198–202 (English text)
Lunsford, Andrea, 4–5
La Luz (The Light), 96

machismo (extreme male dominance), 18
Macías, Anna, 5
Madero, Francisco I., 228nn5–6, 229n12, 230n3
Magnón, Adolpho, 110
Magón, Enrique Flores, 16, 69
Magón, Ricardo, 19, 69
Malinalxóchitl, 10, 186–87, 188 (español), 192 (English text)
Malintzin, 189, 192–93
Manifest Destiny, 228n3
Manresa de Pérez, Concepción, 10, 21, 24–25, 44, 61, 227nn1–2; biography, 53–54

—writings: "La memoria" (Memory), 227n2; "Mujeres de nuestra época" ("Women of Our Era"), 53–54, 55–57 (español), 58–60 (English text); "El trabajo" (Work), 227n2
mappings, 9, 9–14
María (Mary) of Soto la Marina, 189, 194
Marie of Edinburgh, 231–32n4
Marina, 189, 193
Martí, José, 226n9
Mary of Teck, 232n5
masculine dress, 232n3
Ma Soeur, Henriette (Renan), 229n11
Matlalcihuatín, 188–89 (español), 192 (English text)
Melero, Pilar, 5
Mémoires de Madame Roland (Roland), 229n10
"La memoria" (Memory) (Manresa de Pérez), 227n2
Menchaca, Martha, 15
Mendoza, Cirilo, 67
mestizaje (concept), 2–3, 25, 226n9
mestiza rhetorics, 2–3, 226n10
mestizo (term), 2–3, 226n8, 228n3
mestizos, 3, 226n9
methodology, 20–21
Mexican American War, 16
Mexican Congress (El Congreso Mexicanista), 111
The Mexican Feminine League. *See* La Liga Femenil Mexicanista
Mexican Revolution, 15–19, 167
Mexican students, 225n5
Mexican women (mexicanas): *adelitas*, 167; citizenship, 20; rhetors, 2–3, 6–9, 9, 9–14; *soldaderas*, 19, 167; suffrage, 85–86; teachers, 226n18; work opportunities, 19, 54, 226n15. *See also specific women by name*
—writings about: "Mujeres mexicanas notables" ("Notable Mexican

Women") (Anonymous), 3, 10, 186–87, 188–91 (español), 191–95 (English text); *Mujeres notables mexicanas* (Notable Mexican Women) (Wright de Kleinhans), 187; *Semblanzas: mujeres mexicanas revolucionarias y guerras revolucionarias ideológicas* (Portraits: Mexican Women Revolutionaries and Ideological Revolutionary Wars) (Sáenz Royo), 147

Mexico: Anti-reelection Convention, 228n5; Civil Code, 18; civil war, 16; colonial, 225n7; Constitutionalist Congress, 86; gendered ideology, 18; gender roles, 18; history, 15–20, 228n6; Independence Day, 229n7; Indo-Latin approach, 228n3; newspapers, 15–16; *sistema de castas* or caste system, 2–3, 225n7; U.S.-Mexico border, 11–12, 226n11; War of Independence, 231n2

Mexico City, Mexico, 9, 9

El México de Afuera (Mexico on the outside), 2, 154–55, 225n6

"México para los mexicanos" (Mexico for Mexicans) (Sáenz Royo), 146

Meyer, Doris, 17

"Mi Lira" (My lira) (Zapata de Puig), 227n3

Mill, John Stuart, 91, 92, 93, 94, 148, 151, 231n3

Mina, Francisco Xavier, 189, 194

Minerva, 227n3

Moncayo, Hortencia, 111

Montejano, David, 15

Morelos, José María, 230n2

Mota, José Mariano, 43

motherhood, republican, 229n5

Mother Jones, 135

Moya, Paula, 3

"La mujer artista y artesana" ("The Woman Artist and Artisan") (Wright de Kleinhans), 26, 37–39 (español), 40–42 (English text)

"La mujer como colaboradora en la vida pública" ("Woman as Collaborator in Public Life") (Galindo), 86–87, 91–92 (español), 93–95 (English text)

"La mujer de este siglo" ("The Woman of This Century") (Zapata de Puig), 43–45, 46–48 (español), 49–52 (English text)

"La mujer en el pasado, el presente y en el porvenir" ("Women in the Past, Present, and Future") (Xóchitl), 146–47, 148–50 (español), 151–53 (English text), 155

"La mujer en el porvenir" (The woman of the future) (Galindo), 228n2

"Mujeres de nuestra época" ("Women of Our Era") (Manresa de Pérez), 53–54, 55–57 (español), 58–60 (English text)

"Mujeres mexicanas notables" ("Notable Mexican Women") (Anonymous), 3, 10, 186–87, 188–91 (español), 191–95 (English text)

Mujeres notables mexicanas (Notable Mexican Women) (Wright de Kleinhans), 187

"Las mujeres que escriben" ("Women Who Write") (Garza), 10, 146–47, 155, 163–64 (español), 165–66 (English text)

La Mujer Moderna (The Modern Woman), Ciudad de México, 7, 86, 229n4, 231n1; microfilm collection, 20 —articles: "¡Laboremos!" ("Let Us Labor!") (Galindo), 86, 88–89 (Spanish–language transcription), 89–90 (English text)

La Mujer Moderna (The Modern Woman), San Antonio, 7, 135, 229n4, 231n1

—articles: "A qué venimos" ("What We Have Come For") (Villarreal), 135–36, 137–38 (español), 138–39 (English text)
"La mujer moderna y el hogar" ("The Modern Woman and the Home") (Ariana), 167–68, 169–70 (español), 171–72 (English text)
"Mujer revolucionaria" (Revolutionary woman) (D'Erzell), 218
"La Mujer y el Arte: Teresa Farías de Isassi" ("The Woman and Art: Teresa Farías de Isassi") (D'Erzell), 217–18, 219–20 (español), 221–22 (English text)
mulato (term), 2–3, 225n8
multilingualism, 13–14

El Nacional: Periódico de Política, Literatura, Ciencias, Artes, Industria, Agricultura, Minería y Comercio (The National: Newspaper of Politics, Literature, Sciences, Arts, Industry, Agriculture, Mining and Commerce), 15–16
nacionalismo (nationalism): coercive, 155
—writings about: "Por la raza: la conservación del nacionalismo" ("For the MexicanPeople: The Preservation of Nationalism") (Negra), 97, 101–2 (español), 102–3 (English text)
Napiorski, Maria, 155
Nation of Hidalgo (phrase), 231n2
Negra, A. V., 97, 229n2. *See also* Idar, Jovita
—writings: "Por la raza: la conservación del nacionalismo" ("For the MexicanPeople: The Preservation of Nationalism"), 97, 101–2 (español), 102–3 (English text); "Por la raza: la niñez mexicana en Texas" ("For the Mexican People: Mexican Children in Texas"), 3, 97, 98–99 (español), 99–100 (English text)
Netzahualcóyotl, 188–89, 192
Netzahualpilli, 187
New Mexico: historical context, 17; Spanish-language instruction, 196–97, 225n5; Spanish-language newspapers, 17
—writings about: *Folk Dances of the Spanish-colonials of New Mexico* (Lucero), 197; *The Folklore of New Mexico* (Lucero), 197; "Shall the Spanish Language Be Taught in the Schools of New Mexico" (Lucero), 7, 196, 198–202 (English text)
New Mexico Highlands University, 7, 20
New Mexico Normal University (NMNU), 7, 197
New Mexico Normal University Bulletin, 20
New Orleans, Louisiana, 10
newspaper (term), 225n2
newspapers: locations, 9, 9–14; Mexican press, 15–16; Spanish-language, 15–18. *See also specific newspapers by name*
niñez (children)—writings about: "La infancia" (Childhood) (Zapata de Puig), 44; "Por la raza: la niñez mexicana en Texas" ("For the Mexican People: Mexican Children in Texas") (Negra), 3, 97, 98–99 (español), 99–100 (English text)
NMNU (New Mexico Normal University), 7, 197
La novia de Nervo (Nervo's Girlfriend) (Garza), 156

El Obrero (The Worker), 135
Olson, Christa, 4
"Opiniones de algunas de las feministas que han concurrido al Congreso de La Haya en favor de la paz"

(Opinions of Some of the Feminists Who Attended the Congress of The Hague in Favor of Peace) (Anonymous), 177–78, 179–82 (español), 182–85 (English text)
organization, 21
Ortiz de Domínguez, Josefa, 186, 188–89, 191, 193

Padilla de Piña, Ignacia, 24, 44
Palmas Academicas de Francia, 218
Pankhurst, Emmeline, 233n5
"Para la mujer que lee" ("To the Woman Who Reads") (Astrea), 97, 104 (español), 105–6 (English text)
pardo (term), 2–3, 225n8
Partido Liberal Mexicano (PLM; Mexican Liberal Party), 19, 68, 119, 135, 141
Paz, 8, 21, 225n5, 227n1; biography, 61–62; location, 10
—writings: "Carta abierta" ("An Open Letter"), 10, 61–62, 63–64 (español), 65–66 (English text)
Pelletier, Madeleine, 232n2
Peralta, Ángela, 188 (español), 190 (español), 191 (English text), 195
Peralta, Concepción, 24
Pérez, Emma, 5
Pino Suárez, José María, 230n3
Plan of Tuxtepec, 231n6
PLM (Partido Liberal Mexicano, Mexican Liberal Party), 19, 68, 119, 135, 141
poetry: "¡Surge! A la mujer" ("Rise Up! To Womankind") (Ramírez), 119, 120–21 (English text), 120 (español)
political consciousness, 19
Ponciano Arriaga, 68
"Por la raza: la conservación del nacionalismo" ("For the Mexican People: The Preservation of Nationalism") (Negra), 97, 101–2 (español), 102–3 (English text)

"Por la raza: la niñez mexicana en Texas" ("For the Mexican People: Mexican Children in Texas") (Negra), 3, 97, 98–99 (español), 99–100 (English text)
Portraits: Mexican Women Revolutionaries and Ideological Revolutionary Wars (*Semblanzas: mujeres mexicanas revolucionarias y guerras revolucionarias ideológicas*) (Sáenz Royo), 147
El Porvenir (The Future), 16
Pouwels, Joel Bollinger, 5, 13–14, 20, 43–44
Powell, Malea, 4
La Prensa (The Press), Los Angeles: anonymous feminist writings from, 186–87
—articles: "Mujeres mexicanas notables" ("Notable Mexican Women"), 3, 10, 186–87, 188–91 (español), 191–95 (English text)
La Prensa (The Press), San Antonio, 17, 233n1; anonymous feminist writings from, 177–78; circulation, 167; contributors, 96, 135, 154, 167
—articles: "Lo que no es el feminismo" ("What Feminism Is Not") (Ariana), 167–68, 173–74 (español), 173–74 (español), 175–76 (English text), 175–76 (English text); "La mujer moderna y el hogar" ("The Modern Woman and the Home") (Ariana), 167–68, 169–70 (español), 171–72 (English text); "Opiniones de algunas de las feministas que han concurrido al Congreso de La Haya en favor de la paz" (Opinions of Some of the Feminists Who Attended the Congress of The Hague in Favor of Peace) (Anonymous), 177–78, 179–82 (español), 182–85 (English text); "Se acabaron las mujeres musas" (The women muses have disappeared) (D'Erzell), 218

press (term), 225n2
Prieto de Landázuri, Isabel, 190, 194
primary resources, 6
protest colors, 227n1
El Pueblo (The People), Veracruz, 10, 86
—articles: "México para los mexicanos" (Mexico for Mexicans) (Sáenz Royo), 146; "La mujer como colaboradora en la vida pública" ("Woman as Collaborator in Public Life") (Galindo), 86–87, 91–92 (español), 93–95 (English text)
Puig, Catalina de, 8
Puig de Borberena, Albertina, 24
Puig de León, Dolores, 44
Pujol, Ignacio, 24
pulque (drink), 231n1
purple (color), 227n1

Quiroga, José, 154

racial categories, 2–3
Ramírez, Cristina D., 3, 5
Ramírez, Ignacio, 25
Ramírez, Sara Estela, 17–21, 230n2; biography, 69, 97, 110, 119, 167
—writings: "¡Surge! A la mujer" ("Rise Up! To Womankind") (Ramírez), 119, 120–21 (English text), 120 (español)
Ramos-Escandón, Carmen, 6, 18
Ratcliffe, Krista, 12–13
Rayón, Ramón, 193
Rayón brothers, 193
reading—articles about: "La lectura" ("Reading") (Wright de Kleinhans), 25–26, 31–33 (Spanish–language transcription), 34–36 (English text); "Para la mujer que lee" ("To the Woman Who Reads") (Astrea), 97, 104 (español), 105–6 (English text)
The Rebel (Villegas de Magnón), 110
Regeneración (Regeneration), 16
Renacimiento (Rebirth), 16, 156
Renan, Ernest, 229n11

Renan, Henriette, 229n11
Rentería, María, 5, 21, 186, 233n1; biography, 97, 110, 122, 128–29
—writings: "Leona Vicario y Rafaela López," 7, 128–29, 130–32 (español), 132–34 (English text)
La República: Periódico Político y Literario (The Republic: Political and Literary Newspaper), 15–16
republican motherhood, 229n5
resistance movement, 19, 96–97
Revista Femenina (Female Magazine), 204
"Revolutionary woman" ("Mujer revolucionaria") (D'Erzell), 218
Revueltas, José, 68
rhetoric: *mestiza* rhetorics, 2–3, 226n10; strategy of example, 186–87
rhetorical listening, 12–13
rhetors, mexicana, 2–3; locations, 9, 9–14; selection, 6–9. *See also specific women by name*
Richardson, Mary, 233n6
rights: women's rights, 19–20, 111; women's suffrage, 85–86, 230n4
Rimbló, Emilia, 44
Rios, Herminio, 17
Ritchie, Joy, 5
Rivas-Rodríguez, Maggie, 167
Rodríguez, América, 17
Roland, Marie-Jeanne Phlipon, 229n10
Roland de la Platière, Jean-Marie, 229n10
Romano, Susan, 5
Romero, Manuel M., 45
Ronald, Kate, 5
Royster, Jacqueline Jones, 4, 11
Ruiz, Vicki L., 5

Sáenz Royo, Artemisa N. (Xóchitl), 5, 21, 155, 167; biography, 146–47
—writings: *Historia de una vida: del caos a la luz* (History of a Life: From Chaos to the Light), 147; *Historia*

politico-social-cultural del movimiento femenino en México, 1914–1950 (Political, Social, and Cultural History of the Feminine Movement in Mexico, 1914–1950), 147; "México para los mexicanos" (Mexico for Mexicans), 146; "La mujer en el pasado, el presente y en el porvenir" ("Women in the Past, Present, and Future"), 146–47, 148–50 (español), 151–53 (English text), 155; *Semblanzas: mujeres mexicanas revolucionarias y guerras revolucionarias ideológicas* (Portraits: Mexican Women Revolutionaries and Ideological Revolutionary Wars), 147; *El Venustiano Carranza que yo conocí* (The Venustiano Carranza that I Knew), 146

Salles, Virgilinia de Souza, 204

"Saludo y Prospecto" ("Greeting and Prospectus") (Wright de Kleinhans), 24, 27–28 (español), 29–30 (English text), 44

Salvídar-Hull, Sonia, 111

San Antonio, Texas, 10

Sánchez, María, 140

San Juan de Bautista, Tabasco, 45

Sarabia, Juan, 16, 231n5

scholarly foundation and conversation, 4–6

Schwimmer, Rosika, 182 (español), 185 (English text), 233n2

"Se acabaron las mujeres musas" (The women muses have disappeared) (D'Erzell), 218

El Semanario de la Señoritas Mejicanas: Educación Científica, Moral y Literaria del Bello Sexo (The Weekly for Young Mexican Ladies: Education, Science, Morality and Literature for the Fair Sex), 43–44, 227n4

Semblanzas: mujeres mexicanas revolucionarias y guerras revolucionarias ideológicas (Portraits: Mexican Women Revolutionaries and Ideological Revolutionary Wars) (Sáenz Royo), 147

Serviss, Tricia, 5

"Shall the Spanish Language Be Taught in the Schools of New Mexico" (Lucero), 7, 196, 198–202 (English text)

Shaver, Lisa, 4

Sierra, Justo, 19

Sigüenza y Góngora, Carlos de, 186, 190, 193

sistema de castas or caste system, 2–3

Sohn, Katherine Kelleher, 4

soldaderas, 19, 167

Sor Juana Inéz de la Cruz, 68, 186, 233n2

—writings about, 5; "Mujeres mexicanas notables" ("Notable Mexican Women") (Anonymous), 188–89 (español), 191 (English text), 193 (English text)

Sor María de los Dolores, 186, 190, 193

Sor Petronila de San José, 190, 193

Sosa, Francisco, 186, 189, 193

Southwest: Spanish-language newspapers, 17. *See also specific states*

Spanish language, 11–12

Spanish-language instruction, 196–97, 225n5

—writings about: "Adelanto de los mexicanos de Texas" ("Progress of Mexicans in Texas") (Villegas de Magnón), 111, 115–16 (español), 116–18 (English text); "Shall the Spanish Language Be Taught in the Schools of New Mexico" (Lucero), 7, 196, 198–202 (English text)

Spanish-language newspapers: historical context, 17–18; Mexican press, 15–16; in Southwest, 17. *See also specific newspapers by name*

"The Student" ("El Estudiante") (Idar), 96

The Student (*El Estudiante*), 96
students, Mexican, 225n5
"¡Surge! A la mujer" ("Rise Up! To Womankind") (Ramírez), 119, 120–21 (English text), 120 (español)

Tabasco, México, 10
Tabuenca Córdoba, María Socorro, 5
Tapia de Castellanos, Esther, 24, 187, 190, 194
Tartars, 231n4
teachers, mexicana, 226n18
Temple of Minerva, 227n3
Tentáculos de fuego (Tentacles of Fire) (Garza), 156
Texas: historical context, 17; Spanish-language newspapers, 17; women's rights, 111
—articles about: "Adelanto de los mexicanos de Texas" ("Progress of Mexicans in Texas") (Villegas de Magnón), 111, 115–16 (español), 116–18 (English text); "Por la raza: la niñez mexicana en Texas" ("For the MexicanPeople: Mexican Children in Texas") (Negra), 3, 97, 98–99 (español), 99–100 (English text)
El Tiempo (The Times), 24, 26
—articles: "La mujer artista y artesana" ("The Woman Artist and Artisan") (Wright de Kleinhans), 26, 37–39 (español), 40–42 (English text)
Titian, 233n6
"El trabajo" (Work) (Manresa de Pérez), 227n2
Le Trait d'Union (*The Treaty of the Union*), 24
translation, 12–14
Treaty of Guadalupe Hidalgo, 16–17
Trimbur, John, 13
Truth, Sojourner, 5
Tuñon Pablos, Julia, 6
The Two Republics, 23

"¡Unifiquémonos!" ("Let Us Unite!") (Cárdenas), 140–41, 142–43 (español), 144–45 (English text)
United States: Enabling Act, 196; historical context, 16–20; Manifest Destiny, 228n3; Mexican border, 11–12, 226n11; republican motherhood, 229n5; Southwest, 17; Spanish-language newspapers, 17; women's citizenship, 20; women's suffrage, 230n4
El Universal Gráfico (The Universal Graphic), 156
Universidad Nacional Autónoma de México, 20
University of Arizona: Latin American Women Writers database, 20
Uranga, Rodolfo, 155

Vallez Ruiz, Rosa María, 6
Vasconcelos, José, 203–4, 226n9
Venustiano Carranza que yo conocí, El (The Venustiano Carranza That I Knew) (Sáenz Royo), 146
Venus with a Mirror (Titian), 233n6
Venuti, Lawrence, 12
Veracruz, Mexico, 10, 229n13
La verdadera misión de la mujer (The True Mission of Women) (Garza), 146, 155
Vésper: Justicia y Libertad (Vesper: Justice and Liberty), 7, 67–68, 119; location, 9, 9; microfilm collection, 20
—articles: "A los mexicanos" ("To the Mexicans") (Gutiérrez de Mendoza and Acuña y Rossetti), 16, 69–70, 71–74 (español), 75–78 (English text); "¡Ecce homo!" (Behold the Man!) (Gutiérrez de Mendoza), 70, 79–80 (español), 80–81 (English text); "*Vésper* siempre ocupará su puesto" ("*Vesper* Will Always Occupy Its Post") (Gutiérrez de Mendoza), 70, 82–83 (español), 83–84 (English text)

Vicario, Leona, 186
—writings about: "Leona Vicario y Rafaela López" (Rentería), 7, 128–29, 130–32 (español), 132–34 (English text); "Mujeres mexicanas notables" ("Notable Mexican Women") (Anonymous), 189 (español), 193 (English text)
Villaneda, Alicia, 67
Villanueva, Victor, 4
Villareal, Teresa, 7, 135, 229n4
Villarreal, Antonio I., 135
Villarreal González, Andrea, 2, 7, 17, 229n4, 231n1; biography, 135–36
—writings: "A qué venimos" ("What We Have Come For"), 135–36, 137–38 (español), 138–39 (English text)
Villegas de Magnón, Leonor, 8, 19, 21, 96–97, 197; biography, 110–11, 230n1; location, 11
—writings: "Adelanto de los mexicanos de Texas" ("Progress of Mexicans in Texas"), 111, 115–16 (español), 116–18 (English text); "Evolución mexicana" ("Mexican Evolution"), 26, 111, 112–13 (español), 113–14 (English text); *The Rebel*, 110
Violetas del Anáhuac, 10, 43–44, 227n1; name, 25. *See also Las Hijas [Violetas] del Anáhuac*
—articles: "Carta abierta" ("An Open Letter") (Paz), 61–62, 63–64 (español), 65–66 (English text); "La infancia" (Childhood) (Zapata de Puig), 44; "La mujer de este siglo" (The Woman of This Century) (Zapata de Puig), 43–45, 46–48 (español), 49–52 (English text)
voting: women's suffrage, 85–86, 230n4
La Voz de Juárez (The Voice of Juárez), 16
La Voz de la Mujer (The Voice of Women), 140–41

—articles: "¡Unifiquémonos!" ("Let Us Unite!") (Cárdenas), 140–41, 142–43 (español), 144–45 (English text)
La Voz de Mexico (The Voice of Mexico), 24

War of Independence (Mexico), 231n2
Wilson, Margaret, 232n6
Wilson, Woodrow, 228n3
women: *adelitas*, 167; indigenous, 187; rhetors, 2–3, 6–9, 9, 9–14; *soldaderas*, 19, 167; teachers, 226n18; work opportunities, 19, 54, 226n15. *See also* Mexican women (mexicanas)
women's citizenship, 20
women's education, 19, 25–26, 54. *See also* education
Women's Franchise League, 233n5
women's rights, 19–20, 111
women's roles, 18, 54, 86; debate regarding, 146–47
—writings about: "La mujer como colaboradora en la vida pública" ("Woman as Collaborator in Public Life") (Galindo), 86–87, 91–92 (español), 93–95 (English text); "La mujer de este siglo" ("The Woman of This Century") (Zapata de Puig), 43–45, 46–48 (español), 49–52 (English text); "La mujer en el pasado, el presente y en el porvenir" ("Women in the Past, Present, and Future") (Sáenz Royo), 146–47, 148–50 (español), 151–53 (English text), 155; "La mujer en el porvenir" (The woman of the future) (Galindo), 228n2; "La mujer moderna y el hogar" ("The Modern Woman and the Home") (Ariana), 167–68, 169–70 (español), 171–72 (English text); *La verdadera misión de la mujer* (The True Mission of Women), 155
women's suffrage, 85–86, 230n4

"Women Who Write" ("Las mujeres que escriben") (Garza), 10, 146–47, 155, 163–64 (español), 165–66 (English text)
work: opportunities for women, 19, 54, 226n15
—writings about: "Debemos trabajar" ("We Must Work") (Astrea), 26, 97, 107–8 (español), 108–9 (English text); "¡Laboremos!" ("Let Us Labor!") (Galindo), 86, 88–89 (Spanish-language transcription), 89–90 (English text); "El trabajo" (Work) (Manresa de Pérez), 227n2
World War I, 178
Wright de Kleinhans, Laureana, 6–7, 19, 21, 61, 187; biography, 23–26
—writings: "La lectura" ("Reading"), 25–26, 31–33 (Spanish-language transcription), 34–36 (English text); "La mujer artista y artesana" ("The Woman Artist and Artisan"), 26, 37–39 (español), 40–42 (English text); *Mujeres notables mexicanas* (Notable Mexican Women), 187; "Saludo y Prospecto" ("Greeting and Prospectus"), 24, 27–28 (español), 29–30 (English text), 44

writers: "Las mujeres que escriben" ("Women Who Write") (Garza), 10, 146–47, 155, 163–64 (español), 165–66 (English text). *See also* rhetors
Wu, Hui, 13

Xiutlatzín, 186, 188 (español), 192 (English text)
Xóchitl (pseudonym), 146. *See also* Sáenz Royo, Artemisa N.
Xóchitl (Toltec maid who discovered agave juice), 187, 189, 192–93

You, Xiaoye, 4
Young, Vershawn Ashanti, 13

Zapata, Dolores Correa, 44
Zapata de Puig, Catalina, 5, 21, 24–25, 61; biography, 43–45; location, 10, 45
—writings: "La infancia" (Childhood), 44; "Mi Lira" (My lira), 227n1, 227n3; "La mujer de este siglo" ("The Woman of This Century"), 43–45, 46–48 (español), 49–52 (English text)
Zarco, Francisco, 68
Zavala, Gertrudis Tenorio, 190, 194
Zerecero, Licentiate, 189, 194

JESSICA ENOCH, a professor of English at the University of Maryland and the director of the Academic Writing Program, is the author of *Refiguring Rhetorical Education: Women Teaching African American, Native American, and Chicano/a Students, 1865–1911* (2008) and *Domestic Occupations: Spatial Rhetorics and Women's Work* (2019). She is a coeditor of *Burke in the Archives* (with Dana Anderson, 2013), *Women at Work* (with David Gold, 2019), and *Retellings* (with Jordynn Jack, 2019).

CRISTINA DEVEREAUX RAMÍREZ is an associate professor and the director of the graduate program in rhetoric, composition, and the teaching of English in the Department of English at the University of Arizona. She is the author of *Occupying Our Space: The Mestiza Rhetorics of Mexican Women Journalists and Activists, 1875–1942* (2015).

Studies in Rhetorics and Feminisms

Studies in Rhetorics and Feminisms seeks to address the interdisciplinarity that rhetorics and feminisms represent. Rhetorical and feminist scholars connect rhetorical inquiry with contemporary academic and social concerns, exploring rhetoric's relevance to current issues of opportunity and diversity. This interdisciplinarity is transforming the rhetorical tradition as we have known it (upper-class, agonistic, public, and male) into regendered, inclusionary rhetorics (democratic, dialogic, collaborative, cultural, and private). Our intellectual advancements depend on such ongoing transformation.

Rhetoric, whether ancient, contemporary, or futuristic, always inscribes the relation of language and power at a particular moment, indicating who may speak, who may listen, and what can be said. The only way we can displace the traditional rhetoric of masculine-only, public performance is to replace it with rhetorics that are recognized as being better suited to our present needs. We must understand more fully the rhetorics of the non-Western tradition, of women, of a variety of cultural and ethnic groups. Therefore, Studies in Rhetorics and Feminisms espouses a theoretical position of openness and expansion, a place for rhetorics to grow and thrive in a symbiotic relationship with all that feminisms have to offer, particularly when these two fields intersect with philosophical, sociological, religious, psychological, pedagogical, and literary issues.

The series seeks scholarly works that both examine and extend rhetoric, works that span the sexes, disciplines, cultures, ethnicities, and sociocultural practices as they intersect with the rhetorical tradition. After all, the recent resurgence of rhetorical studies has been not so much a discovery of new rhetorics as a recognition of existing rhetorical activities and practices, of our newfound ability and willingness to listen to previously untold stories.

The series editors seek both high-quality traditional and cutting-edge scholarly work that extends the significant relationship between rhetoric and feminism within various genres, cultural contexts, historical periods, methodologies, theoretical positions, and methods of delivery (e.g., film and hypertext to elocution and preaching).

Queries and submissions:

Professor Emerita Shirley Wilson Logan
University of Maryland
Email: slogan@umd.edu

Cheryl Glenn
Department of English
402 Burrowes Bldg.
Penn State University
University Park, PA 16802-6200
Email: cjg6@psu.edu

Other Books in the Studies in Rhetorics and Feminisms Series

*Retroactivism in the Lesbian Archives:
Composing Pasts and Futures*
Jean Bessette

*Feminist Rhetorical Science Studies:
Human Bodies, Posthumanist Worlds*
Edited by Amanda K. Booher
and Julie Jung

*A Feminist Legacy:
The Rhetoric and Pedagogy
of Gertrude Buck*
Suzanne Bordelon

*Regendering Delivery:
The Fifth Canon and
Antebellum Women Rhetors*
Lindal Buchanan

Rhetorics of Motherhood
Lindal Buchanan

*Conversational Rhetoric:
The Rise and Fall of a Women's
Tradition, 1600–1900*
Jane Donawerth

*Domestic Occupations:
Spatial Rhetorics and Women's Work*
Jessica Enoch

Feminism beyond Modernism
Elizabeth A. Flynn

Women and Rhetoric between the Wars
Edited by Ann George, M. Elizabeth
Weiser, and Janet Zepernick

*Rhetorical Feminism and
This Thing Called Hope*
Cheryl Glenn

*Educating the New Southern Woman:
Speech, Writing, and Race at the
Public Women's Colleges, 1884–1945*
David Gold and Catherine L. Hobbs

Food, Feminisms, Rhetorics
Edited by Melissa A. Goldthwaite

*Women's Irony:
Rewriting Feminist Rhetorical Histories*
Tarez Samra Graban

*Claiming the Bicycle:
Women, Rhetoric, and Technology
in Nineteenth-Century America*
Sarah Hallenbeck

*The Rhetoric of Rebel Women:
Civil War Diaries and
Confederate Persuasion*
Kimberly Harrison

*Evolutionary Rhetoric:
Sex, Science, and Free Love in
Nineteenth-Century Feminism*
Wendy Hayden

*Liberating Voices:
Writing at the Bryn Mawr Summer
School for Women Workers*
Karyn L. Hollis

*Gender and Rhetorical Space
in American Life, 1866–1910*
Nan Johnson

*Antebellum American
Women's Poetry:
A Rhetoric of Sentiment*
Wendy Dasler Johnson

*Appropriate[ing] Dress:
Women's Rhetorical Style in
Nineteenth-Century America*
Carol Mattingly

*The Gendered Pulpit:
Preaching in American
Protestant Spaces*
Roxanne Mountford

Writing Childbirth:
Women's Rhetorical Agency
in Labor and Online
Kim Hensley Owens

Rhetorical Listening:
Identification, Gender, Whiteness
Krista Ratcliffe

Feminist Rhetorical Practices:
New Horizons for Rhetoric,
Composition, and Literacy Studies
Jacqueline J. Royster and
Gesa E. Kirsch

Rethinking Ethos:
A Feminist Ecological
Approach to Rhetoric
Edited by Kathleen J. Ryan,
Nancy Myers, and Rebecca Jones

Vote and Voice:
Women's Organizations and
Political Literacy, 1915–1930
Wendy B. Sharer

Women Physicians and
Professional Ethos in
Nineteenth-Century America
Carolyn Skinner

Praising Girls:
The Rhetoric of Young
Women, 1895–1930
Henrietta Rix Wood